EFFECTIVE FAITH

A Critical Study of the Christology of Juan Luis Segundo

Bryan P. Stone

UNIVERSITY
PRESS OF
AMERICA

Lanham • New York • London

Copyright © 1994 by
University Press of America®, Inc.
4720 Boston Way
Lanham, Maryland 20706

3 Henrietta Street
London WC2E 8LU England

Library of Congress Cataloging-in-Publication Data

Stone, Bryan P.
Effective faith : a critical study of the christology of Juan Luis
Segundo / Bryan P. Stone.
p.   cm.
Includes bibliographical references.
Originally presented as thesis (doctoral)—Dedman College of Southern
Methodist University, Dallas, Tex.
1. Jesus Christ—History of doctrines—20th century.   2. Segundo,
Juan Luis.   3. Liberation theology.   I. Title.
BT202.S746   1993   232'.092—dc20   93–3494 CIP

ISBN 0–8191–9105–1 (cloth : alk. paper)
ISBN 0–8191–9106–X (pbk. : alk. paper)

For Karla

*Nothing can separate us or those whom
we love from God's boundless love for all of us.*

Acknowledgments

This book was originally written as a doctoral dissertation presented to the Graduate Faculty of Dedman College at Southern Methodist University, Dallas, Texas. The dissertation was directed by Professor Schubert M. Ogden and I am grateful to him for his counsel and encouragement not only in the course of writing the dissertation, but also throughout the course of my doctoral studies. I also wish to thank Professor Charles Wood and Professor Edward Sylvest for their role as members of my doctoral committee and for their critical suggestions and guidance. Finally, I would like to express my sincere appreciation to my family and to the congregation, friends, and directors of "Liberation Community," the urban ministry which I had the privilege to pastor and direct during my studies at Southern Methodist University. The balance of academic research with inner-city ministry was personally enriching and rewarding also, I think, for my doctoral work.

Table of Contents

INTRODUCTION
THE PROBLEM OF METHOD IN CONTEMPORARY CHRISTOLOGY

PART I. SEGUNDO'S CHRISTOLOGY

Preface

My primary aim in the following study is to suggest for Christian systematic theology an adequate and effective method for critically interpreting the significance of Jesus for human liberation today. I have sought to make this contribution by undertaking a critical analysis of the method of the Latin American liberation theologian, Juan Luis Segundo. Segundo has been chosen as my interlocutor in this study for three basic reasons: (1) For some time now, proponents and interpreters of liberation theology have emphasized that the unique common denominator of various theologies of liberation is not so much their content as their method.[1] Segundo himself is one of the leading advocates for this view and writes,

> I think that the most progressive theology in Latin America is more interested in *being liberating* than in *talking about liberation*. In other words, liberation is not concerned so much with the content as with the method used in order to do theology in the face of our reality (1975b:13).

Again, Segundo writes:

> the only thing that can maintain indefinitely the liberating character of a theology is not its content but its method (48).

If, indeed, the challenge of liberation theology to Christian systematic theology is primarily one of method and if, also, we acknowledge, as I certainly do, that Juan Luis Segundo is one of the most serious and articulate champions of just such a method, it seems to me that any contemporary effort to contribute to the method of interpreting the significance of Jesus might find it exceptionally useful to explore the christological method of Segundo himself.

---

[1]Some, such as Robert McAfee Brown, have characterized its method as a "new way of doing theology" (255). Juan Carlos Scannone refers to it as "a completely new reworking and formulation of theological activity as a whole from a completely new standpoint: i.e., the *kairos* of salvation history now being lived on our continent" (215). Schubert Ogden provides a slightly different perspective and, though he interprets the phenomenon of liberation theology as a unique and distinctive theological movement, highlights instead the place of liberation theology as squarely within contemporary currents of liberal-postliberal theology (1979a:18-25).

(2) Segundo concedes that liberation theologians, to whatever extent they have taken up christological reflection, have not done so merely in order to fulfill a desire to make new contributions to that specialized branch of knowledge known as christology.   For Segundo, however, nowhere is theological method more crucial than when it comes to christological considerations and, thus, we have his recent, massive undertaking, *El hombre de hoy ante Jesús de Nazaret.* This turn to christology by Segundo is not, I believe, arbitrary, but is the logical outcome of his attempt to apply his method beyond the more ethical or programmatic considerations that have heretofore characterized so much of the work of liberation theologians.   One could even say that this turn to christology provides not so much *a* test case as *the* test case for evaluating Segundo's theological method, so much so that Segundo even calls his work an "antichristology."

(3) Finally, in the face of the massive ecological and political crises facing our planet, I consider Segundo's proposal for interpreting the significance of Jesus as one of the most creative and pertinent efforts now available.   Segundo's relevance stems from his interpretation of Christian faith as offering optimum possibilities for giving direction and meaning to human culture in a way that is at once both normative and liberative.   In our own time, as we watch the collapse of communism in the east and the restructuring of entire cultures throughout the world, Segundo's critical appraisal of both capitalism and socialism, his analysis of human existence in terms of human meaning and values, on the one hand, and in terms of the specific means required to implement those values, on the other hand, and his framing of the whole human endeavor in terms of important evolutionary qualities holds great promise, it seems to me, both for bringing Jesus forward 2,000 years in a meaningful and credible way and for enhancing human responsibility in living out an "effective faith" in ever new and imaginative ways.

Despite Segundo's rich analysis of the relationship between faith and ideologies and his application of evolutionary insights to the problem of interpreting the significance of Jesus, however, his christological method is fraught with several deficiencies that cry out for resolution.   It is to the task of providing an alternative to these deficiencies that I will devote myself in Part III of this study.

Though my primary intent in exploring the theology of Juan Luis Segundo is to make a contribution to an adequate and effective method of interpreting the significance of Jesus for human liberation, that in no way should be understood to detract from my secondary aim in this study to provide a tool for better appreciating and understanding the thought of Juan Luis Segundo.   Though Segundo is one of the most prolific writers among contemporary theologians today, when we turn to the literature on him, we cannot help but be disappointed by the relatively meager quantity of tools at our disposal.[2] Even granting the relative novelty of Segundo's christological work and the certainty that his own thought is still very much alive and developing in several areas, his writings are some of the more insightful of contemporary liberation theologians and, by all indications, some of the more widely read; yet very little exists by way of interpretation and critical analysis of Segundo's theology. This is all the more surprising in view of the sheer stature and volume of Segundo's work in comparison to that of other liberation theologians.[3] As little as is written on the theology of Segundo, however, even less has been written about his life and biography. Perhaps the best, though relatively brief, statement of the biographical context of Segundo's thought is provided by Gerald J. Persha in his dissertation, *Juan Luis Segundo: A Study Concerning the Relationship Between the Particularity of the Church and the Universality of Her Mission* (1963-1977) (40-46). I will not attempt to restate Persha's material at this point, though on several occasions throughout this study, as will be noted, I find the biographical information provided by Persha and others indispensable for understanding Segundo.

By word of caution, however, I must say that this study does not pretend in any way to have the scope required by a thorough introduction to the theology of Juan Luis Segundo. For an individual to approach my study as such an introduction would do a great disservice to Segundo and to his theology, which

---

[2]Perhaps the only published work that provides something of a broad overview of the thinking of Juan Luis Segundo is Alfred T. Henelly's *Theologies in Conflict: The Challenge of Juan Luis Segundo* (1979). Theresa Lowe Ching's published dissertation, *Efficacious Love*, captures the essence of Segundo's fundamental dialectic more precisely and accurately than possibly any other interpreter by using the notion of "efficacious love." Marsha Aileen Hewitt's *From Theology to Social Theory: Juan Luis Segundo and the Theology of Liberation* (1990) is a notable recent study that presents Segundo more as a social theorist than a theologian and provides an excellent analysis of Segundo's dialogue with contemporary thinkers outside the field of religion and theology. Other helpful dissertations on Segundo are Gerald Persha's *Juan Luis Segundo: A Study Concerning the Relationship Between the Particularity of the Church and the Universality of Her Mission* (1979), Judith Ann Merkle's *The Fundamental Ethics of Juan Luis Segundo* (1985), Stanley David Slade's *The Theological Method of Juan Luis Segundo* (1979), and Anthony Tambasco's *The Bible for Ethics* (1981). Cf. other monographs and articles listed in my bibliography.

[3]Indeed, of *El hombre de hoy ante Jesús de Nazaret*, Alfred Henelly states that "this monumental work is one more very convincing proof that Segundo is the most profound and creative theologian now working in the Catholic church -- and arguably in the world" (1989b).

I take to be one of the most profound and complicated theological endeavors of our century and one that is, by all indications, still very much alive and unfinished. My goal is much more modest. I do believe, however, that this study has the merit of providing a framework in which we may begin to understand and evaluate his christology.

So far as the criteria are concerned by which the adequacy of both Segundo's and my own approach will be measured, I accept the twin criteria of appropriateness and credibility, as laid out by Schubert M. Ogden (1986:4-6). Ogden's remarks are, of course, directed to the assessment of theological statements and not, specifically, to the assessment of theological method. However, insofar as the task of Christian systematic theology is the critical-constructive interpretation of the witness of Christian faith and insofar as theological method has a particular structure designed to accomplish just that task, I take Ogden's criteria to be applicable to the whole process of theologizing, including both the method and the content of theology. Indeed, as Ogden says, "unlike the special sciences, theology is such that its content and its method are finally not two questions but one" (12). Ogden's criteria, I believe, are especially apropos for this study in light of his own well-known criticism that liberation theologies in general "tend rather to be the rationalization of positions already taken than the process or the product of critical reflection on those positions" (1979a:33). It is my own view that Segundo, perhaps more than any other liberation theologian, asks not only about the appropriateness and relevance of the claims of Christian faith but also about the truth of those claims and, thus, may be fairly said to accept these criteria, at least implicitly, himself. Indeed, as I shall attempt to show, Segundo's dialectic between faith and ideologies is deployed as a methodological device designed to meet these very criteria.

If, however, the "product" (content) of theology is inseparably tied to its "means of production" (method) then, in addition to the above two criteria of adequacy, the question of method is subject to one further criterion that, because it is so obvious, can be easily overlooked -- namely, the criterion of effectiveness. What I mean here is that a method is only as good as its ability to accomplish successfully the task in the service of which it is employed. This is an especially critical distinction in a study such as this because so much of Segundo's work is explicitly "methodological," that is, devoted to a critical reflection on "method." The distinction may seem inconsequential, and yet the difference between what a person wants to do or claims to be doing, on the one hand, and what he or she actually ends up doing, on the other hand, even if those two are never finally separable, is important in theology, just as it is in other areas of life. This, of course, means that we must be clear about the nature and task of christology or we will have very little by which we may judge the effectiveness of the means designed to accomplish the appropriate end.[4] I therefore devote the first part of my study to just such an attempt to make explicit what I take to be the nature and task of christology.

Though I have great appreciation for the available English translations of Segundo's work, all translations of Segundo appearing in this study, unless otherwise noted in my Bibliography, are my own. I have attempted to stay as close as possible to Segundo's own terminology throughout this study, though even an initial reading of Segundo's work reveals how difficult it is to assign strictly single meanings to many of his key terms. Segundo bends and stretches many of his primary words and phrases, assigning them multiple meanings and setting them within numerous contexts. This is largely due to the fact that Segundo's theological probings move in and out of a variety of human dimensions including the religious, scientific, psychological, philosophical, and poetic while his vocabulary is made to encompass this breadth of existence and to serve it.

---

[4]I am not here saying that theology is in some way verified by the criterion of the praxis of faith. The effectiveness I have in mind at this point is not the effectiveness of the praxis of faith but of the praxis of theological method itself as a science, or discipline.

INTRODUCTION

THE PROBLEM OF METHOD IN CONTEMPORARY CHRISTOLOGY

CHAPTER 1

THE NATURE AND TASK
OF CHRISTOLOGY

The fundamental purpose of this study is to contribute to the ongoing discussion of the contemporary significance of Jesus and how that significance is best interpreted by a theology which today seeks to be faithful to the Christian witness of faith, credible to both human experience and reason, and relevant to the contemporary impulse for furthering the struggle for human liberation on our planet. This purpose is to be carried out by means of a critical analysis of Juan Luis Segundo's christological method. In these first two chapters of the study I will set forth what will serve as a background for this study, namely, what I take to be (1) the nature and task of christology, and (2) the contemporary predicament facing christological method. I can only offer an outline of that predicament here, however, since its fullest statement is best developed in the course of my interpretation of Segundo's christology in Part I; indeed, I would argue that what makes Segundo such a worthwhile dialogue partner is his extraordinarily significant restatement of the contemporary constructive problem which faces christology and to which his own work is an attempt at providing a solution.

In this first chapter, I will explore the situation in contemporary theology with regard to christological method along with what I take to be the nature and task of christology in general. The presupposition here is that, apart from determining clearly what it is that christology is supposed to be and to do, no analysis of a particular christological method could make much sense. I find Schubert Ogden's analysis of contemporary revisionary christologies especially helpful in this regard and a useful starting point for this discussion. Then, in the next chapter, using the thought of Segundo, as well as other liberation theologians, I will show that the very nature of the situation in liberation theology with regard to christology makes method extremely problematic, especially in three specific areas: (1) the relationship of theology to praxis, (2) the historical understanding presupposed by and involved in theology, and (3) the role of metaphysics in theology.

At the outset of this study, I would like to draw attention to a fundamental distinction made by Segundo with regard to two different levels of speech about and reflection upon the significance of Christ, each of which often bears the name "christology." One type of christology operates on the level of what we might call "faith," "praxis," "proclamation," or "witness," while the other operates on the level of "theory," "reasoned discourse," or "theology." Segundo makes this

3

distinction by talking about the difference between a "gospel" and a "christology" and writes,

> A christology, like all reasoned discourse, is worked out, studied, and taught. A gospel is preached. . . . Christology, insofar as it is a part of theology, is to be located within the overall effort of the *intellectus fidei*, the effort to understand the faith. A gospel, by contrast, is preached, and in its proclamation, the faith is offered . . . (1982:II:17).

Segundo's distinction here is not dissimilar to that made by Schubert Ogden between "a christology of witness" and "a christology of reflection" (1982:1ff). For Ogden, while a christology of witness is "any and all thought and speech about Jesus who is said to be Christ" (1), a christology of reflection is characterized by its more deliberate and sustained "critical" approach to that witness and, especially, its search for the *meaning* and *truth* of that witness.

The failure to distinguish clearly between these two levels of reflection, as I hope to show in Chapter 6, breaks down the effectiveness of christological method in accomplishing its task and yields especially disastrous results for the relationship between theology and praxis. We will have to return to the question of just what Segundo means by the term "gospel" and the continuity he claims between present day "gospels" and the canonical "gospels" of the New Testament. Suffice it to say, however, that the polysemous nature of the term "gospels" leads me to adopt some other language in this study when referring to this "first-order" level of discourse. Ogden's terminology is helpful, but his distinction is far from absolute, as he himself admits.[5] In this study, I shall use the term "christology" to designate the critico-interpretive inquiry into the significance of Jesus along the order of theological inquiry whereas I will use the term "witness" to designate the religious discourse that is the more immediate expression of the believer's faith and praxis.

The "Revisionary" Consensus

One of the most obvious characteristics of christology during most of the last two centuries has been its project of developing christological responses to what has been perceived to be the problematic nature of the validity of the traditional witness of faith. Schubert Ogden, in his book, *The Point of Christology*, drives to the heart of what contemporary christology intends to be and to do and offers criticism as to how more or less successful christology has

---

[5]For example, Ogden uses the qualifier -- "of reflection" -- to designate the more critically reflective reflection on the christological witness even though both christologies are reflective.

been in its revisionary efforts along with what he sees as the future prospects of revisionary christology. Because of this, Ogden's analysis provides an excellent starting point for determining the situation of christology today as well as the nature and task of christology. I will briefly review Ogden's analysis and then investigate the contemporary situation in liberation theology in the light of that analysis in order to determine precisely what christology is and does.

As Ogden remarks, the "revisionary" efforts of contemporary christology are attempts to "replace or at least reformulate the traditional christology based on scripture and dogma" (5). Ogden singles out two principal reasons for this. The first is the emergence of a modern world-picture and understanding of human existence that renders the conceptuality and symbols of the traditional witness to Christ mythological and problematic in terms of both meaning and truth. The second is difficulty with the doctrine of the incarnation along with the outdated and inadequate metaphysical conceptuality in which it is expressed, its own inner lack of coherence and consistency, and its diminution of the humanity of Christ.

Given these difficulties with traditional christology, the fundamental aims which revisionary christologies are concerned to achieve are, on the one hand, the thorough demythologization of the witness of faith and, on the other hand, the re-expression of "the point of christology" in terms of a more adequate and credible conceptuality and symbolism (11-12). It is to the achievement of these aims that a wide variety of theologians have given themselves and over a sufficient period of time now that it is possible, according to Ogden, to detect three points of consensus shared by contemporary revisionary christologies.

The first consensus point is the identification of the question that christology is supposed to ask and answer as the question "Who is Jesus?" Ogden points out convincingly that, in this respect, revisionary christologies are not very different from traditional christologies because whether a christology focuses on the traditional questions of Christ's dual nature in order to understand how he can be understood to be both God and human or whether a christology goes the route of searching for the historical Jesus in order to know just what kind of life he lived and just what he believed, both are asking about the being of Jesus "in himself" rather than about the significance of Jesus for us. Ogden agrees that the question christology answers is, indeed, the question "Who is Jesus?" but that this question logically implies two other questions:

> On the one hand, there is the question "Who is God?" understood as asking about the ultimate reality upon which we are each dependent for our own being and meaning as human persons. On the other hand, there is the question "Who are we?" or better, "Who am I?" which we are each led to ask more or less explicitly insofar as we are concerned not to miss but to attain our own authentic existence as human beings (28).

To acknowledge who Jesus is, then, entails a particular understanding of his significance for human existence and, so, Ogden refers to the constitutive question of christology as an "existential" question in that "it has to do with the ultimate meaning of one's very existence as a human being" (30). As an "existential" question, however, Ogden argues that the constitutive question of christology -- "Who is Jesus?" -- has both "a metaphysical aspect" and "a moral aspect" corresponding to the two questions above--"Who is God?" and "Who am I?" On the one hand, the metaphysical aspect of the question asks about the meaning of ultimate reality for us, while, on the other hand, the moral aspect of the question asks about the particular self-understanding that is authorized by ultimate reality along with its necessary implications for our moral beliefs and actions. The structure of the christological question, therefore, is inherently complex, and to disregard the complexity of the christological question or to reduce that question to only the one question about the being of Jesus in himself is not simply to leave out part of the whole but seriously to change the question itself. As Ogden says,

> Instead of being the question about the meaning of Jesus for us, given the logically prior questions about the meaning of our own existence and about the ultimate reality by which our existence is determined, it becomes the very different question about the being of Jesus in himself, about *his* existence as determined by ultimate reality, and so on (29).

Just because the christological question is an existential question, however, does not mean that the historical question of who Jesus is becomes irrelevant. According to Ogden, the question of the significance of Jesus could never have been posed in the first place were it not for some particular historical experience of him. Christological inquiry, then, must undertake the historical study of the witness of faith in order to reconstruct the earliest stratum of such witness wherein Jesus' decisive significance is first and normatively communicated. Here, however, we run up against what Ogden specifies as the second point in the revisionary consensus, namely, the identification of the Jesus about which christology speaks as

> the so-called historical Jesus, in the sense of the actual Jesus of history insofar as he can be known to us today by way of empirical-historical inquiry using the writings of the New Testament as sources (16-17).

This point, according to Ogden, presupposes not only a belief in the historical possibility of the quest for and reconstruction of the historical Jesus but a conviction that this quest is also theologically necessary.

We need look no further than to a theologian of the stature of Wolfhart Pannenberg for an example to confirm Ogden's observation. Pannenberg, in *Jesus - God and Man*, claims that all theological statements "win their Christian character" by virtue of their connection with Jesus "himself." Establishing this connection is precisely the task of christology but, as Pannenberg recognizes, the primitive Christian kerygma is clearly stamped by the interests and perspectives of the witnesses to Jesus so that "one cannot simply equate Jesus himself with the apostles' witness to him" (23). What is needed is a christological method that can establish the foundation of our faith, which can only be the historical Jesus of Nazareth. As Pannenberg says,

> Admittedly, this basis of our faith stands the test and must stand the test of our present experience of reality, but it itself lies completely in what happened in the past (27).

Pannenberg then justifies the "possibility" of establishing this foundation as follows:

> One can and must get back to Jesus himself from the witness of the apostles by trying to recognize, and thus making allowance for, the relation of New Testament texts to their respective situations. It is quite possible to distinguish the figure of Jesus himself, as well as the outlines of his message, from the particular perspective in which it is transmitted through this or that New Testament witness. . . . Going back behind the apostolic kerygma to the historical Jesus is, therefore, possible. It is also necessary (23).

If Pannenberg's justification cited above sounds rather weak by way of clarifying the "possibility" of reconstructing the historical Jesus, that is because it is really the theological "necessity" of such reconstruction that, for Pannenberg, drives its "possibility"; indeed, it often appears that, for Pannenberg, simply because something *must* be done, it *can* be done.

Pannenberg believes that any antithesis between Jesus as he actually was and the witness of faith to Jesus is "unsatisfying" and forces christology to take up the task of elucidating the continuity between the two. Furthermore, the necessity of reconstructing the historical Jesus is confirmed, in Pannenberg's view, by his belief that the inner unity of scripture is destroyed if we cannot penetrate behind the manifold witnesses that make up the New Testament to the one sure historical basis for their witness--Jesus as he was. As Pannenberg puts it,

> To go back behind the New Testament text to Jesus himself is unavoidable for another reason. Only in this way is it possible to see the unity that binds together the New Testament witnesses (24).

To Pannenberg's mind, as to many contemporary theologians, there are really only two choices: "Must Christology begin with Jesus himself or with the kerygma of his community?" (22)   But offered only the choice between a faith that has support in the historical Jesus himself or a faith that rests on a kerygma consisting of assertions for which Jesus himself is irrelevant, Pannenberg, like many other contemporary theologians, opts clearly for the historical Jesus.

The third point of consensus, according to Ogden, is a general agreement about the conditions necessary for truthfully asserting the christological predicates of the subject Jesus. Here, says Ogden,

> Jesus can be truthfully said to be Christ, or any of the other things that the christology of witness has appropriately asserted or implied him to be, if, and only if, he himself, as a human person, perfectly actualized the possibility of authentic self-understanding (1982:65).

This third point is obviously a by-product of the second point and focuses on the character, consciousness, and faith of the historical Jesus as the key to interpreting his significance for us.

Method and Complexity of the Christological Question

Perhaps the greatest value of Ogden's analysis of the contemporary christological setting is his compelling argument for recognizing the complexity of the christological question. Rather than being the simple question as to who Jesus is, the question that constitutes christology as such is the more complex question as to what the "significance" of Jesus is, the complexity of that question arising precisely from the nature of the word "significance." To ask about the "significance" of something is to ask not only about the object but about those of us to whom that object is said to be significant. It is to ask about our context, our interests, our relationships; it is to ask not only about the contingent features of our daily world and how we interact and relate to the challenges and opportunities that confront us but also about the very presuppositions of our interaction and existence in any and every case--that is, the features of reality with which we always have to do no matter what happens.

Just how the complexity of the christological question is understood, it seems to me, is absolutely crucial for evaluating the adequacy or effectiveness of christological method. Recent "praxis-oriented" theologies, such as the various theologies of liberation, have much to offer, it seems to me, at precisely this point. Liberation theology, for example, stresses the relationship between theological theory and the concrete praxis that both precedes and follows such theory in such a way as to demonstrate the role of praxis in critically interpreting the significance of Jesus. If Ogden is correct and the question of who we are is implicit in the question of who Jesus is for us, a thorough exploration of how our praxis both determines and is determined by the meaning we give to our existence would seem to be fundamental to the method of any christological inquiry.

We must, of course, be clear as to the meaning of the word, "praxis," at this point. Clodovis Boff defines praxis as "the *complexus of practices* oriented to the transformation of society, the making of history" (6).[6] Boff goes on to explain that this praxis provides the *de facto* milieu for interpreting the significance of Jesus and that our particular interpretations of the significance of Jesus constantly issue forth in ever new forms of praxis. Furthermore, as Boff says, praxis has a fundamentally "political" connotation "inasmuch as it is through the intermediary of the political that one can bring an influence to bear on social structures" (6). The implications of this understanding of praxis for theological method are significant. In the following statement, José Míguez Bonino develops some of those implications while claiming that the realm of praxis today is, more than ever, the socio-political realm:

> the political realm [is] the sphere in which people take responsibility for the world and history. This entails several things: (a) recognizing that theology operates under the conditioning of the political realm with its conflicts and its own kind of rationality; (b) incorporating socio-political instruments and categories in our theological reflection, realizing that the political sphere is the realm of structures, ideologies, and power; (c) abandoning the assumption that theology can prescind from politics and be nontemporal while at the same time taking on and articulating some concrete option: in our case, the struggle for liberation (1979:262).[7]

Praxis, then, is much more than sheer activity but is the process whereby humans shape their reality and are, themselves, shaped by it. If we return to the question

---

[6]See also the definition offered by Paulo Freire -- praxis is "reflection and action upon the world in order to transform it" (36). Many liberation theologians, such as Segundo himself, maintain an implicit dialectic of "reflection" and "action" in the one word "praxis":

> The greek word *praxis*, or *practice* as it is translated into English, is generally used in our language to highlight the notion of a practice grounded in a theory and, at the same time, the way this theory is enhanced and revised by new elements discovered in our experience (1982:II:581).

[7]Cf. also Clodovis Boff who recognizes that a proper understanding of praxis has a "fundamentally *political* connotation . . . inasmuch as it is through the intermediary of the political that one can bring an influence to bear on social structures" (6).

of the significance of Jesus and if we insist that it includes the question not only of who Jesus was but of who we are, surely an adequate christological method must ask about the praxis that both determines and is determined by the meaning we give to our existence.

Of course, much more must be said in the course of this study about the relationship between christological theory and historical praxis and the implications of that relationship for christological method. For example, we will have to consider whether and, if so, in what way and to what extent the theologian's own praxis and commitments impact both the method and content of his or her christology. Then also, we must determine whether and, if so, in what way and to what extent praxis may serve as a criterion of the validity of one's christology. Though I have not explicitly mentioned Segundo's thought at this point, we shall see that he has a great deal to offer on the subject. At least one thing must be said, however, about the relationship between praxis and christology in terms of the complexity of the christological question and in terms of the method that goes about asking and answering that question. For liberation theologians such as Boff and Míguez Bonino, the place of praxis as providing the *de facto* milieu of theology does not mean that theology simply goes about its work and then, afterwards, "applies" its results to concrete socio-political circumstances or specific human practices. Such a procedure treats truth as a commodity and, in the case of christology, never adequately allows itself to "know" the human being for whom Jesus is said to be significant. This it cannot fully do apart from developing and utilizing the tools necessary for mediating the socio-political reality (praxis) in which our witness is born and raised, on the one hand, and into which it must be interpreted, on the other hand. A christological method which today adequately goes about interpreting the significance of Jesus must admit that the human being for whom Jesus is significant is no more readily available, self-contained, and a "finished product" than is the witness of faith simply some kind of "deposit" lying before us ready simply to be "quarried." An adequate christological method today must draw not only from the insights of biblical hermeneutics and biblical criticism but from the social sciences, thereby enabling it to engage in an exploration of the meaning, truth, and relevance of the witness to Christ.

Not unlike the above noted liberation theologians, Ogden also emphasizes that the christological question is a complex question because it does not ask simply about who Jesus is but also about our own self-understanding and the implications of that understanding for our moral beliefs and actions ("praxis"). However, for Ogden, as I have already indicated in a preliminary way, the christological question is even more complex than most liberation theologians allow, having not only a moral (or what I shall call a "praxic") aspect, but a metaphysical aspect as well. This is true, according to Ogden, because to ask about the significance of Jesus for us is to ask about the fundamental and necessary conditions of our very existence and about that basic "faith" by which we all hold, as Ogden says, that "our own existence and all existence are somehow justified or worthwhile" and that, therefore,

> ultimate reality is such as to authorize some understanding of ourselves as authentic, just as, conversely, there is some understanding of our existence that is authentic because it is the self-understanding authorized by ultimate reality (1982:30).

But if ultimate reality is understood as authorizing a particular self-understanding and its implications for praxis, then reflection on the meaning of who we are requires that we also reflect on the meaning of ultimate reality for us, or what Ogden refers to as the "metaphysical" aspect of the christological question.

The dual structure of the faith that underlies our existence, and thereby the dual structure of an adequate reflection on that faith, is further confirmed by Ogden's analysis of religion, where the question of faith and the meaning of our existence is explicitly asked and answered. Utilizing the insights of anthropologist Clifford Geertz, Ogden points out that religion has aspects that relate it closely to both metaphysics and ethics. As Geertz says, religious symbols

> function to synthesize a people's ethos -- the tone, character and quality of their life, its moral and aesthetic style and mood -- and their world-view -- the picture they have of the way things in sheer actuality are, their most comprehensive ideas of order (79).

Each aspect in this synthesis is mutually complementary, as Geertz explains:

> In religious belief and practice a group's ethos is rendered intellectually reasonable by being shown to represent a way of life ideally adapted to the actual state of affairs the world-view describes, while the world-view is rendered emotionally convincing by being presented as an image of an actual state of affairs peculiarly well-arranged to accommodate such a way of life (79).

Religion, then, on the basis of Geertz's analysis, may be said to have aspects that relate it closely to both metaphysics and ethics while remaining, as Ogden points out, using Schleiermacher's phrase, "the necessary and indispensable third" (1982:33).

Given the above analysis of the structure of faith and of religion, which explicates that faith, I propose, for the purposes of this study, to proceed by affirming that the question about the significance of Jesus requires that we answer, on the one hand, the question about the meaning which we give to our existence ("faith") and the praxis which both shapes and is shaped by that meaning and, on the other hand, the question about the ultimate reality that grounds and authorizes our faith and praxis as authentic. I propose that we designate the latter of these two questions as the "metaphysical" question, as does Ogden, and that we designate the former of the two as the "praxic" question,[8] in order thereby to highlight the important role of praxis not only in giving expression to the faith that we take to be authorized as authentic by ultimate reality, but in shaping and determining that faith as well. Far from implying that praxis is thereby the only criterion of truth for christology, this understanding of the complexity of the christological question takes the relationship between praxis and faith as just one aspect of that question and forces us to admit that christologies which conceive themselves as having no other determinations than praxis understood as sheer moral activity are not critical reflection on the faith but a mere reflex of faith. A proper understanding of praxis yields for christology its context, its tools, and the categories of its articulation but, as Adolphe Gesché says,

---

[8]It might seem counterproductive to use a concept as prone to ambiguity and as subject to such a wide variety of interpretation as "praxis" to "clear things up," so to speak. Nonetheless, I believe that it is both possible and necessary to do so. In the first place, much of the confusion about the notion of "praxis" in liberation theology stems from understanding it as mere "practice," "activity," or even "morality." Here liberation theologians are as much to blame as anyone else for the confusion (Cf. Gutiérrez's understanding of praxis as "real charity, action, and commitment to the service of men" (1973:11)). There is, of course, a sense in which praxis is sheer moral activity, or the practice of the faith. But then that is not the sense in which praxis is an aspect of the existential question as to "who we are" nor is it the sense in which praxis can be a criterion of the practical credibility of a theological statement. There is, however, a more adequate understanding of praxis that combines our own self-understanding with the activity that flows from that self-understanding. As Roger Haight says, in his interpretation of liberation theology, *An Alternate Vision*:

> Praxis does not simply mean action, behavior or practice. Rather it means a particular form of historical behavior, not of course blind or unmixed with reason or theory. Its meaning supposes the broad and general truth that history is in some degree in human hands, that it is moved neither by blind fate, nor by a closed set of laws, nor by a predetermined providence. History is open and in some measure can be directed by human beings (1985:41).

In my opinion, what Haight more or less points toward in this statement is the insight that "praxis" is not sheer activity, even moral activity, but activity that is conscious, directed, and expressive of one's basic self-understanding as a human being.

this does not mean that the word "praxis" should sound in our ears like the voice of a fairy godmother, making everything all right. Practice is not the criterion of truth, any more than is any other art, and it is not by being personally committed and "engaged" that theologians create a work of pertinent theology. It is precisely a *science* that theologians must practice. It is as theologians that they must guarantee the conditions for entry into that practice for whose sake they are creating a relevant, operative theory (xv).

In summary, then, given what I take to be the unavoidable complexity of the christological question, I think we must so understand the method of any christology which intends critically to interpret the significance of Jesus for us today as at least asking and answering the following questions:

a) "Who is God?," or alternatively, What is the meaning of ultimate reality for us? This is the metaphysical aspect of the christological question and presupposes the properly metaphysical question as to the structure of ultimate reality in itself.

b) "Who are We?," or alternatively, What is the meaning of our own existence and its relationship to the historical praxis that both shapes and is shaped by the faith which is authorized as authentic by the structure of ultimate reality? This is the praxic aspect of the christological question and presupposes the question as to the structure of our historical praxis in itself, that is, of our moral-political beliefs and actions.

c) "Who is Jesus?" This is the existential-historical question as to who Jesus is in terms of his significance for us. The inclusion of this historical question prevents us from thinking that because the above two logical components of the existential question have been asked, the christological question is thus reduced to merely an existential question. As Ogden insists:

> This, however, it could not possibly be, because even though it is not *only* a question about Jesus, it very definitely *is* a question about Jesus; and this means that it could never so much as arise, much less ever be answered, except on the basis of particular historical experience of the Jesus about whose meaning for human existence it is the question (1982:40).

While this "particular historical experience" is beyond the control of empirical-historical inquiry, that is not to say, however, that the empirical-historical inquiry into who Jesus was understood to be by the apostolic witness of faith ceases to become theologically important. On the contrary, such a quest for the earliest stratum of the tradition of witness lying behind the varied and sometimes contradictory christological formulations of the New Testament is theologically necessary, not in order to arrive at what Jesus actually said or did, but in order to arrive at the normative Christian witness which these and later christological formulations claim to express and against which they are to be tested for appropriateness.

CHAPTER 2

THE SITUATION IN
LIBERATION THEOLOGY

Much like the Franciscan and other "poverty" movements of the 12th and 13th centuries, the movement known as "liberation theology" has been, in an important sense, an ecclesiastical movement -- that is, it has focused on new and unique paths for being the church. Thus, whether liberation theology has taken a more popular form that attempts to provide answers to the problems which surface in the everyday life of Christian people and which they bring forward when they meet in the "Comunidades de Base" that have sprung up throughout Latin America, or whether it has taken a more intellectual approach that attempts to unmask ideologies through various intellectual tools such as the social sciences, thus leading to a new hermeneutic and a new vision of what theology should become, the fundamental vision of liberation theologians has been ecclesiastical and pastoral.

Also like the Franciscans, the liberation movement has had rather mixed success within the official church, sometimes being scorned and rebuked and at other times being endorsed and co-opted. This has only deepened the sense in which liberation theology has been preoccupied with ecclesiastical matters, if for no other reason than that its very existence depended on what it said about the church and what the church said about it.

But even more like the Franciscans, much of the stimulus behind liberation theology is an "image" of who Jesus is. For the Franciscans, this image was a naked, suffering, crucified, and poor Christ without property or possessions and joined up with the ideal of the *vita apostolica* and a commitment to voluntary poverty. For liberation theologians, however, the image is more that of a "Jesus the Liberator" who struggles with and on behalf of the poor and the oppressed -- an activist, revolutionary Jesus. Whereas, for the Franciscans, the image of Jesus on the cross was so interpreted as demanding an identification with those who suffer and the renunciation of power and property, for liberation theology, the image of the crucified Christ is taken as a call to challenge the kind of political power that performed and continues to perform such acts of political and economic execution as we find in the cross.

The Franciscans, of course, had St. Bonaventure, who achieved for the movement an agreed way of expressing, defining, and construing the kinds of images to which Francis had given expression. For liberation theology, however, the "image" of who Jesus is remains rather consistently at the level of "image" and one of the more obvious characteristics of liberation theology is its preoccupation with the proclamation of this image of Jesus rather than with more traditional christological theory. Thus, one often hears the charge that liberation theology has no christology, even from among liberation theologians themselves. As Segundo says,

> Latin American theology, whether or not it is called the theology of liberation, lacks a christology (1982:II:27).

Hugo Assmann, responding to the accusation that liberation theology has no christology says, "this charge . . . is just" (1984:125). Assmann justifies this situation, however, by claiming that the challenge of liberation christology does not lie in any revolutionary new theory but in doing christology under the banner of a particular image of Christ.

> Incipient liberation christology has said nothing to date that the churches themselves do not support, or have not supported--powerfully, at times. Only, it has said it under the opposing ideological sign. . . . The challenging image of Christ the Liberator is ever in the fore, it points ever out ahead of us, for we encounter it only on the frontiers of the future. Its challenge to the liberation of the oppressed implies an ongoing revolution, yes, but a realistic, not an idealistic one (133).

Claus Bussman, in his study of Latin American christologies, likewise confirms that the uniqueness and common denominator of liberation christologies is not primarily their theoretical interest:

> They make their christological study neither as pure historians and exegetes, nor as systematic theologians. Their interest in Jesus is practical (47).

One might draw the conclusion from this situation that what liberation theology really offers is what I earlier noted as a "christology of witness" rather than a "christology of reflection" (Ogden), or a "gospel" rather than a "christology" (Segundo). Segundo would disagree, however, with this assessment and claims that liberation theology does, indeed, critically reflect on and interpret the significance of Jesus and that there is a traceable pattern in the method used by liberation theology to do just this. In fact, the lack of christology in liberation theology, according to Segundo, is best explained not as an accident or deficiency but as a methodological choice taken in order to reverse the illegitimate methods used by classical christologies for so many years.

In many respects, the various christologies of liberation, may be characterized as "revisionary," given Ogden's analysis delineated above. Certainly they are driven by the concern to replace or reinterpret traditional theological statements, though not so much because of the lack of theoretical credibility on the part of those statements as the lack of "practical" credibility -- i.e., their thoroughly ideological use in consciously or unconsciously sanctioning injustice in the world. As Segundo says about the origins of liberation theology,

> de-ideologizing our customary interpretation of Christian faith was, for us, the necessary task in order to get the whole Church to carry to our people an understanding of our faith both more faithful to Jesus' Gospel and more capable of contributing to the humanization of all people and social classes on our continent (1990:357).

Though Ogden, in *The Point of Christology*, does not initially include this problem of "practical" credibility as one of the main issues leading to the development of revisionary christology, he does go on to affirm it as a criterion that any adequate christology today must now meet and goes on to claim that what is now required is a procedure of "deideologizing" and "political interpretation" designed to meet the criterion of practical credibility. This, of course, corresponds to the procedure of "demythologizing" and "existentialist interpretation" designed to meet the criterion of theoretical credibility.

But if liberation theology may be considered "revisionary" because of its desire to deideologize and reformulate traditional interpretations of scripture and dogma, I think we have even more reason to consider it so in terms of the three points of a revisionary consensus outlined in Chapter 1. In the first place, as to the identification of the constitutive question of christology, liberation theologians are fairly consistent in assuming that it is Jesus' own identity, consciousness, character, and "faith" and, thus, the question as to who Jesus actually was in himself that is of primary interest. Of course, some liberation theologians, such as Segundo, would insist that their interest is not in the being of Jesus "in himself" but rather in Jesus' significance for us. Segundo states, for example:

> Both christologies "from above" (dealing with such categories as messiahship and divinity) and those "from below" (in search of those categories from concrete history) respond, then, to one question: *What* (or who) is Jesus? It is a question that Jesus himself rejected and that blocks access to him (1982:II:29).

Segundo believes that the one sure way to misunderstand Jesus and fail to appropriate the meaning of his message for us is to focus simply on "who Jesus is" at the expense of his significance for us.

Even so, however, I for one am not prepared, on the basis of these remarks by Segundo, to conclude that he shares the same concerns as Ogden with respect to the question that christology asks and answers. If I understand Ogden correctly, the real issue at this point is whether the christological question is sufficiently complex to move us beyond a mere description of Jesus to an interpretation of his significance in terms of our own existence as human beings. Ogden criticizes the tendency to ask about who Jesus is apart from what he refers to as the "logically prior" questions about who we are and about who God is. Thus, simply because a christology states that it is interested in the meaning of Jesus "for us" does not exempt that christology from Ogden's criticism. What we find when we come to Segundo is, indeed, a keen and helpful analysis of the logically prior question as to who the human being is for whom Jesus is said to be significant. Segundo provides a great deal of exploration and insight into the process of communicating meaning and values within a culture and lays a solid anthropological groundwork for understanding how the meaning and values adopted are structured and lived out in a human life based on the concrete realities with which we are faced. However, just as in other liberation theologies, there is an express disinterest in, or more correctly, disdain for the "prior question" about the ultimate reality by which our existence is determined and, thus, the meta-physical aspect of the christological question. As we shall have further opportunity to see, Segundo rejects metaphysical analysis as having any essential role at all in interpreting or communicating the significance of Jesus for us, as in the conveyance or adoption of meaning and values, generally. For Segundo, rather, the significance of Jesus for us is interpreted by beginning with the history of Jesus and only then moving to any consideration of ultimate reality:

> in the affirmation "Jesus is God," the information does not move from an already known predicate to the not yet determined and still ambiguous historical figure of Jesus. On the contrary, the concept of divinity, with its special characteristics applicable only to a singular, must be filled with attributes arising out of the concrete history of Jesus. This means that any "cosmic" interpretation of Jesus ought to begin with what we know of his history, and not with what we supposedly know about what God is or might be (1982:II:892).

Segundo is not alone in this judgement as the following quotation from Jon Sobrino illustrates:

> The Chalcedonian formula presupposes certain concepts that in fact cannot be presupposed when it comes to Jesus. [It] assumes we know who and what God is and who and what human beings are. But we cannot explain the figure of Jesus by presupposing such concepts because Jesus himself calls into question people's very understanding of God and human beings.

We may use "divinity" and "humanity" as nominal definitions to somehow break the hermeneutic circle, but we cannot use them as real definitions, already known, in order to understand Jesus. Our approach should start from the other end (1987: 9).

All this is not to say, however, that Ogden proposes a procedure that begins with an already defined concept--"God"--and then proceeds to interpret Jesus in terms of that concept. But what Ogden does make abundantly clear is that no interpretation of Jesus can claim for him the kind of significance for which the New Testament writers argue apart from the *logically* prior question as to the ultimate reality with which we all have to do no matter what else happens, has happened, or will happen.

As to the second point in Ogden's analysis, there is ample evidence of the virtually wholesale agreement among liberation theologians in identifying the subject of the christological assertion as the historical Jesus. There is, of course, a great deal of variety as to just what is meant by the historical Jesus and little attention is generally given among liberation theologians to careful consideration of the historical possibilities of uncovering that figure. There is, however, a consensus among liberation theologians that the appeal to the historical Jesus is not only historically possible but theologically necessary in order to overturn classical formulations that begin with Jesus' divinity and then distort, de-politicize, and de-historicize his historical existence. Jon Sobrino summarizes the situation as follows:

> In Latin America liberation theology has focused spontaneously on the historical Jesus for guidance and orientation. Since it arose out of the concrete experience and praxis of faith within a lived commitment to liberation, it soon realized that the universality of Christ amid those circumstances could only be grasped from the standpoint of the concrete Christ of history. The historical Jesus would serve as a satisfactory midway point between two extremes: turning Christ into an abstraction on the one hand, or putting him to direct and immediate ideological uses on the other (1978: 10).

Sobrino's fundamental justification for appealing to the historical Jesus as a starting point for christology is premised on a comparison between the contemporary situation in Latin America and the situation in which Jesus himself lived. The presence of poverty and exploitation in both situations as well as the way conditions are interpreted as sinful in both circumstances provide helpful points of contact for a method of correlation that gives impetus to a vital expression of contemporary Christian faith in concrete historical circumstances of oppression and injustice.

Gustavo Gutiérrez, like Sobrino, notes how the situations of injustice and revolution in which many Latin American Christians find themselves have compelled them to ask about the attitude of Jesus regarding his own socio-political environment. Gutiérrez claims that the very fact that so many people have to even ask this question is the by-product of a christological tradition that obscures the life and activity of Jesus with a mound of theological meanings and themes.

> The life of Jesus is thus placed outside history, unrelated to the real forces at play. Jesus and those whom he befriended, or whom he confronted and whose hostility he earned, are deprived of all human content. They are there reciting a script (1973: 226).

Gutiérrez insists instead that we must return to a recovery of "the historical Jesus" and, especially, the attitudes and relationships maintained by Jesus with regard to, for example, the political authorities of his day, the Zealots, or other leaders of the Jewish people.

> To approach the man Jesus of Nazareth, in whom God was made flesh, to penetrate not only in his teaching, but also in his life, what it is that gives his word an immediate, concrete context, is a task which more and more needs to be undertaken (226).

With regard to Ogden's third point of consensus among revisionary christologies, here again we find that liberation theologians, in general, are rather unanimous in concluding that, in some form or another, it is precisely the fact that Jesus lives out a meaningful and liberative faith that makes him Christ. Segundo Galilea, for example, undertakes his theological reflection by appeal to Jesus' own commitments and perspectives.

> Instead of taking a point of departure in the rational process of theology and the human sciences, I propose to approach the subject from the gospel --from the attitude of Christ himself toward the political contingencies of his time (93).

For Galilea, this process of examining Jesus' own outlook and deportment yields a norm of Christian activity that compels the contemporary Christian to dedicate himself or herself to the "prophetic proclamation of the kingdom," especially in situations characterized by conflict and politicization, as in Latin America. Like Galilea, Leonardo Boff also shows a keen interest in the relevance of the faith of Jesus for theology in a way that brings together, on the one hand, the significance of Jesus' own faith as that which makes him the Christ and, on the other hand, the significance of Jesus' own faith as that which ought to be reflected in and expressed by Jesus' followers. For Boff, Jesus is "a person of extraordinary creative imagination," an individual with "courage," "a person of extraordinary good sense and sound reason," and, as Boff puts it, "Jesus was an extraordinary believer and had faith. Faith was his mode of existence" (1978: 113).

Sobrino also appeals extensively to the faith of Jesus as that which the Christian is to imitate.

> In his historical life Jesus posed many concrete demands to human beings; but the most comprehensive one was the general demand to reproduce his own way of life in oneself and one's life (1978: 115).

The faith which Jesus demands of us, therefore, is the faith which he himself exhibited and which, thus actualized, orients him to God in such a way as to be the Christ. With regard to Jesus' own experience of faith, Sobrino writes:

> When a systematic reconstruction is made of that experience, it is clear that Jesus was utterly convinced that living means living for others and serving others. Thus it corresponds to the reality of his vision of God. . . . His orientation to the mystery of God certainly makes his life an ex-ist-ence--a life not centered upon itself, but directed to someone else who gives it meaning. Precisely because his orientation is to a particular God, and not to just any divinity, his ex-istence is pro-existence. Existing for others and the conviction that one is thereby related to God is Jesus' fundamental experience (1987: 125).

We will have extensive opportunity in this study to consider Segundo's views on this matter. Certainly his appeal to the historical Jesus is much more complicated and nuanced than that offered by Sobrino, for example. Nonetheless, it is worth noting at this point that, as with Sobrino, so, for Segundo, it is precisely the fact that Jesus himself held the values that he held that makes him interesting and meaningful to us. As Segundo says,

> all of this work and, in particular, this last part, could be described as the methodical acceptance of the challenge contained in this profound and accurate observation from Guerrero: "We would save ourselves much wasted effort trying to gain believers in Jesus if we would try to interest human beings in what was really original in the life of Jesus -- his faith, i.e., the faith of Jesus (1982: II: 803).

Moving on now beyond the three points of consensus identified by Ogden as characteristic of contemporary revisionary christologies, I would like to highlight three central features of the method used by liberation theology to interpret the significance of Jesus, each of which, in its own way, points up a specific problematic with regard to christological method and each of which dovetails with one of the three components of the task of christology as outlined in Chapter 1--the praxic question, the metaphysical question, and the historical question.

Christology and Praxis

The first general feature of the christological method of recent Latin American liberation theologies is the selection of the particular "image" of Jesus, as noted above, based on a prior commitment to the struggle for liberation. Thus, the Jesus of liberation christology is "Jesus the Liberator," the Jesus who struggles with and on behalf of the poor and oppressed. This, of course, is but the christological implication of a more general principle of liberation theology with regard to the relationship between theology and praxis in which, as Segundo puts it, "commitment is the first step."[9]

Thanks to the efforts of liberation theologians over the past few decades, we are coming to a fuller cognizance of just how our "commitments," our respective social locations, and our own historical praxis are the starting point for all that we say and do. It is precisely the concern to show just how this is so that has led liberation theologians to insist on an essential role for the utilization of the tools and data of the social sciences in the process of theologizing. As Gustavo Gutiérrez says of the Latin American Conference of Bishops held in Medellín, Columbia in 1968, where liberation theology is said to have found its official genesis,

> Medellín marks the beginning of a new relationship between theological and pastoral language on the one hand and the social sciences which seek to interpret this reality on the other (1973: 136).

---

[9]This principle typically goes by the name of "orthopraxis" which, here, designates a "prior commitment" to liberation. In its broadest connotations, however, this principle refers simply to the fundamental notion that it is only insofar as it is lived that faith can provide for theology an object that is at once relevant and meaningful. Some liberation theologians extend this more general notion to include praxis as the criterion of theological truth; others extend it to include the idea that theologians must "take sides"; and still others extend it to include the notion that theology must be done through the eyes of the poor as, for example, in the case of Gustavo Gutiérrez:

> It is not enough to know that praxis must precede reflection; we must also realize that the historical subject of that praxis is the poor -- the people who have been excluded from the pages of history. Without the poor as subject, theology degenerates into academic exercise (1978: 247).

Most liberation theologians, however, go beyond the relatively modest lessons from the sociology of knowledge to claim that one particular "praxis"--a praxis that is committed to the liberation of the poor--provides the only legitimate starting point and, itself, serves as a criterion of truth for theology. The result of this procedure for christology is that it becomes a rationalization of a vision for change and the justification of an already existing historical praxis rather than critical interpretation of the significance of Jesus. Thus, the image of Christ chosen becomes little more than a projection of determinate social conditions and ideologies.

Nowhere is this procedure clearer than in the christological work of Jon Sobrino. Sobrino sums up the situation into which liberation theology entered as follows:

> On our continent, faith in Christ has been maintained for centuries without any special christological discussion. We have accepted the dogmatic statements underscoring the divinity of Christ rather than those stressing his humanity, and those emphasizing the individual and transcendent rather than the historical, salvific significance of this divinity. Meanwhile, popular piety has reinterpreted Christ's divinity in its own fashion -- as power in the face of the people's helplessness -- and has sought in its own ways to recover his humanity, especially in the suffering Christ (1987: 4).

Liberation theology, according to Sobrino, entered this situation with the intent of assisting in the historical and ecclesial praxis of liberation into which these powerless Christians had already inserted themselves. These Christians, says Sobrino,

> were searching both for a way to see their historical praxis as consistent with their actual Christian faith and for the support and radicalization that faith lends that praxis. Therefore they went back to the figure of Jesus, and this was the origin of an incipient reflection on Christ (10).

Reflection on Christ, then, is the service that Sobrino claims to provide and this reflection is for the stated purpose of "inviting the church, precisely in virtue of its faith in Christ, to insert itself into a task of liberation that would now be seen to be specifically Christian in form" (10). Christology, then, legitimizes, or as Sobrino puts it, provides an "ecclesial authenticity" to the praxis of liberation.

Sobrino sees the primary danger of his own conception of the task of christology as "the functionalization of Christ" whereby

> the Liberator would disappear behind the liberation. . . the Liberator would be used only when he was relevant for "historical" liberation, ignoring

"transcendent" liberation. . . . the ultimate criteria of liberation, even in its historical aspect, would not be sought in the Liberator, but elsewhere (10).

Sobrino thinks that even though this danger of "horizontalism" exists, liberation theology protects against it sufficiently in three ways. First, liberation theology points to "the historical Jesus" and not to liberation itself or to other liberators that would surpass Christ. This emphasis converges with an evangelistic tenor that calls the believer to the historical person of Jesus rather than to a lesser personage or an abstract conceptuality. Second, because liberation theology presents Christ as the one who himself moves humanity toward liberation by becoming "the prototype of the new human being for whom liberation strives," liberation theology thus utilizes its horizontalism precisely to demonstrate that Jesus is Christ and thus to include a "vertical" dimension in its reflection. Third, according to Sobrino, liberation theology has as one of its basic aims the demonstration of how Jesus is already used horizontally by traditional theology in order to justify the oppression of the poor. A christology of liberation can bring an epistemological suspicion that is required to counteract and correct this tendency in its presentation of a new "figure of Christ" (13).

Each of these points in its own way, however, demonstrates just how problematic is this conception of the method and task of christology. Whether Jesus is presented as "the historical Jesus," or as the "prototype of the new human being," or as some other figure set over against more traditional and, perhaps, oppressive figures, liberation christology, along the lines laid out by Sobrino, has not really moved far beyond proclaiming an "image" of Christ and that image has been selected based on a prior commitment to liberating praxis and the ability of the image selected to justify and legitimate that praxis. In this way, the task of christology as critical interpretation of the significance of Jesus is seriously undermined. Though Sobrino sees the danger of his christological method as "functionalism" or "horizontalism," the real problem is that his method fundamentally consists in a rationalization or justification of a position already taken and, therefore, runs counter to the process of critical reflection.

Segundo's approach to christology is much more nuanced than Sobrino's with regard to the relationship between praxis and theology, though the similarities between the two are still quite clear. There is no question that Segundo makes his turn to christology in order to determine what significance Jesus has for the process of humanization and liberation. For Segundo, it is liberation that draws us to Jesus and not the other way around. In fact, Segundo is quite tempted by the idea of portraying a "Jesus for atheists" (1982: II: 25) by which he means that, rather than starting with Jesus as truth incarnate or Jesus as divine and then moving to the significance of Jesus for liberation, we instead start with liberation and move to what makes Jesus interesting for liberation. There is, of course, a circle here because, for many, it is, indeed, Jesus who points them to liberation in the first place. But why do we listen to Jesus? Because he is interesting for liberation! Segundo's primary point, it seems to me, however, is that it is first and foremost Jesus' relevance for liberation rather than his character as divine that should be of interest to us. Segundo even suggests that when it comes to christology, "a potential atheism is an unavoidable hermeneutic prerequisite" (25).

In fairness, not all liberation theologians exhibit the same tendencies with regard to the relationship of theology to praxis. Clodovis Boff, for example, can say that "the theology of liberation finds its point of departure, its milieu and its finality in praxis" and that praxis is "the fundamental locus of theology, the 'place' where theology occurs" (xxi), and yet Boff takes a position against what he calls the "pragmatism" of theology where theology is no more than "the *voice of praxis*" (15). This version deserves no other name than that of "ideology," says Boff. According to Boff, the notion that praxis is the place where theology begins means that, like any other science, theology

> is inserted in a complex network of material and historical determinations that situate it in a particular location within the socio-historical field. All theory is susceptible of geographical location and historical dating. Consequently, all theory is dependent on multiple conditions of production: materials, cultures, policies, politics, and so on; and hence its results can be directed toward this or that social, political, or other objective, and so on (16).

It is in this way, then, that praxis holds a certain primacy over theory, but that can never mean that praxis is a criterion of the verification of theology. As Boff says,

> From the viewpoint of theological practice, (political) praxis neither is nor can be the criterion of (theological) truth. The reason is simple: political practice is of another order than that of theoretical practice. Thus neither has anything in common with the other. The thesis that praxis is the criterion of truth is theologically nonpertinent. It seeks to compare the incomparable (198; Cf. 199ff).

Christology and Metaphysics

A second feature of christological method found in liberation theologies, generally, stems from their disdain for the traditional preoccupation with the divinity of Jesus at the expense of the humanity of Jesus. This shift, characteristic of revisionary christologies in general, is accompanied in liberation theology by a virtually unanimous rejection of metaphysics as having relevance for interpreting or communicating the significance of Jesus, the argument being that metaphysics tends to steer us away from history and experience toward vague abstraction and otherworldliness. In the case of liberation christology, however, the refocus on the humanity of Jesus (or the historical Jesus) for which it calls is typically accompanied by an uncritical dragging along of classical statements of Christ's divinity, thus undercutting the very humanity which it seeks to preserve. As Sobrino says,

> The christology of liberation, for its part, accepts these statements of the New Testament and the early councils on the divinity of Christ, even though it has not considered it its specific task to undertake an in-depth analysis of these statements. The statements rather subsist in a symbiosis with the specific elements of liberation christology, whose very radicalness in its presentation of Jesus proceeds, in part and not always in thematized form, but nonetheless really, from its acceptance of the divinity of Christ (1987: 23).

What actually happens in this word "symbiosis," however, is, at best, the taking of classical, problematic statements as to Jesus' divinity and suspending them alongside of the historical Jesus for appearance ("ecclesial authenticity") or, at worst, a taking of these classical statements as to the divinity of Jesus and placing them in contradiction with a view which holds that precisely what satisfies the conditions of calling Jesus the Christ is his own perfect actualization historically of the demands of faith so that, as Sobrino says, "his divine transcendency [is] based on his personal history" (24).

The problem, of course, is that a christology that wishes to revise the traditional preoccupation with the divinity of Jesus in order to interpret his significance in a way that is at once more credible and more relevant to human projects and struggles requires something more than concentration on a different "figure" of Jesus, or a different "aspect" of his person (i.e., his "humanity"). It requires some sort of logic and conceptuality which can clarify what makes Jesus the Christ -- i.e., what gives his significance an "ultimacy" -- even if that ultimacy cannot take the form of a retreat either to some sort of divine physiology or some otherworldly reality. But, as already indicated in Chapter 1, it is difficult to understand how such a clarification can be achieved by anything less than an inquiry into the structure and meaning of the general features of reality itself, which is the specific task of metaphysics.

Sobrino and others evidently think that a liberation christology can get by without such metaphysical inquiry, and Sobrino, for example, draws a comparison between his own horizontalism and Karl Rahner's christological method. Sobrino cites the following statement from Rahner:

> We orthodox Christians ought not to dismiss too quickly this sort of [Jesuism] in its diverse variants. It is a perfectly serious question whether a human being with an absolute and pure love without any egoism must not be more than a human being. If the moral personality of Jesus in word and life really makes such a compelling impression on a person that they

find the courage to commit themselves unconditionally to this Jesus in life and death and therefore to believe in the God of Jesus, that person has gone far beyond a merely horizontal humanistic [Jesuism] and is living (perhaps not completely spontaneously, but really) an orthodox Christology. However, orthodox Christology must give its own implications a thorough examination (Rahner and Weger, 1981: 93-94).

Of course, what Rahner attempts to provide in his own christology is not only an account of the basic conviction that Jesus Christ is the particular person to whom alone soteriological significance can be attributed ("historical christology"), but, simultaneously, the necessary conditions that make such a judgment even possible ("transcendental christology"). Thus, while the first task focuses on the man Jesus as the person in history through whom "God's ultimate and irrevocable utterance of salvation to man is made" (Rahner, 1961-1988: XIII: 215), the second task seeks to show, in the words of Bruce Marshall, how the significance of Christ "can be universally meaningful and accessible on the strength of [its] coherence with logically general criteria" (9). But even if Rahner's point cited by Sobrino is overstated, as I believe it is, and even if Rahner is more or less successful at his own attempt to combine historical and transcendental christology, Rahner's method at least has the merit of recognizing that an attempt to recover the historical question as to who Jesus was does not reduce but rather reaffirms the need for some metaphysical, or transcendental, inquiry.[10] But it is precisely this metaphysical inquiry at the heart of Rahner's christological method that is conspicuously absent from the method followed by most liberation christologies.

---

[10]In fact, Rahner's basic anthropology is fundamentally an attempt to show how humans are historical precisely as transcendental subjects so that the relationship between historical christology and transcendental christology is one of mutual presupposition. As Rahner says,

A transcendental christology as such cannot presume for itself the task and the possibility of saying that the absolute savior, whom radical hope in God himself as the absolute future searches for in history, is to be found there, and that he has been found precisely in Jesus of Nazareth. Both of these statements belong to the experience of history itself which cannot be deduced. Today, however, a person would be blind with regard to this actual history if he did not approach it with that reflexive and articulated hope for salvation which is reflected upon in a transcendental christology. Transcendental christology allows one to search for, and in his search to understand, what he has already found in Jesus of Nazareth (1978: 212).

Christology and History

Perhaps no words in the theological vocabulary are as prone to ambiguity and diversity in meaning as "history" and its cognates. Nowhere is this truer than when we come to liberation theology where we find the appeal that the church recognize its "historical" vocation,[11] the claim that theology is reflection on "historical" praxis (Gutiérrez, 1973: 145), the understanding of the Kingdom of God as a "historical" reality,[12] the declaration that it is only in human "history" that we encounter God,[13] the summons for a renewed quest for the "historical" Jesus,[14] and the proposition that "history is one."[15] Even Christian hope is thoroughly historicized for liberation theology and presented as the assurance "that the definitive reality is being built on what is transitory."[16] Perhaps the most concise statement of the liberationist view of history is provided in the following summation of the most fundamental points of the theology of liberation, written by Segundo:

---

[11]Cf. Muñoz, 1979, who means by this phrase: "(1) that the church is a human reality subject to the contingencies, limitations, and conditioning influence of the society in which it lives (i.e., that it really is "historical"); (2) that the church bears within itself a particular impulse and commission which goes back to its origins on the one hand and which is designed to transform society on the other hand, thus opening society to a future of greater peace and justice (i.e., that it has a specific irreplaceable vocation in and for human history)" (152).

[12]Cf. Sobrino, 1978: 43ff; Segundo, 1979b: 247ff.

[13]Cf. Gutiérrez, 1973: 189ff.

[14]Cf. Segundo, 1982; Sobrino, 1978; Boff, 1978; and Gutiérrez, 1973: 225ff.

[15]Cf. Ellacuria, 3-19; Gutiérrez, 1973: 153-168.

[16]Gutiérrez, 1973: 237. Liberation theologians, in general, have a strong aversion to any attempt at splitting history into two parts:
> there are not two histories, one profane and one sacred, "juxtaposed" or "closely linked." Rather there is only one human destiny, irreversibly assumed by Christ, the Lord of history. His redemptive work embraces all the dimensions of existence and brings them to their fullness. The history of salvation is the very heart of human history. . . . All reflection, any distinctions which one wishes to treat, must be based on this fact: the salvific action of God underlies all human existence (153).

that the stress on individual and other-worldly salvation constitutes a distortion of the message of Jesus, who was concerned with an integral liberation for human beings, a liberation which is already at work in the historical process and which makes use of historical means; that the Church does not possess a magical effectiveness with regard to salvation, but rather liberating elements in its faith and its liturgy; that the victory of the Church must not be considered to be numerical or quantitative, but rather functional, insofar as the Church's own proper means manage to exercise a powerful impact on human history; that there is not one supernatural and ahistorical order separate from another natural and historical order, but rather that one and the same grace raises all human beings to a supernatural level and gives to them the means necessary to achieve, in love, their destiny within one and the same history (1975b: 7-8).

This study, of course, is not primarily an attempt critically to interpret or evaluate the theology of history advanced by liberation theology. Nonetheless, many of the features of that view of history have significant implications for its own development of christological method, and especially the historical understanding implied or presupposed in that method. I wish to highlight two such features which have relevance for the purpose of this study: (1) the historical understanding presupposed in the appeal to the historical Jesus, and (2) the role of Marxist social analysis for hermeneutics.

I have already noted that most liberation theologians call for the historical Jesus as a starting point for christology, and I need not elaborate on that point at much more length here. The claim is made that it is the actual history of Jesus of Nazareth, including his activity, attitudes, and faith, that are of fundamental significance for our own praxis today. I do wish, however, to spell out here how this claim is related to the more general view of history espoused by liberation theologians and how this relation is problematic for the development of an adequate and effective christological method.

Jon Sobrino enumerates several reasons why liberation christology does and does not make the historical Jesus its point of departure. In the first place, Sobrino emphasizes that liberation christology does not begin with the historical Jesus in order, thereby, to produce a biography of Christ along the line of the "lives of Jesus" produced in earlier days[17] nor does it focus on the historical Jesus primarily in order to ground or preserve the kerygma of Christ. As Sobrino

---

[17]Indeed, such "lives" continue to roll off the presses as, for example, John Dominic Crossan's recent, monumental *The Historical Jesus: The Life of a Mediterranean Jewish Peasant* (1991), touted by its publisher as "the first comprehensive determination of who Jesus was, what he did, what he said."

says, "it does not return to the historical Jesus in order to solve the general question of the New Testament: the relation between the Christ who is preached and the Christ who preaches" (1987: 65). So too, liberation christology is not primarily interested in finding in Jesus some "once-for-all" core or quality that can withstand the processes of time and history. Rather, as Sobrino says, the reason for beginning with the historical Jesus is "to serve the continuation of his history in the present" (65); that is, to transform our own present reality in the direction that Jesus' own practice transformed his reality. Sobrino sums up his reasons as follows:

> The historical element in Jesus, then, is not primarily simply that which can be situated in space and in time. Nor is it the doctrinal element, in the latter's hypostatization unto itself independently of Jesus' practice. Neither is it the prime finality of a christology that returns to the historical Jesus to be able to learn about his geography and temporality or his pure doctrine. This requires an understanding of the New Testament in general and the gospel narratives in particular, not only, and not basically, as description and doctrine, but as accounts of a practice that are published precisely in order that this practice be continued. For us, then, the historical element in the historical Jesus is first and foremost an invitation (and a demand) to continue his practice--or, in Jesus' language, an invitation to his discipleship for a mission (66).

Here we can see that the primary reason for liberation christology's taking the historical Jesus as its point of departure is an intensely practical reason--to better enable the church to continue Jesus' own practice. Two presuppositions lie behind this reasoning. The first is that the church's primary sphere of operation and place of mission is this world. The second is that it is this history where salvation happens. Thus, the appeal to Jesus' own personal history is so as to join up with our history and to give it direction. The problem here is that historical understanding is largely reduced to historical description for the sake of presenting the historical possibilities of living out a faith that is liberating, active, and politically relevant. Jesus is a witness of liberating faith, and christology has as its task the presentation of Jesus as *exemplum* upon which the possibilities of faith today may be built. But the significance of Jesus is really robbed, thereby, of any true existential-historical significance in terms of making the kind of difference in our own lives that the original witnesses to Jesus claim he does make. In other words, by merely considering, historically, whether and how Jesus was "political" or whether or not Jesus exhibited courage or common sense in this or that situation, I am not really learning the mechanics or preconditions for effectively expressing my own faith in my own unique situations. This essential task, to the contrary, requires a method of true historical interpretation that can translate the significance of Jesus for our own existence.

Sobrino points out that just as European theology has, in general, been a response to the "first moment" of the Enlightenment, symbolized by Kant, where liberation is understood as the freeing of reason from all authoritarianism, so liberation theology is, in general, a response to the "second moment" of the Enlightenment, symbolized by Marx, where liberation is understood as the freeing of reality from suffering. In the first, the basic interest is in rationality, while in the second, the basic interest is in transformation. Notwithstanding the oversimplification of such a schema, Sobrino's distinction does make clear the importance of Karl Marx as a dialogue partner and interlocutor in most liberation theologies.

Liberation theologians, of course, are quite unified in using a neo-Marxist analysis of history because, quite simply, they believe it to be the best in terms of providing the social analysis required by theology today (Cf. Gutiérrez, 1990: 421). As Míguez Bonino says:

> [Marxism] seems to many of us that it has proved, and still proves to be, the best instrument available for an effective and rational realization of human possibilities in historical life. . . . When we speak of assuming Marxist analysis and ideology at this point, there is therefore no sacralization of an ideology, no desire to "theologize" sociological, economic, or political categories. We move totally and solely in the area of human rationality--in the realm where God has invited man to be *on his own*. The only legitimate question is therefore whether this analysis and this projection do in fact correspond to the facts of human history (1975: 97-98).

According to Marsha Hewitt, however, the use of Marx by liberation theology runs much deeper than simply as a tool for social analysis. Rather, the importance of Marx is to be understood in terms of his relevance for the primary goal of liberation theology, namely, to turn theology into a liberating force for social change. Liberation theology, says Hewitt, is grossly misunderstood as merely an interpretation of Christian faith in terms of the concept of "liberation" when, actually, its intentions are much less modest.

> Most North Americans who are interested in liberation theology and are to some extent informed about it are quite familiar with its 'preferential option for the poor', the central place of the Exodus narrative, its use of the Old Testament prophets to underline God's commitment to justice, and its reading of the synoptic gospels as evidence of the solidarity of Jesus with the victims of oppression and suffering. Most approaches to liberation theology are faith-oriented and theological.
>
> However, the meaning of the theology of liberation goes much farther than a basic commitment to social justice. . . . Liberation theology's first concern is not with developing theology in this way, but rather with

constructing a "science" of society, history, politics, and economics (1990: 3).

Hewitt would admit that few liberation theologians contemplate the tremendous contradiction that is inherent in such a development, namely,

> how can a theology, however critical or progressive, seek to become a practical, emancipatory force in the historical process without transforming itself utterly into a theory that is not theology in its classical definition? (4)

As I see it, Hewitt has laid her finger on a central problem in the method of liberation theology and one that, as she says, is hardly ever addressed by liberation theologians themselves, namely, can theology so design its method as to accomplish the goal of historical liberation "without inevitably dissolving theological categories into those of critical social theory?" (9) In general, when liberation theologians take up the famous eleventh thesis of Marx on Feuerbach that "philosophers have only *interpreted* the world, in various ways; the point, however, is to *change* it" (1975: 64), and when they make an analogous claim for their own efforts, it is not at all clear that they are prepared consistently to follow through on the implications of such a shift for theological method or, for that matter, for theology itself as a discipline. As Clodovis Boff says,

> since Marx, it is no longer permissable [*sic*] to theologize as before with regard to social problems. And to the extent that theology continues to ignore an etiological approach to these problems, this critique will be justified. . . . The touchstone of the authentic response of theology to this critique will be whether it will be able to accept the truth it contains without losing out entirely (13-14).

It is this last sentence by Boff, I believe, that points up the real problematic of Marxist social analysis for liberation theology, namely, how does theology go about incorporating social analysis in order to become an emancipatory force in history without becoming, simply, social theory? In other words, how and to what extent does theology come down out of the clouds, abandoning all pretense to possessing a deposit of divine certitudes, thereby situating itself theoretically in history and society, in order both to understand and to impact the complex problems which human beings today face and yet retain the task of theology *qua* theology? The same question, obviously, has to be asked of christology and, really, the structure of this problem is already apparent in what I have suggested as the historical understanding presupposed in the appeal to the historical Jesus. If christology today is to move beyond merely metaphysical descriptions of Jesus' divinity toward interpretations of the significance of Jesus for our own historical and political contexts, what is the role of social analysis (either in the present or in some remote past, two thousand years ago) in making this move and can it be made without turning either ourselves or Jesus of Nazareth into mere social theorists? In other words, how does the method of liberation theology move, as Segundo says, beyond merely "talking about liberation" in order really to "be liberating"? At this point, I agree with Hewitt that Segundo, more than any other liberation theologian, understands this contradiction and deals with it explicitly in terms of constructing a method that attempts to liberate theology for just this task of social transformation, with all the risks and revolutions that it may entail for our conception of the nature and task of theology itself. It is toward an understanding of just how Segundo proposes to accomplish this task as well as an appraisal of how more or less successfully he succeeds in doing so that this study is dedicated.

The Christology of Juan Luis Segundo

Segundo's recent multi-volume work on christology, *El hombre de hoy ante Jesús de Nazaret*, is, in its fundamental aims, consistent with his work as a whole, which, since the early 1960's, has been aimed at trying to ask and answer what he understands to be the most pressing question of our time, namely, how contemporary human beings can grow into mature human beings without losing or abandoning their faith (1983b: 13ff). Segundo wants to show that Christian faith does not have to be merely "noble but ineffective." He believes that "the gravest danger for faith continues to be the divorce between faith and life with its commitments" (1980: 173) and it is to the question of just how this rupture can be overcome that Segundo's life, work, and theology are given. Thus, it is a question arising from the interaction of faith and praxis that motivates and sets the agenda for Segundo's theology and that thrusts the question of the relationship between theology and praxis into the center of his inquiry. In many ways, just as his life and work is devoted to overcoming the divorce between faith and life, so it is devoted to overcoming the gap between theology and praxis or, rather, to revising an insufficiently critical and, therefore, ideological relationship between theology and praxis.[18]

Segundo's work over the last several decades in developing a critical and liberating relationship between theology and praxis is a product of a variety of influences which have given his thought a multi-dimensionality that avoids the kind of superficiality and oversimplification characteristic of so many "praxis-oriented" theologies. For example, existentialism was the subject of Segundo's earliest book in 1948, demonstrating the focus of his studies during his early priestly training at the Jesuit Faculty of San Miguel near Buenos Aires, Argentina,

---

[18]One might well characterize Segundo's work as taking up what Clodovis Boff calls the "ideo-political vigilance" of theology (Boff: 43).

beginning in 1941. Segundo's encounter with the works of Berdyaev were of particular importance during this period and Berdyaev's notion of the human person, on which Segundo wrote his doctoral dissertation, continues to influence him on up to the present. Segundo's existentialist moorings early led him to be impressed with the need for philosophy to interact with poetic language in order faithfully to interpret human existence in its fullness, but perhaps the most important notion that Segundo derives from Berdyaev is that of a human freedom in creative tension with the determinations of nature. Thus, Segundo continuously stresses both the primacy of freedom over nature and the need for every expression of freedom alertly to attend to the mechanisms of nature in order to be effective. It is no wonder, then, given Segundo's dual interest in both freedom and nature, that Segundo's attraction toward existentialism and philosophy has, from the beginning, been combined with an insistence on science and social analysis. Indeed, many of Segundo's earliest writings take the form of social analysis of the problems and struggles of Latin America and reveal the importance early on of the social sciences as a theological tool of as great importance as, if not greater importance than philosophy.

Segundo has also been deeply influenced by the works of Rudolf Bultmann and, especially, the latter's existentialist method of interpreting scripture. Segundo employed that method over several years and a variety of studies on the Pauline concept "flesh," equating the term with "inauthenticity" and applying it to Christendom which, to Segundo's mind, represented a mass, inauthentic approach to Christian faith rather than a minoritarian, authentic one. Segundo's distinction between "masses" and "minorities" has been an especially productive tool, appearing in virtually all of his writings, and has been especially important insofar as it has dovetailed with his study of the evolutionary insights of Teilhard de Chardin.

All of these influences combine in Segundo to produce a remarkably wholistic approach that avoids some of the overly-individualistic tendencies of existentialism, overly-theoretical tendencies of philosophy, and overly-impersonal tendencies of sociology. Furthermore, the way Segundo holds these influences in balance exhibits his general attitude that theology is only impoverished to the extent that it retreats from dialogue with any dimension of human life or knowledge. Thus, we always find Segundo writing in response to some specific problem or in dialogue with some other thinker. Theologians are certainly not his only dialogue partners; rather, he dialogues with a range of subject areas including physics, sociology, linguistics, the sociology of knowledge, literature, and philosophy.

Nowhere is this wholistic approach more evident than in the case of christology, to which Segundo turns because he believes that there is an urgent need of asking what contribution, if any, Jesus of Nazareth can make to the process of humanization in our world and, specifically, in Latin America. Segundo makes it clear in *El hombre de hoy ante Jesús de Nazaret* that the fundamental question in this work has to do with the significance of Jesus, not first and foremost as a savior or divine emissary (or, as Segundo says, not primarily with regard to his "religious" significance) but rather as a real human being who himself had to make calculations of energy and take account of the givens of his social context in order to decide creative methods for exercising freedom and for making faith effective.

In essence, it is a cultural problem that motivates and drives Segundo's christological reflection and gives it its pertinency. This was true, in a more pastoral way, of the individual five volumes of his *Teología abierta para el laico adulto* (recently published in a 3-volume edition entitled, simply, *Teología abierta*), where the persons for whom Segundo writes and about whom he is concerned are the average lay adult believers who, in their attempt to mature as human beings, find little in their faith to guide them. But even though, from the writing of *Liberación de la teología* foreward, there is a noticeable broadening of Segundo's audience to include non-Latin Americans and a more "academic" audience[19], it is still the average lay Christian for whom Segundo attempts to interpret the doctrines of Christian faith in order to produce a more liberating and liberated life and it is on their behalf that Segundo attacks a church that is more interested in preserving orthodoxy and unity than in developing a liberating and effective praxis. Though his own native Uruguay is often singled out by Segundo, it is the entire continent of Latin America that is the point of reference for Segundo's theology, especially insofar as that continent has common problems and a common destiny.

In *El hombre de hoy ante Jesús de Nazaret*, Segundo's turn to christology is driven by a fundamental belief that years of destruction of the Latin American "social ecology" have produced a "disillusionment," "lack of hope," and "despair" among those who live on his continent, especially the youth (1982: I: 336). This situation has resulted in a kind of "epistemological premise"--a way of interpreting reality that is a negative form of faith and the basis for unproductive and destructive attitudes and actions in every sphere of life, especially the political. In Segundo's opinion, this disillusionment is the product of a distorted and confused relationship between "faith" and the vehicles used to implement that faith. Whether it is the allegedly faithless ideology of Marxism, the various repressive and dictatorial governments over a period of decades, or the ineffec- tiveness of Christianity on the continent, Segundo believes that no cultural vehicle has been created that could transmit a meaningful and coherent value-system and meaning-world ("ends") and at the same time allow for and assist in the

---

[19]This is obvious simply from the sheer numbers and character of the groups and thinkers with whom Segundo carries out lengthy dialogue in his more recent works.

production of a variety of effective and creative "means" to express that value-
system and live out that meaning-world. As Segundo says,

> the Latin American experience of life and political activity during a quarter
> of a century has led to a growing *emotional dissociation of means and
> ends* and, consequently, a rationality that has become disaffected in its
> justification of the means by the ends. . . . it is a period where the politics
> we have seen each time has been increasingly devoid of "instrumental
> reward" expressed in terms of human values. Less and less do we feel any
> "ever-imminent but undefined" hope that we are building something
> worthwhile. Horizons were closed off, silencing the "reasons of the heart"
> in many people and unleashing without counterbalance the "reasons of the
> reason." And there has been a resultant loss of "wisdom" and "grace"
> (1982: I: 342-343).

Segundo believes that Christian faith, despite the impotence, failure, and even
destructiveness of the Christian church on the Latin American continent over the
past decades, can provide a creative vehicle for the reconstruction of culture. This
it can do insofar as it can transmit and communicate meaning and value without,
at the same time, sacrificing effectiveness and relevance. What gives christology
its theoretical pertinency, for Segundo, is its task of critically interpreting the
significance of Jesus for just this urgent task of cultural construction.   Furthermore, if it is true, for Segundo, that the task of christology is reflection on the
significance of Jesus for the adoption and concrete, historical expression of faith,
then it is also true, as we shall see, that the very structure of this faith bears
heavily on the method Segundo employs for such reflection.

While Segundo's work is generally classified with other Latin American
liberation theologians who share similar concerns and perspectives, Segundo is
adamant that not all liberation theology has proceeded along the same lines.
Indeed, Segundo exhibits a heightened degree of clarity and critical-mindedness
when it comes to method in christology, disagreeing with the trend among
liberation theologians simply to defend the praxis of existing faith.   In fact,
Segundo would disagree with liberation theologians such as Gustavo Gutiérrez,
Leonardo Boff, and Jon Sobrino at several points with regard to the nature and
method of christology.   Segundo disagrees with the pattern among liberation
theologians who want

> to be in religious matters the "organic intellectuals" of poor and unculti-
> vated people, . . . to understand their function as one of unifying and
> structuring people's understanding of their faith, as well as grounding and
> defending the practices coming from this faith (1990: 360).

On the contrary, Segundo refuses to give up

the first critical function, which comes out of a suspicion that theology, like other all-pervasive cultural features, can and perhaps should be considered an instrument of oppression and, hence, as a non-Christian theology (360).

In addition, Segundo rejects two preconceptions that seem almost fundamental to so many of the most widely read versions of liberation theology:

> The first one is that liberation theology comes out of practice. And the second one is that it makes orthopraxis, instead of orthodoxy, the main criterion for its solutions (356).

Segundo demonstrates an interest in christology that is concerned not simply to explore its content or symbols but systematically to construct a critical method for christology, as for theology in general. Thus, Segundo does not see his own work with christology as itself primarily an attempt to interpret the significance of Jesus; rather, Segundo's effort is one that attempts to point out the preconditions for such interpretation. Two of these preconditions, according to Segundo, are (1) arriving at historical data about Jesus himself, and (2) clarification of our present real-life problems and interests for which Jesus is significant. I will have a more extensive opportunity to examine what Segundo has to say about the possibilities of gaining reliable historical data about Jesus. Segundo repudiates any assumption that we already possess all we need to know about the history of Jesus, and yet he maintains that the history and theology intermixed in the synoptics can be distinguished (as revealed by changes in literary genre, etc.) and the "faith" of Jesus arrived at.

Even so, Segundo is sure that the "historical Jesus" cannot be understood as providing an objective criterion that could pass judgment on various interpretations of Christ's significance. Rather, Jesus must be interpreted with some "key" if he is to have any significance or meaning at all today, and this "key" is something like a link between our interests and his history. In this way, even though the interests of Jesus' interpreters prevent us from reading their gospels as objective, unbiased history, these interests can lead us to that same Jesus rather than shielding us from him. They can, that is, if we pay attention to these interests and understand them as the key to interpretation. As Segundo says, "We can never be completely objective in our reconstruction of the past" (1982: II: 802); we must "cast or project from today toward the past some interpretive scheme originating in the present with which we are involved" (II: 798). This requires, according to Segundo a "hermeneutic wager" (II: 800)--an unavoidable risk that immerses the significance of Jesus in very specific, contingent historical situations.

It is this express desire to interpret Jesus in terms of his historical and human significance rather than in terms of his metaphysical status or relationship to God that causes Segundo to label his christological reflection an "anti-christology"--a term that reveals the centrality of "method" in his thinking. One could, I suppose, even call his theology in general an "anti-theology" inasmuch as he takes a similar approach to other theological subjects and concepts (the church, salvation, etc.), treating them first and foremost in terms of their relevance to concrete historical interests and problems. The following lengthy quotation by Segundo illustrates in summary form, Segundo's concerns at this point with regard to his own approach to christology:

> This work is not a treatise in *theology*. I do not wish it to be thus, at least not in the current sense of the word. Its aim is, precisely, to rescue the question of Jesus' significance for human existence from the discipline that has expropriated the task of interpreting Jesus for many centuries, and that has interpreted him for the exclusive benefit of the members of the Christian religion or its corresponding churches.
>
> Justifiably, then, my stress on methodology, characteristic of this whole work, was considered necessary in order to give back to *any and every* human being the question of the significance of Jesus and the possible richness of the answer. At the very least I want to give back the way of facing existence exhibited by Jesus of Nazareth to those human beings who had an impact on the history that precedes us at any given moment; and I want to show that this way of his, in translated form, can even today interest and humanize people who, due to a cultural misunderstanding or for more profound and considered reasons, claim they do not believe in God.
>
> Now then, it is an historical fact that, from the New Testament on, many formally religious categories have been applied to Jesus. In the two prior parts of this work, I have tried to demonstrate that the human significance of Jesus of Nazareth was not dependent upon the acceptance of those categories, at least not in the form they have taken today. Thus I have remained faithful to the perspective suggested by the title of a book by Milan Machovec [*A Marxist Looks at Jesus*]. I want to offer, in a version as free as possible from esoteric concepts, a *Jesus for atheists*. Of course I do not mean a Jesus for atheists alone, but rather a Jesus who can get beyond the traditional barriers of language and categories and reach the human being who, having rejected the idea of a God (perhaps a distorted idea, cf. *Gaudium et Spes*: 19) or, without thinking about God, are more concerned with what I have called their own *anthropological* faith (II: 625-626).

Even though Segundo claims that his is not a "treatise in theology," this does not necessarily mean that Segundo's work is not theological nor that it should not be judged as theology, though, for example, one of his interpreters claims that he is more of a critical social theorist than a theologian (Hewitt, 1990: 165)[20] and another claims that, in Segundo's hands, the question must be asked, "is liberation theology still recognizable as theology?" (McCann, 1981a: 230). When Segundo says that his work is not "theology," he is engaged in a polemic to distance his own method from other more classical theological methods and believes that his so radically reverses these latter, especially with reference to the role of *theos* in theology, that it may not even be appropriate to class the two different methods under the same term--"theology." Whether Segundo's brand of liberation theology still deserves to be called theology, however, will be taken up in my own critical appraisal of his method.

Segundo devotes considerable time in his christological reflection to an exploration of three christologies -- the "historical Jesus" of the synoptics, the "humanist christology" of Paul," and the christology of the *Ignatian Exercises*. His purpose in using this method is not simply to broaden the content base of his christology, for he in no way desires, or even thinks it is possible, to provide a more complete and total picture of the significance of Christ by exploring a variety of christologies.

On the contrary, Segundo opposes all efforts to mix christological data from various sources in order somehow to complete, "round out," or finalize the interpretation of Jesus. According to Segundo, christologies that traditionally try to bring together all that has been thought or said about Jesus in the authoritative sources (such as the *Diatessaron*) uproot the individual christologies from the particular historical contexts out of which they developed in order to make them more timeless and useful. But this process is severely destructive of the christologies themselves and is unhelpful to those who continue to attempt new christological reflection.

The approach that Segundo instead fashions in order to interpret the significance of Jesus attempts to expose the mechanics of just a few christologies

---

[20]Hewitt is over-impressed with Segundo's dialogue with non-theological thinkers in his later works to the point that she seems to think he has made a shift in his theology toward strictly secular, non-theological social theory. Hewitt fails to recognize that Segundo's interpretation of human existence in a thoroughly secular, politicized, and historical way is a fundamental premise of even his more explicitly theological writings as, for example, his *Teología abierta para el laico adulto*. There, for example, Segundo interprets the church in a way that gives it a functional significance vis-á-vis the world rather than some supra-mundane significance. Like many other explicitly theological doctrines, the starting point for understanding the church today is fundamentally anthropological in terms of what any and all human beings, simply as such, are called to be and to do. Thus, the church is the community of those "who know," i.e., the community that makes explicit the answers to the important questions that we all ask.

on their own terms in order to learn their own creative method and to discover their own "key" by which the significance of Jesus is unlocked for their day. In each christology Segundo wants to analyze the writer's effort to interpret the significance of Jesus in such a way that faith can be effective in his own context and to point up how such an effort must be made over and over again in any and every context. Here again, we find grounds which, in Segundo's opinion, demand calling his method an "anti-christology."

Segundo, for example, finds a "political" key operating in the christology of the synoptics while he finds an "anthropological" key in Paul's christology. Every key has its own limitations, not simply or even primarily the "political" key, which is more obviously time-bound and culture-bound. Even the anthropological-existential key, discovered by Segundo in Paul's literary device of personifying the conflicting forces which characterize all of human existence (such as "Sin," "Flesh," "Grace," or "Spirit"), has its own limitations.

> We have, in effect, the impression that the key employed by Paul largely overcomes, at least in great part, the limitations of the political key of the historical Jesus. This latter key forced Jesus to involve himself in conflicts dividing groups of human beings and to use means (ideologies) that framed his activity within a context determined by those conflicts. This, while it heightened his concrete significance, reduced his universality.
>
> The opposite, however, seems to come to pass with Paul's anthropological key. It is presented as valid for every human being in any context. . . . Paul's anthropological key only has the *appearance* of being less limited than the political key of Jesus of Nazareth. Limitation is not peculiarly characteristic of the political, as is commonly thought by those who attempt to minimize the key of the history of Jesus *in the name of that which is universal or unlimited about his message* (1982: II: 568-570).

The point is that no interpretation of Jesus can be freed from ideologies, and no key frees a message that is transmitted in history from its limitations; rather, by paying attention to the key, one can point up where those limitations are most visible. Segundo, therefore, asks for the key that each christology uses to unlock the significance of Jesus within a specific historical problematic.

Fundamental to Segundo's christological method, then, is a precaution against determining in any way what the specifically Christian contribution to liberation might be ahead of time. Rather, Segundo seeks only to understand the "logic" of making a Christian contribution to liberation and the kinds of mechanics that must be employed to make such a contribution possible in our contemporary world. This means paying close attention to the kind of bridge that must be built between the person of Jesus and our own historical situation.

As we shall see, this bridge, for Segundo, is the spiraling evolutionary bridge comprised of the twin strands of "faith" and the "ideological" mediation that every faith requires. Segundo rejects any attempt simply to get back to the "historical Jesus" in some kind of "fundamentalist" way so as to arrive at a once-for-all significance for Jesus that has only to be applied to any and every situation. But neither is Segundo trying simply to construct one particular interpretation of Jesus' significance for present-day humanity. Segundo is laying out the preconditions for building any bridge between the Jesus of history and our own historical context and his answer to the fundamental question of Jesus' significance is not so much a "quantity" of information that would inform us of that significance as a "way" of getting to that significance -- a "method."

It is no wonder, then, that Segundo's so-called "anti-christology" takes on a very unconventional structure which begins with a lengthy volume on the relationship between faith and ideologies. Segundo wants his readers to understand that the significance of a historical figure is not to be interpreted by compiling piece after piece of historical data, one on top of the other. What Segundo wants to demonstrate and what he understands to be the one indispensable historical truth that can be determined about Jesus is that Jesus was a human being whose faith had to be expressed in terms of ideologies to be effective.

So, in order for Segundo to answer his fundamental question as to the significance of Jesus for concrete and contemporary human projects and human maturity on our planet, he cannot settle for a simple or straightforward exegesis of biblical texts or conciliar definitions and documents, but rather an existentialist analysis of the structure of human valuing, communicating, decision-making, and bearing witness that can help us travel backward in time and view more adequately how others (Paul, Ignatius of Loyola, etc.) surrendered themselves to the values to which they understood Jesus to bear witness while at the same time translating those values into "mechanisms" that would make their faith in Jesus "effective." Such an analysis can also help us more adequately understand the context in which we now live and to which we must respond if we are to live out an "effective faith."

Given some of the more general features of Segundo's thought offered above, it should be evident why I choose to interpret his theology under the notion of "effective faith."[21] An effective faith is, for Segundo, the most urgent commodity for the task of cultural reconstruction on his continent. No longer can

---

[21]I find Theresa Lowe Ching's identification of "efficacious love" as Segundo's "unifying principle" (2) to be making much the same point as I make here. Her doctoral dissertation, *Efficacious Love: Its Meaning and Function in the Theology of Juan Luis Segundo* tends to confine itself more to the themes rather than to the method of Segundo's theology, though her work is quite helpful and on target, I think.

Christians risk a faith that looks good on paper, so to speak, but has no practical relevance. As a single concept, "effective faith" best specifies Segundo's most basic concern, namely, the exercise of freedom in terms of concrete expressions that incarnate nothing less than God's grace itself and the gift of God's salvation in history. But if "effective faith" signifies, for Segundo, the challenge of a liberating praxis in history, it also points to the dialectic characteristic of Segundo's theological method at every level, whether the epistemological dialectic between faith and ideologies, the linguistic dialectic between digital and iconic types of language, the sociological dialectic between masses and minorities, the existentialist dialectic between freedom and necessity, the physical dialectic between entropy and negentropy, or the theological dialectic between sin and grace. Finally, and most relevant for this study, "effective faith" points to what gives Jesus his primary significance for contemporary human beings. As Segundo says,

> The Gospels do not offer us a solely minoritarian Jesus, who ignored the weight and the necessity of mass mechanisms. Without succumbing to them, his love inserted itself, honestly, humanly, within an economy of energy (1973c: 104-105).

An Overview of the Present Study

In Chapter 1, the complexity of the christological question was emphasized and it was noted that, if christology is seriously interested in interpreting the "significance" of Jesus for human beings, then its method must reflect that complexity. In this chapter, I highlighted three problematic areas with regard to the method typically followed by Latin American liberation christologies which correspond to the above methodological complexity, namely, the historical, metaphysical, and praxic dimensions of the christological question. It is the exploration of these three problem areas and how they function in the method of Juan Luis Segundo's christology that will occupy the bulk of this study. Part 1 will provide an interpretation of Segundo's thought and method with regard to each area; Part 2 will provide a critical appraisal of Segundo; and Part 3 will provide some indications of how I myself propose to solve some of the problems inherent in Segundo's thought and thus attempt a contribution to the critical interpretation of the significance of Jesus for human liberation today.

PART I

SEGUNDO'S CHRISTOLOGY

CHAPTER 3

THE DIMENSION OF PRAXIS: FAITH AND IDEOLOGIES

I have already attempted to describe the complexity of the christological question and to give indications of how contemporary christologies, in general, and liberation christologies, in particular, more or less adequately express that complexity in terms of the method with which christology is pursued. I have also attempted to provide a rough sketch of some of the more predominant concerns and interests of Juan Luis Segundo himself in order to provide a general framework for analyzing his own method of critically interpreting the significance of Jesus. One of the notable values of Segundo's work is that the contours of his christological method are shaped by the complexity and depth of the christological question itself. In this first part of the study, I will attempt to provide an exposition of Segundo's christological method with special attention to his treatment of the three aspects of the christological question specified above--the praxic, metaphysical, and historical aspects.

As I have already indicated, the fundamental context for understanding Segundo's christology is the dual process in every human life of adopting a faith and of expressing that faith concretely in one's life-praxis. At the heart of Segundo's christological method, therefore, and prior to any and all reference to the significance of Jesus of Nazareth, is a phenomenological analysis of human existence that points up the universal presence of what, to Segundo, are two fundamental human dimensions: faith and ideologies. "Faith," for Segundo, is the meaning-structure, or valuational-structure, that humans give to their existence, while "ideology" is the system of means we choose in order to give expression to our values and meaning-world so as to make them "effective." Thus, while faith structures a human life around some specific meaning or scale of values, ideology, just as universal, is more concerned with effectiveness and method. It is crucial to understand this less pejorative and somewhat unusual use of the word "ideology," for Segundo, which, as he says, refers to "all systems of means, natural or artificial, employed to attain an end" (1982: I: 30).

It is precisely in the context of this important dialectic of faith and ideologies that the question of praxis arises for Segundo, and it is here that we find the context for understanding our human condition and, in Segundo's mind, the only adequate framework for interpreting the significance of Jesus. Segundo's examination of the twin dimensions of faith and ideologies also presents us with a rare glimpse of the philosophical foundations of his work while, at the same time, raising crucial questions about christological method.

Adopting a "Faith"

Segundo's most fundamental statement about faith is that it is essentially a living and dynamic commitment on the part of the human being rather than a "possession" or "deposit" consisting of formulas and creeds which require preservation and to which the individual returns for repeatable solutions when confronted with the struggles of life. Segundo believes that the most pressing dangers to faith are classically perceived by the church as having to do with orthodoxy. This is so because

> it is supposed that faith is something that, on a par with the sacraments, has a kind of *ex opere operato* efficacy, which means that it is, up to a certain point, like a church possession, as if the church *owned* the truth
> . . . .
>   I believe that this is the greatest danger: to think that faith is a kind of possession of the church that is best preserved when the formulas are repeated in a strictly orthodox way and when the Christian stays far away from dialogue with others who do not keep the faith in the same orthodox way (1980: 173).

For Segundo, faith is primarily a "lived" reality--a "process" rather than a "content"--by which individuals interpret their existence and structure their praxis.

For Segundo, in order to understand what faith is, we must first understand the process of how we, as human beings, come to adopt a faith as our own. This process is neither simple nor mechanical and hinges on the reliance of human beings on each other. In the first place, Segundo's analysis of human experience discloses a universal inability to know on our own what way of living will turn out to be the most satisfying in life. We can only travel "one road," so to speak, in determining the meaning that we will give to existence and we can never predict with absolute accuracy whether the values we adopt will, later on down the road, be the most satisfying. We can never choose the road to follow beforehand from actual experience because we do not and could not have such experience. This necessary limitedness in any and every human life forces us to structure our lives *as if* we knew ahead of time the full range of possibilities available to us. As Segundo says,

> every human being must gamble on existence, choosing as his or her supreme goal something whose value is not known personally or experientially. . . . It is not possible to jump to the end of existence to see what is

worth the trouble to realize and then, with this certain knowledge, return to the beginning and resolve to do it (1982: I: 17).

According to Segundo, however, the choice of which road to follow is not purely arbitrary. Human beings inevitably fall back on the experiences of others in order to decide what path might be the most satisfying. Values that have been effectively realized by our fellow human beings -- Segundo calls these people "referential witnesses" -- are communicated to us in a variety of ways and we adopt them as our own. Thus, this basic dimension of all human experience, which Segundo calls "faith," is a necessarily "social" dimension.

In every human life, on the basis of the faith adopted, values form a "scale" in which some values are preferred over others. Segundo says,

> every option, every act of preferring one thing to another, involves the implementation of a faith. Extending this to all the acts of "preference" in a human life, we can say that faith *structures* an entire existence around some specific meaning. Life is valued, is considered meaningful, to the extent to which concrete valuations converge towards that which has been chosen as predominant in terms of value, in terms of what ought to be (I: 20).

To say that this dimension of faith, including the selection and prioritization of values, is a universal dimension in human beings is not, however, to say that this faith is always a conscious dimension. Often (especially as one becomes older), faith takes on something like the role of a "conscience" and, rather than being called into question, is more likely, instead, to be the source of a manipulation of one's perception of reality. Thus, faith is more than simply a selection of what we ought to do, it is a way of perceiving reality -- it is a "cognitive principle which enables us to perceive certain things rather than other equally obvious things" (I: 28).

Within this realm of faith, or valuing, Segundo discovers what he calls "absolute value." This is something akin to the traditional Aristotelian "highest good" in that it is the value that serves no other values but is preferred by a person solely for itself. As Segundo says,

> every value-structure, however elementary it may be, must be crowned by something that is not a means toward something else, but that rather turns everything else into a means towards it (I: 34).

These values, though considered "absolute" and "unconditioned" by Segundo, may or may not include reference to God; indeed, both the theist and the atheist adopt values and commit their lives to the implementation of values, which are to be considered "absolute."

The absolute, as one can see, has nothing to do with something infinite, perfect, or metaphysical. . . . The way in which the most simple or superficial human being conceives happiness is that person's "absolute" (I: 34).

Rather than locate the "absolute" in human life within a strictly religious frame of reference or in an uncompromisingly God-oriented way, Segundo argues for the recognition that every human being simply as such develops a scale of values that is dependent on nothing else, preferred solely for itself, and, thus, absolute.

It is true that in ordinary language, the word "absolute" is used more with reference to decisions than to factual entities, to realities. But what easily introduces itself here, especially when we wish to move toward a more refined and philosophical language, is an uncritical habit that has become a commonplace, generating a number of confusions: the old axiom that the order of values and the order of being are to be identified. The more [perfect] the being, the more valuable it is. Therefore a conditioned being could not possibly have anything absolute about it. And since the only being whose reality is absolute would be God, the word "absolute" is reserved for divine values when one intends to speak properly. By the same token, it is ruled out for human beings, against everyday experience which shows us that human beings value as absolute things or persons they know to be imperfect and perishable (I: 82).

There is, to be sure, such a thing as "religious faith," for Segundo--in other words, some human beings do relate their meaning-structure to God and interpret their values on the basis of revelation--but this is only a particular instance of a more basic "anthropological faith." Segundo, then, does not rule out religious language *a priori* for the communication of faith, but believes that "human beings ought to communicate their respective meaning-worlds slowly, amply, and deeply before they begin to discuss whether or not they share a 'religious' faith" (II: 11-12). Just how we come to a religious faith, however, is critical for understanding Segundo's entire christological reflection and method. According to Segundo, there are really only two ways of looking at the subject. Either, on the one hand, faith is related to God by displacing human witnesses in favor of divine revelation (what Segundo sees as the "classic" approach in theology) or, on the other hand, faith is related to God when, in Segundo's words, "it perceives in a particular series of human witnesses a certain quality which, logically or not, it attributes to God" (I: 83). According to Segundo, the first choice is extremely problematic because we can never simply separate out the revelation which is purported to be from God and the messengers which both communicate that revelation and purport it to be from God. Rather, as in the case of Jesus' disciples, it is the witnesses themselves who become the object of faith because it is they who interpret an historical happening as somehow decisive or revelatory. As Segundo says,

It is certain that the disciples of Jesus, insofar as they were able to explicate what they had understood about him, perceived that Jesus--and not, for example, the religious authorities of Israel--offered a revelation about God, about the values that God himself was elevating to the plane of the absolute. Despite that fact, or rather precisely because of it, each one of us must today have *faith* in the disciples of Jesus, and not only because they were eyewitnesses--i.e., because the concrete events are transmitted to us by them--but also because it was their evaluational judgment of those events that is a decisive element for our "faith" directed at or in Jesus (I: 85).

According to Segundo, Jesus was not and could never have been understood as somehow decisive for human existence by just anybody, but rather only by those who had "eyes of faith." In other words, Jesus could be recognized as the revelation of God only by those people who already had the values which were understood to be elevated to the level of absolute in Jesus. This, for Segundo, is precisely the gratuitousness of faith.

the values upheld by human beings enabled them to recognize in Jesus the revelation *of a God* who declared precisely those values to be his own divine, absolute values (I: 85).

Thus, believing in God's existence is not really the primary issue, but rather "being in agreement with God." The important role of witnesses has to do with the fact that no one starts with belief in God and then determines which values are the best for their life; rather, they start with certain values which then enable them to interpret certain events rather than others as revelatory of God. That is not to say, however, that the witnesses to Jesus, for example, simply reiterate their own values or project them onto Jesus, or even that they profess Jesus to be the Christ because he preaches the same values that they already have. Rather, there is a "conversion" to which the witnesses of Jesus are called and religious faith not only confirms pre-existing values but corrects and deepens them by virtue of "transcendent data" to which Jesus appeals.

I will examine Segundo's concept of "transcendent data" in greater detail further in this chapter, but suffice it to say at this point that Segundo believes an anthropological faith becomes a religious faith by virtue of two features: an adherence to a specific tradition and a dependence on certain key "transcendent data." For Segundo, every values-structure, or faith, is chosen or preferred on the basis of what he calls "the ultimate possibilities (or limits) of the universe and the human being" (I: 97). No experience or experiences that we could possibly have could confirm or deny these possibilities; rather, they are presented to us as "transcending" experience, by which Segundo means that they exceed the limits of our direct experience and verification. Segundo calls these possibilities transcendent "data" because language requires some such handle to express the reality of what is being communicated. Segundo warns, however, that transcendent data are often confused with or reduced to ordinary empirical data and, though that should not keep us from using the term "data," there is a difference in the kind of language used to communicate each type of data. The adoption of transcendent data by a human being does not rule out or displace the basic processes of anthropological faith; rather it can contribute to and deepen that faith. As Segundo says,

> by building on anthropological faith, and only by building on it, can we construct a faith in these transcendent data about which I have been speaking. Thus, it still remains irrelevant whether this faith is accepted explicitly or not, or whether one consciously yields to this overall limit of experience. Much more decisive is determining what values or what meaning-structure those "data" support, correct, develop, or deepen. What is important is their potential contribution to anthropological faith (I: 98).

As essential as transcendent data are for developing "religious faith," however, so also is the role of the tradition of witnesses in that development. Segundo understands a religious tradition in a dynamic rather than a static sense. A tradition is not the location of a "deposit" of faith or a "pool" of data to be learned and obeyed. Rather, it is a living and vital process of "learning how to learn" in which we put our faith in others who have learned how to make their faith effective in ever new and creative ways. Segundo calls this kind of learning-to-learn "deutero-learning" in contrast to "proto-learning," which is a simple accumulation of data. Segundo understands theology, like the Bible itself, as a process of "deutero-learning," through which we learn from the way others have learned and thereby accumulate not a reservoir of data but a reservoir of experiences to which we could not have had access by ourselves. In this way we can recreate contexts that are not ours and learn from the way that others have creatively developed liberating solutions (ideologies) to their various crises. Thus, Christian faith, as an example of a religious faith, is a succession of faith-ideology complexes rather than one single faith-ideology complex. Segundo sums up the characteristics of a religious faith as follows:

> a faith which defines values, not because those values are revealed or communicated to a human being who has been without them up to that point, but because this faith constitutes a system of learning-apprenticeship transmitted by historical witnesses. This faith enables people to recognize and discern genuine transcendent data which, themselves, in turn, become determining factors of existing meaning-structures (I: 101).

Returning now to Segundo's concept of basic anthropological faith, it is important to note that, for Segundo, faith is not a kind of basic existential trust in reality as such or some kind of underlying confidence in the worth of life, and he explicitly distinguishes his view from that of David Tracy at this point. Faith, according to Segundo, is much more concrete and differentiated than what he thinks Tracy allows and his critique of Tracy is highly instructive both for understanding what Segundo means by "faith" and for understanding the implications of this notion of faith for his christological method.

As Segundo affirms, there is considerable agreement between himself and Tracy in several areas. James Hawks analyzes Segundo's critique of Tracy and makes the observation that both Segundo and Tracy approach human experience with a perspective that, interestingly enough, causes them to find themselves more in solidarity with committed secularists than with many of their Christian contemporaries with whom they share only a tradition along with its texts, symbols, rites, and structures. As Hawks notes, both have in common "the affirmation of the significance of our lives in the world" with "no time for a Christianity which discourages or negates the value of intra-mundane action for human development" (277). Both are led to attempt descriptions of the relationship between faith and human experience that emphasize the place of faith as a universal dimension in every human, whether one is religious or not, and both identify the most worthwhile values as being just as often characteristic of the non-religious as they are uncharacteristic of those who quite openly claim to be religious.

Notwithstanding the similar perspectives shared by Segundo and Tracy with regard to the universality of faith, there is a fundamental difference, to Segundo's mind, as to how that dimension of faith is to be understood and, more importantly, as to the relationship between faith and religion. One of Tracy's primary concerns in *Blessed Rage for Order* is to provide some account of the meaningfulness and truth of the cognitive claims of religion (91). Tracy is not concerned with trying to come up with some universal definition of religion, given what he takes to be a thoroughly pluralistic situation, and yet he does find certain "family resemblances" among religious perspectives that converge on their expression of a "limit-to" all ordinary human experience (whether moral, scientific, political, aesthetic, etc.) and their disclosure of a "fundamental trust in the worthwhileness of existence, our basic belief in order and value" (also referred to by Tracy as a "*fundamental* faith") that is the "limit-of" or ground to "our more ordinary ways of being-in-the-world" (93). Segundo basically agrees with Tracy's identification of a limit-realm common to all human experience that is, as Segundo says, "the necessary basis of everyday experiences of all types" (1982: I: 52). Segundo, however, criticizes Tracy, first, because he believes that Tracy's understanding of faith is too abstract and indeterminate--a general trust in the worthwhileness of existence--while Segundo presses for the importance of the "decision" whereby each human being determines just what is worthwhile in existence (I: 53). Segundo goes on to say that "Tracy's formulation seems a-critical precisely to the extent that it is generalizing" (I: 53).

To Segundo's mind, the more decisive criticism made of Tracy at this point has to do with the motivations which Segundo suspects are inherent in Tracy's linkage of faith with *religion*. To be sure, Tracy states that this dimension may be either explicitly or implicitly religious (93), but Segundo sees in Tracy's method a clear preference going to those who have succeeded in explicating the religious dimension of their existence over against those who have not, especially when these former are able to identify the objective ground in reality of this faith as God. Segundo believes that his own concept of faith is much more "radical" in that the crucial distinction with regard to faith is not whether or not, or to what extent, one is able to explicate one's faith but rather what specific scale of values one ends up choosing. Thus, as Segundo says, it is the "human" element in faith, not the religious, that is of crucial importance. The fundamental line of demarcation is between the values which individuals hold, whether they are religious or not, and this is confirmed, according to Segundo, by the fact that the same set of religious beliefs and practices can be compatible with completely conflicting sets of fundamental values (1982: I: 55ff). Hawks summarizes the difference between Segundo and Tracy at this point as follows:

> It is clear that Segundo, like Tracy, collapses together religious and secular experience. However, there is a fundamental difference. While Tracy does this with a view to demonstrating the religious dimension inherent in secular experience, Segundo wishes to point out the 'secularity' of religious experience. Where Tracy tries to demonstrate that secular faith and religious faith are both religious, Segundo follows a precisely opposite course. He wishes to show that both are equally human (284-285).

The importance of "referential witnesses" at this point is crucial. Even though faith is a dimension present in all human beings, what Segundo wants to guard against is any understanding of faith that is so general and basic that all human beings can be said to have the same faith (e.g., a fundamental faith in reality as such, a basic trust in the worthwhileness of existence, or a basic belief in order and value). The real danger in taking the concept of faith that direction, according to Segundo, is that it opens the door to viewing "religion" as a universal anthropological dimension and God as the universal referent of faith when, in fact, religion most commonly serves an ideological function -- as an "instrument" for "any class of values" (1982: I: 55). Thus, to identify religion with the dimension of faith would not only be confusing, but, as history has shown us time and time again, often results in the worst forms of idolatry.

> Those who make the mistake of thinking that the religious realm as such has to do necessarily, or the majority of the time, with the plane of

meaning, in other words, those who thus absolutize the religious because it is "religious" and hence refers to the "Absolute," do nothing less than close themselves off to the understanding of the Christian gospel itself (I: 57).

Segundo is not always fair to Tracy at this point and, in several respects, he and Tracy are in more agreement than Segundo seems to allow. For example, Segundo does acknowledge the existence of a "real *anthropological dimension*, a precondition of the very possibility of human life and activity at all" (I: 74). This common dimension "directs" people to adopt some kind of values-structure. So also, Tracy's understanding of faith, though he can call it a "religious dimension," is really prior to all religious reflection and has primarily to do with human value. As Tracy says,

> reflective beliefs--whether theist, agnostic or atheist--are not the basic issue. The first and abiding issue for human beings is their faith or un-faith, commitment to value or failure to live a human life (187).

The problem for Segundo, however, is that Tracy defines the basic human value that underlies all more or less reflective beliefs as faith in the worthwhileness of existence or some other general trust in order and value. This may sound similar to Segundo, but Segundo claims that such a formulation cannot specify the content of faith; though it is formally prior to all existential choices, it is too general and of no critical significance.

> Faith (or unconditioned trust, if you wish), to the extent that it is the meaning-structure of *each* human being, cannot have as its object reality, in other words, the whole complex of circumstances, things, and persons; its object can only be specific persons (I: 48).

Hawks attributes the source of Segundo's criticism of Tracy at this point to Segundo's Marxist influences and, specifically, to the Marxist perspective on the debate between materialism and idealism. On this interpretation, Segundo's motivation in attacking too close an identification of faith with religion stems from something like the Marxist criticism of Hegel[22] for reading the abstract and universal back into the concrete and particular. Thus, to call faith the "religious dimension," as Tracy does, is to invert the relationship between the subject and the predicate; to take a concept that ought only to express the predicate of the real, existing object and make of it a subject in its own right, while the real subject,

---

[22]See "Contribution to the Critique of Hegel's Philosophy of Right" (Marx: 43-59).

faith, is turned into a manifestation of the concept--a predicate of the predicate (Cf. Hawks: 279ff).

Hawks is no doubt correct in identifying one of the primary sources of the criticism of Tracy by Segundo in the latter's Marxist perspective, but one could just as well identify the roots of that criticism in Segundo's overall "hermeneutics of suspicion" derived not only from the Marxist attempt to expose the inversion of the material and the conceptual, but also from the Freudian effort to demystify and unmask a false consciousness that fails to accept reality. Hawks goes on to add (correctly, in my opinion) that Segundo's criticism does not arise primarily from philosophical but from practical considerations.

> Marx's philosophical attack on the Hegelian system was motivated by a very practical dissatisfaction. It did not provide him with a basis for the critical judgements he wished to make about the unsatisfactory nature of existing reality and the need to change it. . . . it is crucial to realize that [Segundo] too is not motivated by some merely abstract preference for one system of philosophy over another. Like Marx, his motives are intensely practical (280).

Here, I believe, Hawks moves closer to the heart of Segundo's motivations, though he only partially identifies the kind of practical urgency that is fundamental to understanding Segundo's work. Hawks does recognize the role of Segundo's criticism of Tracy in terms of establishing, in the first place, the proper practice of theology. Segundo believes that concrete choices with regard to human values are the precondition, not the result, of authentic theological reflection and that, therefore, theology is a "second step." But the practical urgency that drives Segundo to criticize an over-easy identification of faith with religion is not confined simply to the practice of theology and to the need for theology to begin with the material conditions of suffering and the oppression of the poor, as Hawks suggests. Rather, Segundo's criticism of Tracy is rooted, in the second place, in the urgency which he assigns to the process of cultural transformation on his continent and the potential role of either religion or faith in that transformation.

Segundo maintains an energetic hope that Christian faith can provide a normative and "energy-saving" meaning-system and set of values that will guide and propel the transformation of culture, but this hope is rooted in his belief that it is only Christian faith *qua* faith and not *qua* religion that can do this. To be sure, the Christian faith is a "religious" faith, but, for Segundo, a "religious faith" and a "religion" are two different things. Segundo believes that too often religion disguises itself as faith when it is actually a set of instruments, or an "ideological system," for virtually any set of values. Religion, while it provides an abundance and variety of "means" for the transmission of values, is one of the most dangerous ideological tools because it tends to impose itself as "endowed with a power which is assumed to be sacred, and, thus, effective for the realization of values whose attraction derives from other sources" (1982: I: 396).

The implications of Segundo's criticism of Tracy are decisive for his theological method, in general, and his christological method, in particular. For Segundo, if faith is more than a general trust in reality as grounding the meaning of our beliefs and actions, but is, instead, the adoption of concrete values based on the testimony of specific referential witnesses, then a critical method is required that employs an analysis of human existence and is attentive to the various levels of faith and their relationship to subsequent reflection, expression, and implementation. If theology is critically to interpret the meaning and truth of faith, that critical task calls for the ideological unmasking of that faith, i.e. the determination of just what is normative in terms of meaning and values and just what is functional for the expression of the faith. Theology is called to engage in a hermeneutic suspicion which will change the way the witness is itself mediated to the practice of theology--not now merely with an eye to the literary, form, and historical criticisms that assist us in interpreting the meaning of the witness to faith and not now merely with an eye to the philosophical criticism that assists us in evaluating the truth of the witness to faith, but now also with an eye to the ideological criticism that assists us in demystifying and desacralizing certain ideological elements in the witness to faith in order to reinterpret that witness in terms of new and more relevant ideologies.

Christologically, this means that a truly adequate method for interpreting the significance of Jesus must begin with an analysis of the process whereby human beings communicate, adopt, and live out faith prior to the religious interpretation of that process. In fact, according to Segundo, it is precisely a "religious" starting point that all too easily distorts or deflects the significance of Jesus. As Segundo says,

> those who are not disposed to set up certain human values as criteria prior and superior to any particular religion are incapable of recognizing the importance and significance of Jesus (II: 25).

It is in this context that Segundo affirms the possibility of depicting "a Jesus for atheists" (II: 26). The absolute values that go to make up what Segundo terms "faith" are the factors by which decisive distinctions between people occur and the acceptance or rejection of the significance of Christ is dependent on such distinctions, not vice-versa. Religious faith is but one instance of the more general, universal faith.

The Language of Faith

Segundo recognizes the difficulty in trying to conceptualize and express the values underlying the faith of an individual and communicated by specific referential witnesses. This is partly because values are primarily expressed in symbolic form and partly because these values are inseparable from the concrete system of means ("ideologies") used to express the values. Fundamental to Segundo's christological method is a rigorous analysis of the kind of language appropriate to faith and required socially for the effective transmission of faith from one human being to another. At this point, Segundo is greatly influenced by Gregory Bateson's book, *Steps to an Ecology of Mind*. That book attempts to build a bridge, as Bateson himself puts it, "between the facts of life and behavior and what we know today of the nature of pattern and order" (xxvi). This emphasis on "form" and "order," for Bateson, stands in stark contrast to the predominant emphasis on "matter" and "substance" in the behavioral sciences but yields a more comprehensive and complete understanding of the human being.

Utilizing terms borrowed from Bateson, Segundo claims that faith, or values, are not communicated in the way that facts or empirical data are communicated ("digital" language), but rather through "iconic" language which is able to communicate "images" of the satisfactions that can be experienced by living one way as opposed to another or by holding one set of values as opposed to another. These images not only point to satisfactions but "evoke" them in others. Thus, while digital language is the accumulation of information by addition along the lines of a "proto-learning" already mentioned above, iconic language multiplies information by "learning-to-learn," or "deutero-learning"--the acquiring of an attitude or mentality. Perhaps the most important feature of iconic language, for Segundo's christological method, is that it is the language of witness and the basis for communicating one's faith. The language of scripture is iconic language and must be understood as such if we are to adequately comprehend the Christian faith and its most primary witness, Jesus of Nazareth.[23] All this is not to say, of course, that faith cannot be expressed in formulations that have all the characteristics of digital language; only that such digital language is based on premises that are largely iconic, such as testimonies, images, and actions.

The ability of iconic images to call forth faith in certain values is, in part, independent of reality, according to Segundo. The values in question do not admit of empirical verification or falsification for validation and, in a sense, are self-validating. But this should not be taken to mean that when human beings communicate or adopt faith in certain values, they do so just for the sake of mere whim. As Segundo says

> they are convinced that reality is on their side. What they want to say is that in the *ultimate instance* one will see that this way of acting rather than some other will prove to be satisfying. They are appealing to an

---

[23]Theresa Lowe Ching, on the basis of Segundo's language analysis rightly refers to Jesus, for Segundo, as "the Christian 'icon' *par excellence*" (55).

experience that we could well call "eschatological," taken here not in a religious sense, but in a merely human sense. The judge will be some *ultimate instance* of reality (1982: I: 192).

Here we move close to the core of Segundo's understanding of the structure of faith-language and why Segundo claims that "iconic" language such as poetry is the most adequate to communicate the satisfactions linked with particular value-systems or meaning-worlds. This does not mean, however, that Segundo believes theology should use such "iconic" language. Though iconic language is the language of values and witness, digital language is required for explicitly expressing, for example, transcendent data.

> the human being is the only *cultural* being. And this possibility of explicitly expressing transcendent data arises from the fact that it is possible for the human being *to mingle the two types of language, iconic and digital*. Without the first, the second would not communicate with the world of values. . . . Without the second, the first would not communicate in an explicit way about the conception of reality on which the realm of meaning is built . . . (I: 199).

It would be worthwhile to examine, in "digital" format, so to speak, the formal structure of the language of faith which Segundo states as follows:

> given this *fact*, which the limitedness of every human existence prevents me from verifying (for myself), *in the end* it will be seen that it was better to act *thus* (II: 18).

Based on the above, the three structural components of the language of faith are, for Segundo, (1) "the ontological premise" reflected in the word *thus*, (2) "the epistemological premise" reflected in the word *fact*, and (3) "the self-validation of those premises" reflected in the words *in the end*.

The "ontological premise," according to Segundo, is the notion of how we should live based on the reality with which we have to do. The word "thus" in the above quotation points to, for Segundo, "the structuring of activity in accordance with what is of value in reality, with its 'ought-to-be'" (II: 18). In other words, faith language always includes a built-in picture of the way things should be and a drive toward transforming reality through historical praxis. The "epistemological premise," on the other hand, is the appeal by faith to key "transcendent data" in calling for the above "ought to be." We have already seen that these data, are nothing less than our idea of how reality "in the ultimate instance" is, though we can never empirically validate the premises based upon such data. According to Segundo, we must accept these premises on the basis of a "wager" that "in the end" the rightness of acting on those premises will be proved. Apart from the self-validating nature of these premises, faith would be unnecessary, according to Segundo.[24] The important thing here, of course, and the reason why such premises are termed "epistemological" by Segundo, is that they are our means of seeing what we want to see, as it were. According to Segundo, we "punctuate" events in our lives in accordance with our faith so that we see some things that others do not see and we fail to see things which are equally as obvious as those things which we do see.

So, for example, the primary example of a christological transcendent datum, for Segundo, is the notion that "the cross of Jesus is not a closed door but rather an open one, through which life, justice, and love are already beginning to transform historical reality" (II: 20). This transcendent datum, which no amount of empirical verification can validate, becomes the "epistemological premise" by which we interpret our lives and act accordingly. It is a "wager" that we believe will be validated "in the end"--i.e., eschatologically. For Segundo, the eschatological verification to which this particular transcendent datum appeals is the resurrection of Jesus.

I have already pointed out that, if we look closely at Segundo's transcendent data, we find that they are not arrived at by individual experience but by experiences "taken as a whole" or the "sum-total" of human experience. They are, as Segundo says, "data referring to things which we cannot personally experience and which, in that sense, are beyond us" (I: 38); they "cannot possibly be verified by ordinary experience" (II: 935). By this, however, Segundo does not mean that these data are supernatural or "metaphysical."[25] Appealing to this kind of transcendent data is not equivalent to postulating a "heaven," a future life beyond death, or the immortality of the soul. As Segundo says, "I might simply be talking about some possibility of a satisfaction capable of being realized by a human being if the world as we know it changes or if that same individual changes things, by inserting himself or herself in the possibilities and conditions of this world" (I: 193).

Segundo is here attempting to establish a "logic" of values -- a criterion or criteria that can help us communicate and evaluate expressions of value without placing them under the microscope of empirical verification, on the one hand, and

---

[24]The idea of "wagering" involved in faith is clearly quite important for Segundo and he contrasts his view with those of others, such as Walter Kasper, who, in Segundo's estimate, attempt to validate faith utilizing a "reasoning process with an empirical base" (II: 19).

[25]I will have a considerable amount to say about Segundo's understanding of "metaphysics." Here already, however, it becomes clear that "metaphysical," for Segundo, carries the connotation of that which transcends the world, or experience.

turning them into mere poetry, not subject to any kind of objective validation at all, on the other hand. It is clear that "transcendent data" are precisely these criteria. The language of faith, then, is a dialectic involving our notions of how things "ought to be" and our notions of how things "in the ultimate instance" really are. Thus, all faith statements necessarily conjoin a particular interpretation of reality with the implications of that interpretation for concrete human life and praxis.[26]

Segundo does not, then, believe that the language of faith is above and beyond all need for validation. He insists that logical positivism's universal measure of the veracity of language in terms of its empirical verifiability or falsifiability belongs to a day gone by. Segundo points to the distinction between the words *denote* and *connote* and makes the observation that connotations are often expressed in language that, on the face of things, may be taken for denotation. Segundo then asks,

> Doesn't the same thing happen when people pronounce affirmations or negations such as "God exists" or "God does not exist"? (I: 187)

For Segundo, what language "connotes," just as surely as what language "denotes," can be verified and falsified even though, in the case of the former, "the demonstrations are less direct and precise" (I: 188). The important thing is to know what type of language is being used so we will know its own peculiar logic. When we cross the border into the language of meaning and values (the language of "faith"), we must use different criteria of verification than we would use in the case of science. As Segundo says,

> It is a kind of ethical--or if you prefer, existential criterion. In other words, a language has sense and meaning to the extent that I am different in one way or another because of it or of what it says and insofar as my whole way of acting and living *depends* on it or on what it says (I: 189).

This kind of validation is not simply applicable to language that announces what the basic premise of our conduct is going to be but also to claims that others

---

[26]One cannot help but notice here the remarkable similarity in structure between Segundo's understanding of faith and that expressed by Schubert Ogden insofar as faith, for both of them, presupposes a confidence that reality itself authorizes a particular self-understanding as authentic and that this self-understanding has implications for our moral beliefs and deeds (Cf. Ogden, 1982: 30ff). In the case of Ogden, of course, the reality upon which faith is premised can be explicitly described in an adequate way only by metaphysics, while Segundo rejects metaphysics as having any significance for interpreting or communicating faith.

should live in accordance with our premise. It is important to realize, at this point, that much of what Segundo has to say about religious language is a polemic against the danger of adopting or measuring such language on the basis of its sheer sacredness or piety rather than by utilizing basic criteria of human meaning and value to detect whether people mean the same thing just because they use the same words. This is an especially important principle, for Segundo, when applied to the development of an adequate christological method insofar as it is not the person of Christ in himself that provides the content for what it means to be a "Christian" but rather the basic human meaning and values to which Christ gives expression.

In summary, then, it is clear that, for Segundo, the language of faith is a language of values and meaning. As such, the language of faith is not verifiable or falsifiable in any empirical way. Indeed, there are only two ways such language can be measured: (1) by an ethical criterion whereby language has sense and meaning to the extent that we act *as if* it does (I: 188-189), and (2) by an eschatological criterion whereby, in the *ultimate instance* of reality, we will see that this way of acting rather than some other will prove to be satisfying (I: 192). Thus, we can see why Segundo claims that "iconic" language--and, especially, poetry--is the most adequate to communicate the satisfactions linked with a particular faith.

Segundo's analysis, at points, seems to be not too far removed from that of language philosophers such as R. B. Braithwaite or R. M. Hare who preserve the meaning of religious statements only at the expense of their cognitive function. Hare, for example, in meeting the challenge of Antony Flew, who claims that there are no true religious assertions,[27] argues that religious statements are not intended to be "explanations" or "assertions" but that they instead express an outlook on life, a kind of basic attitude, for which he coins the term "blik." Segundo, however, claims that his account of religious language does not yield what Hans Küng refers to as language that is "notably inexact and lacking in binding force, as if 'religious truth' were similar to 'poetic truth'" (Küng, 1976: 87).[28] Instead, Segundo claims that the kind of "inexactness" that characterizes his account of faith-language is

---

[27]Cf. the "theology and falsification debate" in *New Essays in Philosophical Theology*, edited by Antony Flew and Alasdair MacIntyre (96-108).

[28]Segundo says, of Küng's statement, that it "proves again how theology has unwittingly been moving farther and farther away from the eminently poetic fonts of its knowledge; the Bible, patristics, and the church tradition of the saints and mystics" (1982: II: 54).

nothing more than the space needed by all individuals in order to create their own way of living out that meaning-world within their own unrepeatable coordinates; in other words, thanks be to God, the same poetry and inexactness we find in the canonical Gospels (1982: II: 20).

Ideologies and Effectiveness

If every human being lives according to a certain scale of values called "faith," he or she also gives structure to that faith and implements it in some way. This implementation and structuring is, for Segundo, the second universal anthropological dimension which he calls "ideologies." In a sense, it is the move to this second dimension that is the real challenge of Christian living, and it would be no exaggeration to say that it is to this challenge that Segundo directs the bulk of his life's work and writing.

Segundo is here using the word "ideology" in a more neutral sense than its usual pejorative one which would refer to a system of ideas that serve the interests of a group by rationalizing their behavior. Segundo gives very little theoretical background as to his adoption of this more neutral use of the term "ideology" and one can easily come away from his work with the impression that his usage is somewhat arbitrary. This is all the more true in view of the fact that the relatively small amount of discussion Segundo does provide with regard to the development of his own conception of ideology takes the form of a dialogue with the writings of Karl Marx, who maintains a strictly exclusive identification of ideology and domination. Segundo's conception of ideology as at least a neutral, if not a potentially progressive and constructive force in society is not, however, a shot out of the blue. One only need to read a work such as *Hermeneutics and the Human Sciences: Essays on Language, Action and Interpretation*, by Segundo's dissertation director, Paul Ricoeur, in order to discover a much more positive assessment of ideology which has undoubtedly had an impact on Segundo. Ricoeur interprets ideology in the context of the human need to produce symbols or other interpretive structures that assist individuals or groups in understanding their identity in the greater scheme of things. Ricoeur writes,

> It is necessary, it seems to me, to escape from the fascination exercised by the problem of domination, in order to consider the broader phenomenon of social integration, of which domination is a dimension but not the unique and essential condition. If it is taken for granted that ideology is a function of domination, then it is assumed uncritically that ideology is an essentially negative phenomenon, the cousin of error and falsehood, the brother of illusion (1981: 223).

Ricoeur further influences Segundo in the latter's formulation of the relationship between ideology and knowledge, insisting that all knowledge is conditioned by human "interests" and that it is impossible to sever that relationship expressed in the form of ideologies. Ideology, then, is "the grid, the code of interpretation" within which we come to know anything whatsoever. That is not to say that one cannot evaluate the validity of the truth claims of ideologies or that one cannot critique another ideology. On the contrary, Ricoeur proposes a process of "distanciation" which, by bringing to light the interests and "belongings" of the subject, exposes those interests and makes possible deeper forms of understanding.

But, while Ricoeur's influence on Segundo with regard to the sociology of knowledge is significant, Segundo especially takes this view of ideologies and demonstrates the power and role of ideology in transforming society and bringing about cultural reconstruction. When Segundo speaks of ideologies, what he is talking about are simply the methods of implementing our goals -- that is, the price we have to pay to live the way we choose. For Segundo, the implementation of a faith is, in a sense, independent of faith even if it is itself a by-product of that faith. In *Liberación de la teología*, Segundo emphasizes that "ideologies" are the bridge between faith and history. He believes that "there is a void between the conception of God (that we receive in faith) and the problems that come to us from a history that is always in the process of change" (1975b: 133) and that ideologies are precisely what fill that void. Strangely enough, however, Segundo here defines ideology as "a system of means *and ends*" (133, 175, emphasis mine). In *El hombre de hoy ante Jesús de Nazaret*, however, Segundo stresses the functional character of ideology and defines ideology as "all systems of means, natural or artificial, employed to attain an end" (1982: I: 30). To the extent that ideologies--Marxism or liberalism, for example--propose ends or values to be realized, Segundo says that what are actually offered, whether their proponents admit to it or not, are two different, though complementary elements:

> Some features originate from anthropological faith, and others from a systematization of objective knowledge about efficacy which I here call ideology (I: 42).

This intertwining of ends and means, however, should not lead one to conclude that the lines are blurred between the two, for Segundo. The complementarity is just as real as the difference between the two and, as he says, "a value can never be indissolubly tied to one specific technique for its realization" (I: 160). Thus, faith, while it provides a scale of values by which an individual structures his or her life, never provides the means for implementing those values. Segundo, for example, reacts to Dom Helder Camara's statement that "whoever has Jesus Christ does not need Marx" by replying that revelation, the object of Christian faith, "does not teach us prefabricated things, recipes, or modes of conduct--that is, ideologies" (I: 161). Rather, revelation teaches us a way of "learning to learn," a way of creating and implementing ideologies that will make our faith effective in history.

Because these two realms--faith and ideologies--are so different, there is a great deal of difference between how we adopt a faith and how we choose ideologies. When I decide to live according to a certain set of values ("faith"), I do so by relying on the experiences of others in order to decide which path in life will be the most satisfying in the long run, even though I myself could never know that ahead of time. When it comes to implementing that faith, or putting it into practice, however, I am forced to choose means and methods on the basis of factors that are beyond my control. I am faced with external, objective limitations, and some methods will simply work more effectively than others. Thus, ideology, for Segundo, is always subject to two criteria. The first is its relationship to the values it is expected to realize, i.e., its consistency or coherence with "faith." The second criterion is extrinsic to faith and is simply the objective reality within which the ideology must function.

As I have already pointed out, religion, according to Segundo, belongs properly to this realm of instruments and methods called "ideology." Here, however, religion is distinguished from "religious faith" which, as I mentioned, is a quality of basic anthropological faith and not the property of some specialized plane labelled "religious." Religion, on the other hand, is one of several cultural expressions of faith and, rather than have a defining impact on human values, human values have a defining impact on religion. This is crucial because, in Segundo's estimate, a critical theology today must avoid any false absolutization of the religious which would prevent us from considering what purposes are actually served by the religious beliefs and practices upon which we reflect. This procedure, important for theology, is also the one followed by Jesus himself, according to Segundo, whose gospel took the form of a relativizing of religion and assigned no value to religion in itself but only a functional value. In fact, according to Segundo, one of Jesus' greatest contributions is the "ideological suspicion" to which he subjects a religion which cloaks itself in the disguise of faith. To identify faith with religion is to make an idolatrous use of what is a tool for expressing almost any and every class of values - namely, "religion."

Here, Segundo reveals the significant influence of Karl Marx on his thought. Like Marx, Segundo believes that religion can legitimate oppression and domination, as an ideology. But Segundo argues that the oppressed may struggle toward liberation through the construction of alternate ideologies and, thus, ideology is a potentially liberating force on both the practical and theoretical levels. One would expect Segundo to break with Marx at this point, since the latter understands ideology solely as a repressive form of "false consciousness" and religion as a manifestation of ideology (Marx and Engels, 1975: 66). As Marx sees it,

Religion is indeed man's self-consciousness and self-awareness so long as he has not found himself or has lost himself again. But *man* is not an abstract being, squatting outside the world. Man is *the human world*, the

> state, society. This state, this society, produce religion which is an
> *inverted world consciousness*, because they are an *inverted world*. . . . The
> struggle against religion is, therefore, indirectly a struggle against *that
> world* whose spiritual *aroma* is religion (1963: 43).

Rather than make this break with Marx, however, Segundo attempts to reinterpret
Marx as allowing for a certain degree of neutrality in ideology (especially
"religious" ideology) as, for example, when Marx writes that "religious suffering
is at the same time an expression of real suffering and a protest against real
suffering" (43). But even though Segundo can see in Marx's writings an opening
for viewing the term "ideology" as neutral with regard to value, he finally
concludes that "even in those passages where it seems to be neutral, the term
'ideology' carries with it for Marx at least a negative connotation, if not the sense
of something artificial" (1982: I: 124).

Segundo is convinced that Christian faith must develop a corresponding
ideology by means of which it can practically accomplish that end. Ideologies
can, obviously, work in a reverse way, by preserving and sustaining the existing
social structures of oppression and alienation in society. Christianity has often
functioned in just such a negative ideological way as a form of "false consciousness." Rather than give up on ideology, however, Segundo uses ideology against
ideology both to critique the old superstructure and build a new one. Theology,
of course, is not exempt from this criticism.

Faith and Ideologies

The relationship between faith and ideologies is neither simple nor
mechanical, for Segundo. This is partly due to the fact that "objective reality is
often more complicated than it seems" and that what serves as means for one end
may block other more or equally important ends, or that what serves as means for
one end may "in the long run" destroy that very end (I: 317). Segundo is not
always consistent in articulating the complicated nature of this relationship. In
Liberación de la teología, for example, he emphasizes that "the end justifies the
means" and that "a 'means,' precisely because it is nothing more than a means,
cannot have any justification in itself. It is the end for which it is employed that
gives the means its value" (1975b: 195). But Segundo moves well beyond this
relatively near-sighted evaluation of means when he begins to consider the end-
means relationship in terms of *ecology*, especially within an evolutionary
perspective (Cf. 1982: I: 316ff). On an ecological plane we discover more and
more that our planet is a delicately balanced equilibrium and that relationships are
complex and organic rather than simple and mechanical. Segundo cites as an
example the "eschatological" hope of certain Marxists that the expropriation of
private property would bring about a radically different and pleasurable form of

life. What was not taken into account, however, was the relationship of means to ends within a complex social organism. When we examine the problem of a faith that attempts to express itself in terms of an adequate ideology in the context of the insights of an evolutionary social ecology, we discover that at a certain threshold, humanity enters a real crisis in calculating the ends served by various means:

> What has somehow been slipping through our fingers is the capacity to compare the means with the end, and to decide, on that basis, as to their potential harmony (I: 320).

The crucial consideration with regard to the relationship between faith and ideologies is that even though they are, in a sense, independent of one another and rely on entirely different criteria for their adoption, separating these two planes can prevent people from undertaking the important task of analyzing faith from an ideological standpoint and from re-expressing that faith in terms of a new and liberating ideology. Such a separation can also prevent people from critically assessing the relationship between the means that they use and the values that they seek to attain. Ideological expressions of faith force that faith, so to speak, to come to terms with reality and prevent faith from becoming simply evasion. Thus, Segundo maintains simultaneously the "necessity" and "complexity" of the relationship between faith and ideologies (I: 321).

For Segundo, the significance and complexity of the dialectic between faith and ideologies is exemplified by the dialogue he moderates between Christianity, as an example of religious faith, and Marxism, as a primary example of ideology today. Segundo initiates this dialogue by, first, "neutralizing" both faith and ideologies in order to show that both are universal features of all human beings. By this procedure, Segundo is able to counter the reductionistic conception held by a "one-dimensional" scientific mentality which holds that faith is sheer illusion or religious piety and, at the same time, counter the negative identification by faith of ideology as simply a rigid system of thought that is basically a distortion of reality.

In essence, then, Segundo offers a two-pronged attack against, first, faith without ideologies and, second, ideologies without faith. In the first place, Segundo criticizes those who hold that because they are Christian, they are, therefore, exempt from utilizing any ideology either because Christianity comes ready-made with its own ideologies or because Christianity, as an "absolute value" cannot be made to be dependent on any "relative value" (1979b: 242). Segundo believes, however, that the truth expressed in the statement, "the Sabbath is made for humans, not humans for the Sabbath" inverts any attempt to start with transcendent or absolute values and then move to historical or relative values. Segundo claims that this latter kind of thinking results not in a lack of ideology but rather in an uncritical ideology. The way this phenomenon usually works is that one will simply repeat an ideology that in another context was effective but that now may actually produce the opposite results. This is especially true in the interpretation of the significance of Jesus. That significance is never a finished and complete significance independent of the real needs and experiences of persons and societies.

In the second place, Segundo criticizes those, such as Marxists or scientific positivists, who believe they can reject all faith in favor of ideologies or methodologies. According to Segundo, no ideology can completely relativize faith without becoming counterproductive and contradictory. Segundo shows that there is an "economy of energy" which keeps within positive limits the relativization of beliefs. Faith and ideologies, then, must ever be maintained in a complementary relationship without ever asserting the self-sufficiency of one over the other.

A values-system which ignores the complex problem of its effective realization will end up serving different values. An efficacy-structure which forgets the values it is serving and gets carried away by its presumed autonomy will lose the achievement oriented efficacy it exhibited at the start (1982: I: 217).

Segundo's analysis of faith and ideologies probes equally into the ideologies of capitalism and socialism, demonstrating the surprising similarity between the humanist "faith" behind each and the dehumanizing systems of effectiveness that characterize each. As Segundo points out, a confusion between, or equating of, faith and ideology yields a tendency to identify the dehumanizing effects of the ideology of one camp with the values (faith) of that same camp. In our own time, as capitalism in the West watches the dismantling of communism in the Soviet Union, Segundo's distinction between faith and ideologies is a call for self-examination and caution on both sides of the political fence:

> one of the most habitual "ideological" (in the pejorative sense) mechanisms used by people in the face of these types of systems consists of an inadequate comparison: they emphasize the *ends* of their own system as compared with the *means* of the opposing system. In other words: they talk about their own *faith* and pit against it, as if they were treating the same thing, the *ideology* of the other. Their own thinking is analyzed in terms of meaning or values and that of their opponent, in terms of the costs required for carrying out that thinking (I: 305).

Before moving on to considering some specific implications of the above analysis for christological method, I would like to briefly highlight the fundamental role of Segundo's concept of the human person that grounds the faith-ideologies dialectic. Here, the influence both of existentialism in general and of the philosophy of Nicolas Berdyaev in particular is considerable. I would like simply to point out three principal features of that concept that seem to be most pertinent for this study.

The first feature of Segundo's concept of the human person is that human beings are fundamentally constituted in liberty by God himself. This liberty, for Segundo, both in relation to the world and in relation to God, is real as opposed to merely apparent. Segundo puts the matter this way:

> only two possibilities exist: either liberty can produce something unexpected, add something original which is lacking, in which case it is *creative*; or else it is merely something which sadly and inexplicably separates the human being from its natural finality, in which case it is a *test* with no value for the world and a worthless cruelty toward the human being (1983b: II: 132).

There is no "integral" human nature, conformity to which marks authentic Christian existence. Rather, through liberty, human beings are creative not only of themselves, but of the world and of God. Segundo believes that this notion of human freedom is not only compatible with the Christian notion of God, but fundamental to that notion. Segundo follows Berdyaev's thought at this point in holding that free human activity is created by God in order to provide God with creative and novel responses, something absolutely new which even God cannot give to himself (1963a: 127-128; 1983b: II: 127ff).[29] For Segundo, God both creates us in freedom and calls us to freedom. To become enslaved to nature or law, or to acquiesce to the world or to others is a violation of God's very creation and our own authentic selfhood. Furthermore, this view of human freedom can only lead us to conclude that every good deed, every expression of love, performed by human beings is "supernatural" in that it is the operation of God's grace through human freedom that is its ground and first cause.[30]

---

[29]Segundo believes that Christianity provides the best form of existentialism and, contrary to those existentialists who think that human liberty is something opposed to God, he writes:

> The second religious revolution of Christianity seems, in a certain sense, like that of Prometheus: taking the world from the gods in order to give it to the human being. Only here no one takes anything from God. It is God himself who has given it . . . (1971f: 111).

[30]Gerald Persha's biographical information on Segundo gained from his own personal interview with Segundo reveals the source of this idea for Segundo in Leopold Malevez, one of Segundo's professors while in seminary. Malevez stirred an interest in Segundo in the reality of grace and its presence in non-Christians. Segundo went on to take up a study of the decretals of the Second Synod of Orange, concluding, in the words of Persha, "that every good act is supernatural in so far as it serves others" (41). Essentially, of course, this view is consistent

The second feature of Segundo's concept of the human person follows from the first, namely, that human liberty is nothing apart from its realization in human history.[31]   Here again, Segundo relies on the thought of Berdyaev for whom a clear distinction must be made between, on the one hand, our faculty of free will and, on the other hand, freedom itself, for which our free will is only the condition (Cf. 1963a: 104-105). For Segundo, freedom is something we choose and is a conscious construction, a life-project that fashions history and contributes to God's own life. In Segundo's first writing, *Existencialismo, filosofía, y poesía: ensayo de síntesis*, Segundo describes human existence as a "self-construction through love" and argues that human freedom is inherently social in that it is only by means of existential contact with others that we can, indeed, construct ourselves. It is here that Segundo already hints at what we have just seen to be the case with regard to his view of faith-language, namely, that the cognitive dimension of existence is subordinated to the affective dimension expressed by the need "not to explain life but to communicate it" (1948: 42ff).

Where Berdyaev's influence appears most sharply in Segundo's thought is the third feature of Segundo's notion of the human person which has to do with the limitations and conditions of human freedom imposed by external objective reality. Berdyaev is often referred to by Segundo as a "philosopher of the spirit" inasmuch as Berdyaev argues for the primacy of the human being and human liberty over against the constraints of nature and "being." Human existence is characterized by a dual experience of freedom and necessity where the liberty of the human being threatens to be dragged down or depersonalized through the determinations of the material world which "go their own way," so to speak. Segundo takes over this philosophical problem from Berdyaev and argues for struggling against the enslaving, alienating forces of reality and by so understanding them as to be able to use them as instruments for making love concrete and effective. As we shall see, the significance of Jesus of Nazareth, in this respect, is as a witness to the possibility and challenge of authentic human existence in the face of dehumanizing and depersonalizing forces and, specifically,

---

with that taken typically by Roman Catholic theology in holding that the possibility of human faith expressing itself in love is not a "natural" but a "supernatural" possibility, even if every human existence is graced with this supernatural possibility.

[31]This notion, of course, is fundamental to most liberation theologians as, for example, Gustavo Gutiérrez:

> The social praxis of contemporary man has come to adult status. He now has a clearer picture of the way his life in society is conditioned, but he is also more conscious of being an active participator in history (1974: 135).

as a model of effective love. As Theresa Lowe Ching notes, in her interpretation of Segundo:

> In effect, the understanding of true love is basically in continuity with the Old Testament revelation of God's love. Where the novelty of Christianity enters in, according to Segundo, is in throwing the emphasis on the efficacious aspect of genuine love (28).

Faith and Ideologies--Considerations with regard to Method

Having explored the relationship between faith and ideologies, as Segundo sees it, we are now in a position to begin to grasp just how dominantly that relationship impresses itself upon the character and complexity of the christological question and how it manifests itself in the structure of Segundo's own unique method for interpreting the significance of Jesus. Especially important at this point is the relevance of the faith-ideologies dialectic for the praxic dimension of the christological question and for the relationship between theology and praxis in general.

From the above analysis, it should be clear that faith and praxis are closely interwoven dimensions of all human existence, for Segundo. Just as surely as every human being adopts some world of meaning and values, so every human being expresses that meaning and those values in terms of some system of concrete praxis--ideologies. Segundo is not always as clear, however, as to the relationship between theology and praxis which grows out of and expresses the above relationship between faith and ideologies. In his analysis of various types of liberation theology, including a contrast and comparison of his own version with that of others, Segundo identifies two liberationist misconceptions about theology. The first is the notion "that liberation theology comes out of practice" and the second is "that it makes orthopraxis, instead of orthodoxy, the main criterion for its solutions" (1990: 356). This is startling language coming from a major liberation theologian and represents a serious departure from what Segundo identifies as some of the more simplistic and less critical accounts of the relationship between theology and praxis. In yet another writing, however, Segundo advocates, in similar fashion to Gutiérrez[32] and others, a fundamental commit-

---

[32]Cf. the following statement from Gutiérrez in *A Theology of Liberation*: The annunciation of the Gospel thus has a conscienticizing function, or in other words, a politicizing function. But this is made real and meaningful only by living and announcing the Gospel from within a commitment to liberation, only in concrete, effective solidarity with people and exploited social classes. Only by participating in their struggles can we understand

ment to liberation as a presupposition both for understanding the message of Jesus and for doing theology (1975b: 95-104). In like manner, he elsewhere states that "not one single dogma can be studied with any other final criterion than its impact on praxis" (1979b: 250).

How, then, do we account for the apparent contradiction between these two views? I think the most helpful way to answer this question is by recalling two very fundamental assertions which Segundo makes regarding the relationship between faith and ideologies. The first assertion has to do with the relationship of complementarity between the two while the second has to do with the relationship of relative autonomy between the two. Each of these, without contradicting the other, yields a slightly different insight regarding the relationship between theology and praxis.

First, we must recall Segundo's fundamental assertion that faith without ideologies is abstract, ineffective, and dead (1979b; 1982: I: 156ff). The theological consequence of this assertion is, of course, that theology, as critical reflection upon faith, can never avoid the question of ideologies and must, therefore, incorporate into its own method the results of the social sciences insofar as they not only yield the contours of the very praxis out of which faith arises but insofar as they cast light on the mechanisms whereby human beings structure their lives in terms of ideologies and the relationship, even if disguised or unrecognized, of those ideologies to systems of meaning and values. Every witness to faith, however absolute or unconditional its claims, is expressed under the influence of concrete, historical, and relative factors. A theology which thinks that it is dealing strictly with absolutes is really making absolutes out of things that are not. Theology, according to Segundo, must vigorously address issues that are typically relegated to other disciplines and must pass judgment on matters that it has traditionally avoided because of their relative and historical nature. Segundo makes his point this way:

> Here theology faces an enormous task. It must pinpoint the frustrated evangelical experiences that lie at the roots of this ecclesiastical insecurity. It must try to discover the criteria governing the authentic historical functionality of the gospel message. It must also try to determine the limits of any such functionality, since every incarnation has limits. We are led once again to the same conclusion. If people decide that the gospel message has nothing to say about such a critical human issue as the choice between capitalism and socialism, then it is obvious that the gospel message can only have an absolute value, a non-functional value. In other words, its value is nil (1979b: 245).

the implications of the Gospel message and make it have an impact on history (1973: 269).

One result of this view is Segundo's rejection of the methodological notion that questions regarding ideologies--such as the above option between capitalism or socialism--belong properly to *moral* theology. Segundo believes that theology, for some time now, has served a primarily "conservative" function not so much because it has proposed "conservative" dogmas as that it has claimed for itself an autonomy from practical considerations leaving them "on a secondary plane" and subjecting them to criteria that are "independent of the faith." This, in Segundo's estimation has given rise to a moral theology "behind dogma's back" that is "remarkably similar to the civic morality required by the established society" (250).

Segundo argues that the question of the choice between capitalism and socialism is a question that, though it forces theology to rely on contingent and relative data furnished by the social sciences, is not outside the domain of theology, precisely because theology is critical reflection on the faith and faith is inseparable from ideologies. Thus, one should not conclude that the question of ideologies, however much it is determined by an objective science, is outside of and beyond the question of faith. In other words, if the significance of Jesus is only an absolute significance, unchanging with time and circumstance and eternally established by virtue of Jesus' divine nature, then Jesus has no significance. For Segundo, the significance of Jesus must first and foremost be a "historical" significance--one that connects with and gives guidance to historical praxis. A great deal of the misunderstanding on the part of both liberation theologians and their critics relative to the relationship between praxis and theology (and, by the same token, between the social sciences and theology), stems from a failure to grasp the complexity of that relationship vis-á-vis the structure of human existence as a dialectic of faith and ideologies.

Segundo is especially critical of European "political theologies" or "theologies of revolution" at precisely this point in that, for all their talk of the political implications of the gospel, they "leave us disoriented when we are confronted with the political and revolutionary option par excellence" (245). Segundo notes that, for J. B. Metz, theology must insist on an agnosticism with regard to any possibilities or options for the future other than a stalwart hope in the inevitable triumph of the eschatological kingdom. Theology, then, stands against any tendency by some political program to present itself as absolute or, as Jürgen Moltmann puts it, as a "premature and untimely anticipation of the kingdom of God" (Moltmann, 1969: 129-147). While Segundo himself sympathizes with the call for the relativization of specific options within history, he finds in the deabsolutizing tendencies of Metz and Moltmann a subordination of the relative to the absolute which leads inevitably to their divorce. Says Segundo,

> The revolution envisioned by that theology seems much more akin to the Cartesian theoretical revolution based on methodic doubt than to a real practical revolution. If you like the term, it does revolutionize our way of

Effective Faith

focusing on socio-political systems from our secure installment within them; but it does not choose between one system and another. If there is any tendency to take sides in the theology of revolution, it is a tendency to opt against whatever system is existing *today*. . . . all forms of "eschatological" criticism tend to relativize all that exists. The relativization is revolutionary in name only (1979b: 247).

In Segundo's opinion, German political theology so divorces the relative political order and the absolute eschatological order that the former can only be called an "anticipation" (Moltmann), an analogy (Weth), or an "outline" (Metz). Segundo responds,

But who dedicates their life to an "analogy"? Who dies for an "outline"? Who motivates a human mass or a people in the name of an "anticipation"? (247)

The key issue here, for Segundo, is the degree of "causality" which can be attributed to historical-political options insofar as the coming of the kingdom of God is concerned; Segundo believes that the common denominator of the various "theologies of liberation" is a shared belief that "human beings, both as individuals and as political beings, are already building up the kingdom of God here and now in history" (247). It is this affirmation of causality which, in Segundo's opinion, is denied by German political theology, grounded as it is in the Pauline doctrine of justification by faith alone and not by works. But lest Segundo's complaints sound like a simple case of anti-Protestantism on his part, it is clear from his writings that he is primarily responding to the usage made of Paul's doctrine by German political theologians such as Rudolf Weth. Nonetheless, Segundo seems quite content to accept as characteristic of political theology in general, those interpretations of both Luther and Paul that rule out any role for socio-political systems in contributing to the building of the kingdom of God in any causal way.

There seems to be little question in Segundo's mind that contemporary European theologies of the political--both Protestant and Roman Catholic--so reject any idea of causality in the relationship between political options and the kingdom of God as to effectively rule out any assistance on the part of theology in making the practical political options which human beings must make in their daily lives. Segundo intends for theology to be of more practical relevance than this. In order to establish such relevance, Segundo begins with a conception of theology as *fides quaerens intellectum*. He goes on to explain what he means:

I mean "faith seeking understanding" in order to give guidance and direction to historical praxis. I maintain that not one single dogma can be studied with any other final criterion than its impact on praxis (250).

Segundo, at this point, follows a method that gazes directly at the Bible for examples of those, such as the prophets or Jesus, who do not hesitate to pass theological judgment on political reality and who do not leave concrete political options to some "eschatological reserve." Thus, for example, Jeremiah confronts the situation of the exile with clear instructions that are not diminished by either their possibility of political failure or their relativity when compared with the absoluteness of the kingdom of God. Jesus also interprets concrete acts of liberation, such as the lame walking or the sick being cured, as "signs of the kingdom," regardless of the relativity of such acts measured in terms of their historical finality or long-term success.

Here, Segundo, with his straightforward appeal to "the way Jesus did theology," might seem to open himself up to the criticism made by Schubert Ogden against liberation theologies that "these theologies typically are not so much theology as witness" (1979a: 33). Segundo at least recognizes this danger and warns that his appeals to Jesus and the prophets "might seem to be some sort of gospel proclamation rather than a serious study of theological methodology" (1979b: 256). But even though Segundo wants to develop a critical and modern theological method, he finds much in the method of biblical witnesses that theology should imitate or at least parallel:

> for some time now theological methodology has been looking to other scientific disciplines rather than to gospel proclamation to find analogies for its own underlying criteria. It prefers the categories and certitudes of the other human sciences to the seeming simplicity of the thinking of Jesus and the primitive church (256).

Segundo is not here advocating a retreat from critical rigor or methodological discipline in theology. The theological endeavor is not so easy as simply asking, "What would Jesus do?" in this or that circumstance. What he is trying to emphasize, however, is that despite the critical posture which an adequate theology must maintain, a sensitivity to what liberates human beings here and now, even though we cannot guarantee future success for any given historical step, is a necessary function of theology. Thus, though theology cannot be "the science of the immutable in the midst of human vicissitudes," it may, nonetheless, "like the theology of the gospel message . . . get back to being the theology of *fidelity*" (257). This it can do not by sacralizing any historical possibilities, but by linking present historical praxis to the absolute for the sake of effectively mobilizing human beings.[33]

---

[33]A liberative event, as Segundo notes, "however ambiguous and provisional it may be, stands in a causal relationship to the definitive kingdom. The causality is partial, fragile, often distorted and in need of reworking; but it is a far cry from

One of Segundo's primary concerns, in this regard, is that theology not preoccupy itself with looking for divine efficacy in life apart from historical efficacy as, for example, when the assent to dogmatic formulas or participation in the sacraments becomes more important than comprehending and living out the truth. This is what Segundo intends when he claims that any orthodoxy that does not point toward orthopraxy is "magical." So, too, when we turn to christology, Segundo wants to show that the significance of Jesus is not an already finished and complete significance independent of the real needs and experiences of persons and societies; that is, from praxis. Thus, if Segundo claims that theology does not "arise" from praxis, that does not mean that theology is independent of praxis. Because human beings express their faith, especially when they theologize, in a thoroughly ideological and, thus, political way, the question of praxis, i.e., the question of who we are politically, historically, and socially, is logically prior to the question of who Jesus is and demands a method that, on the one hand, approaches all ideological expressions of faith with the intent of stripping away their false pretense to be that faith itself and that, on the other hand, reinterprets the faith politically in terms of some new ideology.

Just as surely as faith without ideologies is dead, however, so also we have seen that, for Segundo, while a faith is adopted on the basis of a wager in response to the testimony of referential witnesses, ideologies are chosen based on their capacity, in the face of objective reality, effectively to realize that faith. In this way, though faith and ideologies are inextricably linked together, they yet retain a great deal of autonomy from one another. Therefore, even though theology cannot dismiss questions of praxis, or ideology, either by moving them out of the orbit of theology altogether or by relegating them to moral theology, so also theology is not simply to be reduced to the social sciences nor is it to be practiced as a mere reflex of praxis. There is a strong current in Segundo's thought that runs against the desire for "orthopraxy" if by that is meant there is a "correct" way of acting based, for example, on how Jesus acted. To that extent, Segundo would no doubt agree with Clodovis Boff's statement that "praxis as such is not a theological category. It is 'theologically opaque'" (103). T h u s, even if the question of praxis is inherent in the christological question and even if our own asking and answering of the christological question calls us to a new and liberating praxis, it is clear from Segundo's own christological method that

---

being nothing more than an anticipation, outline, or analogy of the kingdom" (1979b: 257). Elizabeth Lord agrees with Segundo and offers the following example:

> To take a concrete issue, no one would refer to the ending of racial segregation in South Africa as a mere anticipatory sign or analogy of the kingdom in its entirety; but what is involved here is the kingdom manifested in its attribute of justice and peace (301-302).

he does not think the importance of the concrete and historical situation lies in our "starting" there. In fact, Segundo devotes the bulk of his first volume in defining and linking terms and concepts and, only after that, does he turn to the specific situation in Latin America. He says,

> The apparent omission of any concrete circumstance as a starting point has its reasons. Too often we overestimate the advantage, for *committed* reflection, of starting with problems as they present themselves concretely and consciously in the life of human beings and, above all, in their practice (1982: I: 304, emphasis mine).

Thus, while any human reflection is always preceded by some praxis, it is nonetheless true that prior experiences constitute a reality independent of our present practice. Segundo even goes so far as to say that we must bracket our own pragmatic urgencies long enough to grasp as carefully as we can the total historical complex that comes to us almost gratuitously as it were. Even though our reflection on the significance of Jesus will never be neutral--guided as it is by our own set of problems and, thus, grounded in praxis-- that significance does not simply "arise" from our praxis. As I shall show in the next chapter, Segundo believes we must give Jesus the room to speak to those of his own day before we begin to pose our own problems to him. In this way, believes Segundo, our own problems will be better served.

The consequence of this relationship between praxis and theology, for Segundo, in terms of christological method, drives him to examine a variety of christologies on their own terms, rather than synthesize them into one christology. Segundo hopes, thereby, to strike a balance between (a) the connection of a given tradition with the particular context in which we live, and (b) the richness and autonomy of the tradition itself as it has utilized, quite independent of us, various approaches to the interpretation of the significance of Jesus. By taking his christology down this path, Segundo claims that he is not trying to create a new christology, not even the Latin American christology. God reveals himself in Jesus Christ as the ultimate meaning of human existence but this revelation is attested to by scripture or through such formulas as the Chalcedonian definition always in a penultimate and historically conditioned way. Thus, there can only be "christologies," that ever and anew reexplore the significance of Christ in the light of new and changing historical situations. Rather than try to present a collection of timeless truths about Jesus which require hiding or bracketing the historical situations in which people have been "interested" in him, Segundo's "anti-christology" takes the form of exposing precisely these "interests" and subsequently immersing Jesus into the relativities and historically-conditioned situations in which we human beings find ourselves. Any kind of supra-ideological, neutral, or impartial interpretation of the significance of Jesus, rather than helping us to recognize his importance, would be closer to the attitude of the kind of people who failed to recognize that very importance in Jesus' own day.

With regard to theology's employment of the social sciences in its method, here, too, Segundo advocates for a necessarily high degree of autonomy in terms of the internal method, logic, criteria of verifiability, and language used by each. That autonomy does not mean that theology can do without the social sciences any more than it can do without philosophy. But, theology must always understand that it stands as critical reflection on praxis. Just as theology requires the social sciences to mediate the reality of historical praxis to it, so also, theology is distinct from that praxis as reflection upon it. Segundo would surely agree with Clodovis Boff who says,

> Praxis must therefore be understood as located on the side of the *real*, as object of faith and of theology, and not on the side of the awareness they represent (102).

Finally, the relative autonomy between theology and the social sciences allows room for the kind of ideology-critique of the former by the latter insofar as theology functions regressively as a legitimator of the status quo.

CHAPTER 4

JESUS AND HISTORY

Method, as Segundo understands it, is not simply an organizational concept referring to the structure of how theology develops or the order in which topics are treated. It is much deeper than that. Rather, it is the very way one comes to know or to understand theologically and how this way of knowing comes to bear on the sources of Christian theology. It is not simply an approach to a certain content. Method informs, influences, and shapes the content itself. In a very real way, Segundo's theological method as a whole and christological method in particular is the systematic attempt to allow a particular understanding of history to make precisely this kind of thorough impact on both the method and content of theology. As Gustavo Gutiérrez says about the early theology of development or theology of revolution,

> Efforts to further development or revolutionary action were regarded as the *application* of a certain process of theological thought to certain aspects of the political world this time, but there was no question of a new kind of apprehension of faith. It was not theological thought in the context of the process of liberation. It was not critical thought from and about faith as a liberating praxis. To theologize from this later standpoint certainly involves a change of perspective (1974: 139).

Segundo takes up something like the task called for in Gutiérrez's statement above. Rather than simply provide a discussion relative to the liberationist view of history, Segundo incorporates that liberationist "change of perspective" into a unique method of interpreting the significance of Jesus.

Historical Knowledge and Christological Method

Segundo makes a distinction between, on the one hand, knowledge of a "pinpoint" event in history which relies on documentary proof supplied by an unbiased observer and, on the other hand, knowledge of a more complicated historical reality, such as a person whose meaning for today we wish to comprehend and which, though it must be faithful to the history of the person in question, requires some sort of interpretive lens. In the case of this latter form of knowledge, "objectivity" and "neutrality" are not necessarily in direct proportion to one another. On the contrary, the pretense of "neutrality" only serves to clutter the history of the individual in question with the subjective interests of the observer disguised as scientific fact. As Segundo says,

> *historical comprehension* of a more scientific and objective nature requires that we cast or project from the present toward the past an interpretive scheme that originates in the present with which we are involved (1982: II: 798).

It is the case with this latter kind of knowledge that we should not even pretend to be "neutral" or "completely objective" in our reconstruction of the past but that we begin with a "commitment" and a "wager," not unlike that which Segundo claims to be at the very basis of faith itself, as we have seen. This is especially true when we come to reflect on the significance of a historical person such as Jesus of Nazareth and the only option other than beginning with "commitment," for Segundo, is that Jesus be placed at the mercy of a christology, whether "from above" or "from below," that raises him above any and all ideological alternatives, thus turning him into the Jesus who is "the most unarmed in the face of the most transparent ideological mechanisms" (II: 798-799) and the least sure basis for faith.

It is in the context of this consideration of historical knowledge that Segundo expresses discontent with the christological method of those, such as Bultmann, who believe, according to Segundo, that they have gone beyond fundamentalism in an attempt to make Jesus more meaningful and his message more comprehensible through processes such as demythologizing. Mythical conceptions are replaced with modern categories, but, in Segundo's opinion, the criteria for determining those categories are more subjective than objective (II: 800). The process boils down to replacing what would be meaningful for persons in Jesus' day with what would be "acceptable" for us today. To Segundo's mind, this method "lacks critical-mindedness" and

> the necessary boundaries between the objective problematic of today's human being (geographically, culturally, and socially situated), on the one hand, and the effort to make the meaning of Jesus easy and painless, on the other hand, are erased with too much ease (II: 801).

The process of adaptation ends up in a "reductionism" in which "the conflictivity unleashed and deepened by Jesus of Nazareth . . . is exorcised in the name of what shocks the human being of today" (II: 801).

Segundo believes that the historical understanding and hermeneutic presupposed by an adequate christological method must be guided by a view of modern humanity that goes beyond the relatively new demands for rationality, pragmatism, or even secularity and that does not give in to every demand of the "modern" human being, especially if that modern human being has trouble accepting "transcendent data," which, as Segundo reminds us, defy empirical verification. Unless we allow for the radical "strangeness" and "difficulty" of Jesus' message, says Segundo, that message "will call into question nothing because it will mean nothing" (II: 802).

Though Segundo's criticism of Bultmann at this point is arguably rather wide of the mark, he does admit the possibility that Bultmann's method may mean "existential translation" rather than "elimination" (II: 54). Nonetheless, while Segundo is surely correct that Jesus has often been interpreted in ways that dilute or mask the "difficulty" of his message, Segundo here seems predisposed toward a kind of "trade-off" mentality that tends to maintain the "strangeness" of Jesus' message at the expense of its coherence and comprehensibility and that tends to achieve the practical credibility of the witness of faith at the expense of its theo-retical credibility. Segundo's reference, for example, to "Bultmann's straight-forward suppression of the mythical" tends toward hyperbole and hides the fact that the task of demythologizing is every bit as important as the task of deideologizing; indeed, the failure to accomplish the former can even hinder us in accomplishing the latter.[34]

At any rate, despite the caution that Segundo verbalizes with regard to the dangers of demythologizing, he is still in basic agreement with the core of Bultmann's hermeneutic method and sides explicitly with Bultmann against the christological work of others such as Wolfhart Pannenberg, Hans Küng, and Walter Kasper. The debate at this point is quite instructive for helping us to grasp the contours of Segundo's christological hermeneutic and the implications of that hermeneutic for his christological method as a whole. As we shall see, Segundo undertakes a new search for the "historical Jesus," but just what he means by this phrase and how he goes about arriving at that quantity does not fit neatly into any preestablished labels or camps and requires a careful and thorough interpretation of his argument.

As Segundo sees it, the two main alternatives supplied by contemporary christology with regard to interpreting the significance of Jesus are to seek out either the Jesus of history or the preached Christ of the kerygma. Pannenberg states the dilemma this way:

> it does make a fundamental difference whether we seek to understand the present proclamation of who Jesus is and what he means for us in terms of what happened at that time or whether, conversely, we speak of what happened then only secondarily, that is, only in the light of what the

---

[34]For example, the failure to demythologize certain eschatological symbols traditionally used to express Christian hope (the second coming, immortality of the soul, etc.) can today quite easily be taken in such a way as to compromise our concern for this world and our responsibility for it.

proclamation says about it today. The question is: Must Christology begin with Jesus himself or with the kerygma of his community? (21-22)

As I have already mentioned in Chapter 1, Pannenberg clearly opts for the former of the two and believes not only that getting back to Jesus as he was is "possible," but that reconstructing the historical Jesus is also "necessary" in order, first, to establish the continuity between Jesus as he was and the early Christian kerygma about Jesus and, second, to establish the unity of the New Testament witnesses to Jesus. Segundo vigorously criticizes Pannenberg at this point, but not so much because he disagrees with Pannenberg's appraisal of the historical possibilities of reconstructing the historical Jesus. Rather, Segundo rejects Pannenberg's desire for christological unity and sees in it a sacrifice of the soteriological diversity of the various witnesses to Jesus and, thereby, the unique needs and problematics of those same witnesses.[35] But while Pannenberg's approach to the historical Jesus smooths over the variety of soteriological interests that characterize the New Testament witnesses so that our faith may be based on something historical rather than a product of faith, Segundo finds an equally disastrous approach to the historical Jesus in the method of Hans Küng who smooths over *our* own interests and motivations as human beings today, in the name of a warning against "ideologies." Segundo responds,

> What seems so inconceivable to me is that anyone thinks *ideology* can be avoided at such a low cost. . . . How can they even suggest that not *desiring* anything (consciously or explicitly) vis-à-vis Jesus is a possible, necessary, or sufficient condition for understanding him, interpreting him, and recognizing his significance two thousand years later! (1982: II: 46)

Segundo points out that the one sure sign of the presence of "ideology," in its most negative sense, is where we find a predominance of claims to neutrality or unity in theological method.

We thus find Segundo rejecting any quest for the historical Jesus taken up as an attempt to uncover historical facts about a person who lived two thousand years ago and thereby "to build on the basis of objective reality, and not on the basis of our own (ideological) desires, a credible discourse about Jesus" (II: 48). According to Segundo, such a procedure is doomed to "theological failure" because

---

[35]Cf. Pannenberg's denial that the starting point for christology is the relevance of Jesus to our individual and varied desires for salvation. Pannenberg says, "The soteriological interest cannot, however be the principle of Christological doctrine" (38).

if theology consists in understanding the faith, then the historical Jesus provides a very poor handle for that faith. Facts about him are merely facts, *facta bruta* (II: 48).

Much more interesting, says Segundo, would be the "Christ of faith." At least that Christ, though certainly not historical, connects up with problems that are more comprehensible and relevant to us because

> according to his interpreters, he was occupied with problems similar to mine and, moreover, he offers me more wide-ranging, comprehensible, and multifaceted access to the human problematic (II: 48).

In the end, however, Segundo believes that the "Christ of faith," is also inadequate for christology and he is unwilling to be satisfied with "an ideological plurality of christologies without objective criteria of discernment" (II: 48). Segundo may seem ambivalent at this point, but in a very real sense, what he is dissatisfied with more than anything else is precisely the way the contemporary statement of the central christological problem is itself posed, as well as the methodological alternatives that way of posing the problem yields.

Segundo believes that he can avoid both extremes and, instead, wants to build

> a valid bridge between christology and soteriology that does not improperly mix the historical Jesus with the Christ of faith, objective data with human desires, but somehow combines both (II: 49).

This he believes he can do by energetically pursuing a hermeneutic method that is more in line with that of two of Martin Heidegger's students, Rudolf Bultmann and Karl Rahner, insofar as they both take up an anthropological-existentialist approach to interpreting the significance of Jesus. Segundo describes the value of both theologians for christology:

> these two clearly seek to establish a dialogue with Jesus in terms of what Jesus has to say to human existence. In this way, Jesus' interest *for the human being* shows up as prior to the establishment of his relationship with God or the inclusion of his divinity. If we use my language, we might say that both Bultmann and Rahner begin by asking about the content and significance of an *anthropological faith* in Jesus (II: 52).

What Segundo means here is that both Bultmann and Rahner take pains to lay out the essential anthropological "preconditions" for adequately interpreting the significance of Jesus--i.e., the necessary and prerequisite conditions underlying human existence that enable what Jesus said two thousand years ago to confront

us with meaning and urgency today. Indeed, we now see that the entirety of
Segundo's own painstaking analysis of "faith" and "ideologies" as two universal
dimensions in all of human existence is an attempt to provide just such an
anthropological infrastructure for developing an adequate christological method.

In the case of Rahner, of course, this approach takes the form of a
"transcendental anthropology" and I will take up Segundo's dialogue with him
more fully in the next chapter. Segundo feels an especially close affinity to
Bultmann, however, and, though he disagrees with him on several points, believes
that Bultmann's method "is the one which best integrates, in principle, the present-
day interest of the human being with the summons issued to us by the Absolute
in Jesus" (II: 58). This it does, according to Segundo, primarily through its
clarification of the role of the "preunderstanding" involved in all historical interpretation.

Bultmann's application of the principle of preunderstanding in the
hermeneutic endeavor and especially the resulting "circle" whereby the preunderstanding is modified and deepened is a point of departure for Segundo's methodological discussion in *Liberación de la teología* where he emphasizes the circular
character of the interpretive process--the dynamic and complex interaction between
the reality to be interpreted and the preunderstanding of the individual doing the
interpreting. In *El hombre de hoy ante Jesús de Nazaret*, Segundo extends this
notion of the "hermeneutic circle" to christology and believes that an adequate
christological hermeneutic absolutely cannot avoid the question of the interests and
desires--call them "ideologies"--either of the New Testament interpreters of Jesus
or of human beings of later times or our own present day. Just as Bultmann
desires to improve our preunderstanding through a circle that brings us back again
and again to the person, text, or message being interpreted, each time with a set
of interests and desires altered by our previous reading, so, for Segundo, this
means that there can never be simply one christology that merely "presents," once
and for all, the significance of Jesus.

> I think that the only valid approach to Jesus of Nazareth is that of the New
> Testament, that is, of a process of successive readings that start out from
> the concrete, historical interest he aroused in his own time and place and
> move on to the human problems of later times and our own present day.
> . . . only one kind of christology is valid and dovetails with the way Jesus
> himself posed issues. It is a christology that starts off from the historical
> data about Jesus and *multiplies* the readings of his message, each time
> *modifying* the *preunderstanding* that is brought to the next reading. A
> complete and finished christology, consisting of one single reading of all
> the (biblical and/or dogmatic) material having to do with Jesus of
> Nazareth, is a dead-end street and, in truth, is not Christian (II: 63-64).

This process of "successive" or "multiple" historical readings is precisely the approach that Segundo takes in his own christology in which he begins with the synoptic reading, moves to that of St. Paul, and concludes with a relatively more recent historical reading--that of St. Ignatius of Loyola. The several volumes of Segundo's christology, then, should not be regarded as lengthy digressions into unrelated or, at best, superfluous matters. All of these, on the contrary, pave a path for Segundo's own formulation of Jesus' significance for our own contemporary problems and challenges in present-day, evolutionary terms. In every case, Segundo's analysis of the fundamental anthropological dimensions of human existence, faith and ideologies, provides the required structure--the "time tunnel," so to speak--that allows us to move back and forth between the Jesus of history and our own contemporary situation. So also, it is the relationship between faith and ideologies that renders impossible any attempt to combine all of our information about Jesus into one single christology and that, instead, demands a christological method that traverses successive interpretations of Jesus utilizing a "hermeneutic circle." Segundo can now come closer to explaining the importance--indeed, the necessity--of his analysis of faith and ideologies for his overall christological method:

> This presupposition of the basic intelligible unity of the human species, an inevitable axiom of all the human sciences (just as the rationality of the universe constitutes the necessary springboard for all physical investigations), is essential to our effort to approach Jesus of Nazareth. . . . thanks to faith, human beings transmit to one another data that are central to the human meaning-world and, so, faith, in this general sense, more or less serves as a species-memory and as the deepest bond of its unity (II: 52).

According to Segundo, this prerequisite anthropological footing provided by his existentialist analysis permits us to take up two fundamental tasks with regard to christological method. First, despite the mistaken motivations that have characterized past studies of the historical Jesus, we must, indeed, travel back to the historical Jesus in order to comprehend his own responses to the desires and interests of his listeners. Here, Segundo is not so much interested in historical facts about Jesus as in his "meaning-world" and the "transcendent data" to which he appeals. Second, we must return to our own present situations and link up the desires and interests to which Jesus did respond with our own desires and interests. This latter task I will explore in the next chapter, but at this point I turn to an examination of Segundo's own distinctive quest for the historical Jesus.

The Quest for the Historical Jesus

So far in this chapter, I have attempted to interpret Segundo's understanding of the structure of historical knowledge insofar as that structure informs and shapes christological method. If that interpretation is accurate, we are faced with what is apparently a contradiction in Segundo's evaluation of the prospects for and relevance of reconstructing the historical Jesus. Segundo, for example, rejects Pannenberg's quest for the historical Jesus and yet his own method explicitly calls for some sort of similar quest. Just how are we to understand these seemingly opposed tendencies in Segundo's thought?

I noted in the first chapter that Segundo accepts, for the sake of argument, the often-made claim that liberation theology lacks a christology. Segundo explains this state of affairs by making the following point, with respect to method:

> every *logia*, here as in whatever other branch of knowledge, presupposes a certain objectification or reification. Every science studies its object under some aspect, treating it as the subject matter of a "rational discourse," of a reasoned effort to grasp something of universal validity. That science makes of its object a category, thereby permitting the science to avoid singular facts (II: 28).

Sticking with a rigid attention to word-etymologies, Segundo comments that "christology" implies, by definition, a *logia* about the category "christ," while the actual object of Christian faith is a single person. To Segundo's mind, this entails a tremendous problem. In order to do "christology" we would have to find "the specific category that would make it possible to go beyond the mere description of facts, introduce the reasoning process, and draw conclusions" (II: 29). But such a category is logically impossible when we are dealing with a single person.

Because what we are asking for is the significance of *a person*, we must let Jesus speak to us as we listen to how Jesus spoke to those who encountered him. In Segundo's opinion, classical christologies reverse this procedure in that "they formulate questions for Jesus of Nazareth for which he clearly and explicitly said he had no answers to offer" (II: 50) -- questions, for example, like what Jesus' relationship to God was or in what way Jesus is soteriologically decisive.

Segundo wants to take a different course that attempts to avoid getting lost or side-tracked in defining who Jesus is theologically or soteriologically ahead of time at the expense of being faced as a human being with the world of meaning and values witnessed to by him. This is why Segundo is concerned to get Jesus out of "the grip of theology," as he puts it, by which he means rejecting any method that purports to approach Jesus free of ideologies or subjective interests and that, instead, pretends to interpret his significance in terms of universal categories. Segundo would rather interpret Jesus in terms of the concrete historical reality (the religio-political context, as we shall see) in which Jesus lived and breathed and with which he interacted, in order to determine historically why he was interesting to his interpreters. Segundo states the essential issue of christology in this way:

There would never have been any christology if the human being named Jesus of Nazareth had not powerfully *interested* some of his contemporaries. From where did that interest originate, and can it reach to us? (II: 30-31)

Interest in Jesus was aroused, so Segundo maintains, not once people "in some more or less confused and incipient way recognized him to be God or, at least, an envoy close to God" (II: 32). Rather, if people somehow came to see Jesus as in some way a divine revelation, it was because "that human being was interesting, because he was humanly significant" (II: 32). Segundo concludes that if people today understand Jesus as somehow revealing God to us it will also be because he is humanly significant to them today. In this way, Segundo believes he has made a methodological shift from focusing on who Jesus is "in himself" to what it is that is "interesting" about Jesus that, for him, warrants calling his christology an "anti-christology." One might well ask at this point, however, if the shift Segundo proposes really is a shift from who Jesus is "in himself" to what is "interesting" about Jesus or whether, instead, Segundo has only shifted his identification of the Jesus who is interesting to us from Jesus the revealer of God to Jesus "the ordinary human being." As I hope to show in Part II, it is not at all clear that Segundo has here really moved the question of the significance of Jesus "for us" very far beyond the form in which it is typically expressed by revisionary christologies in general.

Nonetheless, if Segundo's method drives him to begin with the "human" rather than the "religious" significance of Jesus, that does not mean that Segundo embraces some ostensibly impartial rehearsal of the historical facts surrounding Jesus' life, as if this bundle of facts could somehow be transubstantiated into meaning for us. But even though Segundo believes no headway can be gained by an empirical inquiry that attempts to reach back behind any and all witnesses in order, thereby, to lay its hands on a "historical" Jesus, that does not prevent Segundo from beginning with the "historical coordinates" (II: 63) of Jesus, understood as the historical interest he aroused among his contemporaries. As Segundo says, "Jesus speaks to us through the answers that *others* received from him regarding their own respective problematics" (II: 33). On this basis, Segundo believes it is both possible and important to uncover what we can and should call the "historical Jesus."

Segundo wants to distance himself, as we have seen, from the motivations that guide other quests for the historical Jesus. For Segundo, the importance of a study of the historical Jesus is not conditioned upon some need to arrive at an objective reality that can (1) impartially judge the values and projects of every age once and for all, (2) secure our faith from all ideological trappings, or (3) ground our faith on historical fact rather than the product of faith. Rather, it is necessary in order to uncover how, historically, Jesus' values impacted the values and projects of the people of his own day and, thereby, infer how Jesus' values can impact our own values today. In Segundo's opinion, other christologies do not allow the human needs or desires that were satisfied by Jesus to provide the context for historical understanding; rather, they look for either theological or historical indications of Jesus' oneness with God. Segundo wants to follow a different procedure. He writes,

> Is it not possible to allow ourselves to be interested by that ordinary human being -- however extraordinary he may have turned out to be -- who began to act and to teach in Palestine in the first century A.D.? . . . we must necessarily question Jesus *in terms of the questions* to which historically he was willing (and able) to respond. Travelling through a kind of time tunnel, we ought to join ourselves up to the desires and expectations with which Jesus entered into dialogue (II: 30-31).

Of course, Segundo recognizes that Jesus never speaks directly to us but only through witnesses. What christology must first uncover, then, is the significance of Jesus for these witnesses. In this way, Segundo believes that it is possible through historical research to reconstruct the way Jesus' faith interacted with the interests and desires of those who came into contact with him. Thus, so Segundo believes, even if it is impossible to get to the historical Jesus *apart from* human interpretation, it is possible to get to the historical Jesus *through* human interpretation.

Segundo recognizes that, in the past, theology did not possess the critical means for separating the "history" of Jesus from its "interpretations." In fact, interpretations were not understood for what they were: interpretations. However, with the development of historical criticism and the discovery that all the New Testament writings are interpretations based on faith, the possibility of recovering Jesus "as he actually was" became extremely problematic, if not impossible. Segundo is quite aware of the problems involved in trying to recover the "historical Jesus." He says,

> It is exceedingly interesting and essential to note that we have nothing *directly* from Jesus. Jesus of Nazareth *always* reaches us already *interpreted* by persons or groups *interested* in him. That is the same as saying that we have no access to him except by passing through, in some way, *those interests* (II: 32).

Segundo maintains a very sober assessment of the possibilities of reaching an "uninterpreted" Jesus and admits frankly that "the Jesus interpreted by no one does not exist" (II: 35).

Segundo considers two possible methods that might be pursued in response to the apparent impossibility, historically, of reconstructing the historical Jesus. The first method begins with the admission that we are actually exaggerating when we say we believe in Jesus of Nazareth. It is actually the interpreters of Jesus in whom we believe, each of whom has his or her own individual bias, interests, and expectations. The second approach insists, against the first, that our faith must be in Jesus himself and not in his interpreters. This position wants to get back to the deeds Jesus actually performed and the words Jesus actually spoke. While Segundo does not agree completely with this line of thought, he does, however, believe that there is still much about the historical Jesus that can be gleaned from what he believes an adequate historical method can discover with the help of various forms of literary and textual criticism as well as a thorough knowledge of Jesus' socio-religious milieu. He believes that biblical studies can determine words and deeds that can be attributed historically to Jesus with "reasonable certainty" (II: 34). In fact, the bulk of his reading of the synoptic gospels in *El hombre de hoy ante Jesús de Nazaret* is given to providing a reconstruction of just what can be known with "reasonable certainty" about the historical Jesus.

If Segundo is closer to this second line of thought than the first, however, he still wants to caution against forgetting that the historical Jesus is not speaking to us but to others and it is this recognition, he believes, that distinguishes his own approach to the historical Jesus from others. Thus, the fact that Jesus always comes to us "interpreted" does not entail the historical impossibility of reconstructing the historical Jesus, for Segundo, but requires that we approach Jesus in the light of the questions that he actually was willing and able to respond to as revealed in his interpreters. As Segundo says,

> The solution is to be found, it seems to me, in the perception that the study of the historical Jesus, far from detracting from the importance of the *interpretation* of each witness (Paul, Matthew, etc.), gives it its real value and its future relevance (II: 34).

The *distance* between Jesus and his interpreters allows us to see the interests with which they approached Jesus and how Jesus shed light on those interests. Thus,

> Matthew, Mark, Paul, are turned from being mere screens placed between Jesus and ourselves into witnesses in and of themselves, not just to Jesus. They become real people with their own significant content, which itself becomes, in turn, interesting to us (II: 34).

In this way the question as to who correctly interpreted Jesus disappears because there simply is no uninterpreted Jesus by which to judge interpretations. As Segundo says,

> Even that which can be historically attributed to him with reasonable certainty is interpretation. Not only because the documents at our disposal

for that task are interpretations; nor only because we ourselves must interpret in order to distinguish between what Jesus himself said and what others attribute to him; but rather because of Jesus of Nazareth's own involvement in self-interpretation, making use of the interpretative traditions of his own people and thereby defining his destiny and his mission (II: 19).

But despite the fact that one can never get to Jesus without interpreters, Segundo yet believes that, through the various sciences of biblical criticism, we can, nonetheless, point out when and in what direction Jesus' interpreters are exercising their creative work upon him and to what extent their own sets of problems and interests guide what is said about Jesus. Segundo believes that the "gap" between interpretation and the one interpreted can make Jesus interesting to us since it leaves room for us, as Segundo says, "*to infer, to derive,* from the decisions and the evaluations that he made with respect to other things" (II: 36) how he might respond to what interests us.

In essence, what Segundo is advocating here is a rather unique approach to the historical Jesus. If we recall the distinction made by Schubert Ogden between the "empirical-historical Jesus" (Jesus "in himself") and the "existential-historical Jesus" (Jesus "for us"), I would propose that we refer to the subject of the christological question, as Segundo understands it, as something of an "ideological-historical" Jesus. What Segundo is stressing, is that values are never transmitted in a vacuum, but rather meet up with the desires and interests of those to whom they are communicated, incarnating themselves in the form of ideologies. So it was in the case of Jesus and his followers. Thus, it is only through the ideologies of those who interpreted Jesus that we come to know who Jesus is and, even though Segundo is not interested in a Jesus "in himself," he is interested in a Jesus "for us," insofar as the "us" in this phrase refers originally to the historical witnesses to Jesus but also, most certainly, to all other human beings. Segundo reminds us, however, that it is only as the meaning and values of Jesus are reinterpreted in terms of new and creative ideologies today that Jesus can now be a Jesus "for us." I would argue, then, that Segundo's christological method is fundamentally to be understood as one that takes up the task of "de-ideologizing" and "re-ideologizing" the witness of faith. In other words, we must work backward *through* the interests and desires ("ideologies") of Jesus' interpreters so as to discover precisely who Jesus is, not in the sense of a pristine, uninterpreted "Jesus in himself,"[36] but rather in the sense of a Jesus who is ever and always

---

[36]In this respect, the task of deideologizing is somewhat different in its structure from the task of demythologizing. For whereas demythologizing clearly attempts to express the meaning of mythical assertions in literal, nonmythical language (Cf. Ogden, 1963:118), any claim to ideological neutrality would be, as

interpreted in the context of particular problems and interests. Segundo's method plugs us into a "hermeneutic circle" in which our real-life projects and concerns, just as those of Jesus' immediate followers, can interact with Jesus' own world of meaning and values and thereby participate in a process of "learning to learn" that contemporary human beings need so desperately in order to make faith effective in the world.

What I have shown thus far is that the possibility and the necessity of reconstructing the so-called historical Jesus are understood by Segundo as two sides of one coin. On the one side, the possibility of finding the historical Jesus is predicated upon a theoretical process that moves "through" the interests and desires ("ideologies") of Jesus' contemporaries in order to arrive at Jesus' own historical witness to a specific world of meaning and values--i.e., Jesus' own faith. On the other side, the necessity of studying the historical Jesus is so that, by disclosing precisely how Jesus expressed his faith in terms of the interests and desires of his contemporaries, we may thereby infer how his world of meaning and values may impact our own interests and desires.

Segundo's Christological Hermeneutic

The importance of Segundo's analysis of the structure of human existence for christology and, specifically, for both the possibility and necessity of reconstructing the historical Jesus should now begin to become clear. Because all human beings adopt a faith and then express that faith in terms of ideologies, we may use the complementarity as well as the distance between faith and ideologies not only to connect up with who Jesus was but to reinterpret who Jesus is for us today. But if Segundo's christological method is guided by an analysis of the structure of human existence in terms of faith and ideologies, so also is it guided by a particular approach to historical understanding summed up in the term, "hermeneutic circle," whereby the Jesus to be interpreted and the interests and problems of the one who is doing the interpreting are placed in a dialectic. I now turn to a consideration of how, exactly, Segundo conceives of this hermeneutical dialectic and the relevance for it of human existence understood in terms of faith and ideologies. In other words, if our existence is, indeed, best understood in terms of the historical process of adopting a faith and expressing that faith in terms of creative and liberating ideologies, how does our understanding of that

---

Segundo claims, "the worst form of idolatry." Segundo asks, "to what extent can more direct expressions of the Christian faith, such as the Gospels themselves, be considered free of ideologies?" (1982:I:151) His answer is that no "faith" can be expressed apart from ideologies and that "any meaning-structure which does not structure anything outside the person, anything in the real world has no value or worth" (I:157).

historical process condition and inform the hermeneutical relationship between the interpreter and *interpretandum*?

Perhaps the best place to begin in answering this question is with Segundo's description of his own theological method as a "hermeneutic circle" (1975b: 11ff), a four-step dialectic which stresses the need for a critical, dynamic process that, christologically considered, entails two fundamental tasks: (1) interpretation of Jesus in scripture, and (2) interpretation of our own socio-historical situation. The circular nature of Segundo's method stems from his belief that each encounter with reality, if reflected upon in a sufficiently critical way, pushes us to read the Bible in a fresh way and then to return to change our reality accordingly. The cycle begins again from there. When we start with the experience of human suffering, says Segundo, we are led to an "ideological suspicion" that is then applied to all ideological superstructures, the relevant one here being theology. This demands an "exegetical suspicion" with regard to how biblical interpretation has been undertaken and whether or not certain data have been taken into account. Finally, a new hermeneutic is developed that interprets scripture in a fresh way and that enables us to change reality accordingly. According to Segundo, this hermeneutic circle is imitative of Jesus' own approach and avoids thinking and acting in a way that is simply supportive of the status quo.

For Segundo, each of the dual hermeneutical tasks, of course, requires its own specialized tools--the tools of biblical criticism in the case of the former and the tools of the social sciences in the case of the latter. Indeed, Segundo claims that what separates the liberation theologian from the traditional academic theologians is that the former "feels compelled at every step to combine the disciplines that open up the past with the disciplines that explain the present" (12). However, what is not always given the central attention it deserves, in various studies of Segundo, is the mediating role of existentialist analysis as the common tool that unites the two tasks and makes possible a meaningful dialectic between them.[37] I contend that it is precisely the anthropological footing provided in

---

[37]Thus, for example, Alfred T. Henelly's *Theologies in Conflict*, published before Segundo wrote *El hombre de hoy ante Jesús de Nazaret*, only marginally treats the whole relationship between faith and ideologies, even though that relationship does play a central role in *Liberación de la teología*. When Henelly does treat the subject, he does not explicitly connect it to Segundo's method. Theresa Lowe Ching's analysis of Segundo in terms of "efficacious love" drives to the heart of his theology, but she fails to provide a thorough analysis of his method, not to mention "christological method" in terms of this concept, confining herself almost solely to consideration of Segundo's sources and major categories of thought. Her analysis of the "structure" of Segundo's method does not move significantly beyond an exposition of Segundo's hermeneutic circle nor does it

Segundo's existentialist analysis and expressed in the phrase "effective faith" that provides the key for understanding not merely the content of Segundo's christology but also his method. In other words, the phrase "effective faith" just as aptly characterizes the significance of Jesus for human beings today, for Segundo, as it does the appropriate method for going about critically interpreting that significance.

We have already begun to see just how this is so in the motivations behind Segundo's quest for the historical Jesus. Even though Jesus could never have considered the urgent questions which concern us today and thereby propose specific ideological expressions of faith for our own context, Segundo believes that an adequate christological method can build a spiralling hermeneutical bridge that will span two thousand years of history using the material of faith and ideologies. As Segundo says,

> only when standing on a solidly built bridge of *anthropological* faith, does the religious question about Jesus takes on relevance and precision (1982: II: 23).

By using this bridge, we may yet derive from the interest generated twenty centuries ago by Jesus' own effective faith how we ought also to express our faith in terms of a creative and liberating praxis.[38] But the application of this "bridge" is not a fundamentalist or mechanical one. The christological task is complex and multi-faceted, requiring the integration of a variety of disciplines.

The disciplines required for an adequate christological hermeneutic, however, are but the methodological tools of a more fundamental methodological principle, for Segundo, namely, the principle of "suspicion." The whole of Segundo's application of ideological suspicion to theology and exegetical suspicion to Biblical interpretation that we noted in the hermeneutic circle is designed to get theology in touch with praxis and, beyond that, to get faith in touch with reality. Perhaps Segundo's greatest contribution to theological method

---

demonstrate how the faith-ideologies dialectic really informs that structure.

[38]In Chapter 5, I deal more fully with Segundo's dialectic between "masses" and "minorities." I would point out here, however, that this dialectic runs parallel to that between faith and ideologies as the key for comprehending Segundo's hermeneutic method; indeed, Segundo refers to the problematic of masses and minorities as "a new *theoretical* hermeneutical key," which, taken together with a "new *practical* hermeneutical base" (the political commitment to the oppressed that we saw in the previous chapter), provides the proper method for theology (Cf. 1973c:110).

is his insistence that "erudition be replaced by analysis" and that future theologians be trained with

> analytical instruments of suspicion . . . designed to discard, insofar as possible, the commonplaces, the tranquillizing escapisms, the false explanations, and the false problems that are presented to them in good faith (1979a: xvi).

In studying Segundo's work, one can readily perceive the permeating presence of Marxist ideological suspicion, especially in *El hombre de hoy ante Jesús de Nazaret*, but James G. O'Donnell makes a strong case that it is the influence of Freud, as interpreted by Segundo's teacher, Paul Ricoeur, that is also quite deeply at the basis of Segundo's theological method. Ricoeur, in his book, *Freud and Philosophy: An Essay on Interpretation*, claims that Freud's psychoanalytic approach is a "healing through consciousness" (35). The transformation of a human being from a state of alienation and false consciousness to a state of freedom and happiness is the result of an "expansion of consciousness" that focuses on demystifying and unmasking the interpretation of one's situation and, thereby, assisting one in "accepting reality." As Ricoeur says,

> Psychoanalysis seeks to replace an instinctive, deceitful conscience dominated by an inner darkness with a reflecting consciousness that is guided by the reality principle (43).

Ricoeur understands this process as a "hermeneutic of suspicion"[39] and, as O'Donnell says, "Segundo adopts this hermeneutic of suspicion as the essential basis of his theological method" (31).

---

[39]According to Ricoeur, the hermeneutic of suspicion is a cornerstone for a number of Western thinkers.

> Three masters . . . dominate the school of suspicion: Marx, Nietzsche, and Freud. It is easier to show their common opposition to a phenomenology of the sacred, understood as a propaedeutic to the "revelation of meaning" than their interrelationship within a single method of demystification. . . . If we go back to the intention that they all had in common, we find in it the decision to look upon the whole of consciousness primarily as "false" consciousness. . . . All three clear the horizon for a more authentic work, for a new reign of Truth, not only by the invention of an art of *interpreting*. . . . Beginning with them, understanding is hermeneutics (32-36).

As important as the influences of either Freud or Ricoeur are on Segundo, however, one can hardly overemphasize the influence of Marx,[40] especially with regard to the hermeneutical task involved in theology. Segundo often admits this influence not only on his own theology but on theology as a whole.[41] The judgment of Marsha Hewitt is, I believe, no exaggeration at this point when she says, "I propose that on the level of methodology, Marx is the primary influence on Segundo, and that Segundo's work in general is a kind of polemical 'dialogue' with certain aspects of Marx's thought, especially in the area of ideology" (1990: 65).

Segundo is typical of other liberation theologians for whom Marx has been instrumental in developing a critical stance toward both society and toward traditional theological positions. As in the case of other liberation theologians, Marx's social analysis assists Segundo in exposing much of traditional theology to be a religious rationalization for the self-interest of dominant groups and a legitimation of the suffering and oppression in the world by promising hope in an afterlife in another world. As I have already noted, Segundo is well aware of theology's need to engage in a critical social analysis if it hopes to meet the criterion of practical credibility for its claims and, so, theologians "must accomplish the task of introducing the most rewarding elements of the social sciences into their own daily work of theologizing" (1975b: 79). In the case of Segundo, the "most rewarding element" of Marx's social analysis is its contribution toward recognizing the relationship between the material conditions of human existence and the ideological superstructure and, thus, the illusion of constructing any supposedly "neutral," "pure," or objective theological system, for example. That is not to say that Segundo finds Marx's concept of ideology clear-cut and indisputable. As Segundo says,

> At times it seems that Marx's texts say that the economic structure *determines* the ideologies; at times it seems that it *produces* the ideologies; at times it seems that it *conditions* them; and sometimes it even seems to say that it *is conditioned* to some extent by them (21).

---

[40]This influence must also be extended to include other principal Marxist writers such as Milan Machovec, George Lukacs, and Louis Althusser, so that when we refer to the influence of Marx on Segundo, we must implicitly include these other contemporary Marxists.

[41]Segundo, for example, says:
it is difficult to include Marx among the theologians, and he himself would be the first to protest such inclusion. At the same time, however, there can be no doubt about the influence of Marx on contemporary theology, especially in its more imaginative and creative forms (Segundo, 1975b:19).

But Segundo extends this willingness to allow for a certain degree of ambiguity in Marx as to the relationship between ideology and its material base to a willingness to allow for at least an equal amount of ambivalence in Marx as to the function of ideology in relation to the transformation or preservation of social structures. In her review of Segundo's work, Marsha Hewitt points out convincingly, however, that Segundo's handling of Marx with regard to this latter issue is unjustified and based on an identification of ideology with class consciousness that, in Marx's own usage, are not interchangeable. As Hewitt says,

> Marx understood ideology and class consciousness as completely different phenomena. Ideology positively reflects the ideas which correspond to the existent structures of society, i.e., the relations of material production and their ensuing social relations. Class consciousness emerges when that segment of the exploited classes, the proletariat, sees through the ideological mystification that misrepresents the true nature of class society with the result that the proletariat becomes self-conscious of its role in that society and the necessity for its own self-negation in order to abolish class society (1990: 66-67).

By thus "blurring the boundary lines between ideology and class consciousness" in Marx, then, Segundo is able to suggest that Marx might have left room for a more positive function for ideology rather than merely as a mechanism which sustains domination in class society.

Hewitt, however, claims that Segundo misinterprets Marx at this point because of Segundo's more fundamental desire "to rescue religion from the realm of ideology *in the pejorative sense* that Marx ascribed to it, so that he can claim religion to be ideology in the emancipatory sense" (67). Hewitt, therefore, cannot comprehend why Segundo engages in such an extensive polemic with Marx, trying to make Marx agree with his own views about ideology, rather than simply break with Marx at this point. While I must agree with Hewitt that Segundo does bend Marx's concept of ideology to fit into his own mold, it seems to me that Segundo's reason for doing this and for thus engaging in such an extensive dialogue with Marx is not aimed so much at restoring religion as the form through which Christian faith today may best be implemented, but at analyzing precisely the potential of Marxism as itself an "ideology" in relation to "faith," and this not so much for the sake of Marxism as for the sake of opening faith up to whatever ideology is most appropriate for its own circumstances.

It is clear, of course, that Segundo differs from Marx as to the potential of religion serving human liberation precisely by virtue of the difference between the two as to the function of ideology and, therefore, of religion. Segundo severely criticizes the inconsistency which characterizes Marx's application of the concept of the ideological superstructure to religion. If religion is truly a part of the ideological superstructure then there is no explanation as to why, under the conditions of a more humane social order, there could not be a "new and improved" religion. Marx, however, simply calls for its abolition as a precondition for the transformation of society. But Segundo's criticism here should not be taken to mean that he wants a more privileged or "sacred" role for religion. Segundo understands religion, precisely as ideology, as belonging to the realm of "instruments" and "tools" that human beings use to attain their goals and, as such, as being available for the attainment of almost any set of human values whether liberating or exploitative. In fact, religion is, by its very nature, one of the most dangerous and idolatrous forms of ideology because of its tendency to absolutize itself and, in terms of its potential for the emancipation and reconstruction of culture, comes in a distant second behind "religious faith" (1982: I: 396-413) which, as I have pointed out, is, for Segundo, quite different from religion.

Segundo believes that Marx's historical criticism is not necessarily opposed to faith as such and, in fact, requires the energy of faith in order to accomplish its task. Segundo distinguishes between the "intention" and the "mediation" in Marxist thought, the only really scientific aspect which could benefit theology being the method, or mediations which Marxists use to realize their goals. If Marx's historical criticism is opposed to a "religious" faith, that, according to Segundo, is only because faith is understood erroneously as faith in a certain set of instruments (so that faith is something like what Peter Berger calls a "sacred canopy"). In such a case, then, historical criticism would certainly be hostile to such a "magical" faith.

In Segundo's opinion, the conflict between Christianity and Marxism is largely unnecessary and misguided. As to whether or not Marxist ideology is necessarily atheistic, the answer Segundo arrives at is "no." The "core" of Marxism -- its irreducible minimum -- is its scientific analysis. Segundo wants to salvage the nucleus of Marxist ideology insofar as it relates to faith and that means, for Christians, insofar as it can help Christian faith and Christian theology accomplish its goals. Marxist analysis of the relationship between praxis and ideologies can assist Christian faith in moving from the sheer adoption of empty, dead values to a living and effective expression of those values in historical praxis. Marxist analysis of the relationship between praxis and ideologies, however, can also assist Christian theology in interpreting the sources of Christian witness through its process of ideological suspicion (or what has been previously referred to as "de-ideologizing").

This is not to say, however, that Segundo's use of even the supposedly objective and scientific elements of Marxism is without criticism. On the contrary, Segundo insists, for example, that with respect to the causal relationship between the mode of production and ideology by which the latter is, in a sense, determined by the former, the mode of production is not nearly as materialist as is often assumed but of necessity incorporates the multi-dimensionality of human relations. In other words, the "material" that materialism begins with is complex -- it is both material and spiritual. For Segundo, this means that materialism is not an alternative to the "spirit" but rather an effort to create a new world through a praxis in which the spirit begins with the concrete.   Segundo goes even further to point out that the causal relationship mentioned above is not "immediate" but operates in what he calls "the last instance" and thus results in only a relative autonomy for that causality. Segundo is severely critical of Marxists who cling to the idea that the material base immediately determines everything that is essential on the plane of consciousness. According to Segundo, that line of thinking fails to take into account the fact that the ideological superstructure itself creates the material base in accordance with its desires. For Segundo, revolutionary transformation is not best served by a strictly unreserved determinism that is posited among many Marxists between economic structure and ideological superstructure. Segundo illustrates this point by pointing out that a hammer would not be more effective in driving a nail by stripping away all autonomy from the arm that uses the hammer and instead insisting that the arm is determined in the first instance by the hammer itself.

Despite these objections from Segundo, however, Marx's historical materialism leads him to the important recognition that if all thought is ultimately conditioned by the interest arising from a mode of production, then that means that no ideology is *prima facie* invalid simply by virtue of its being, in some sense, "caused." Ideologies (in Segundo's more neutral sense of the word) have only one criterion by which they are to be judged -- namely, their instrumentality in achieving our chosen meaning or value. Segundo believes that historical materialism best enables us to uncover what reality is like and then to transform it. As such, it is "scientific" and does not exercise jurisdiction over a coherent faith.   It may, indeed, unmask a faith for what it is by showing where the mediations that faith uses actually lead. Again, however, historical materialism cannot determine for us what Segundo calls the "ought-to-be," the value.

CHAPTER 5

THE EVOLUTIONARY "KEY"
TO CHRISTOLOGY

We must recall that Segundo sees his own contribution to christology as primarily a challenge in the area of method by laying out the "preconditions" for interpreting the significance of Jesus. These preconditions take the threefold form of, first, pointing up the structure of human existence in terms of the faith and ideologies that express the freedom and limitedness of every human life; second, a recovery of the faith of Jesus himself; and, third, the clarification of present real-life problems and interests to which we wish to relate Jesus' faith in order thereby to mature and deepen our own existence. It is this third precondition, however, that Segundo believes provides the "key" for unlocking the significance of Jesus in any particular situation or era. Thus, if the problem facing the people of Israel to whom Jesus' message was originally addressed was fundamentally a political problem, a political key is required to interpret the significance of Jesus in that context. Similarly, if Paul restates the significance of Jesus less in socio-political terms and more in anthropological terms in order to move the significance of Jesus out of the Jewish world and into a broader context of meaning, an anthropological key is required.

In Segundo's mind, the key required to interpret the significance of Jesus for our own day is an "evolutionary" key. This is true, first and foremost, because the situation in which human beings now find themselves and to which the evolutionary process has brought them, is a situation of actually sitting in the driver's seat of that very process. As Segundo says, evolution is not now merely a scientific hypothesis; it has become a moral task:

> In effect, we are faced with the challenge of steering this evolution on our planet. To take consciously and deliberately the reins of evolution . . . (II: 805).

Understanding reality in terms of the process of evolution presents a real challenge for us, according to Segundo, in that this process moves slowly and is subject to chance and complexity, even though there is also purpose and probability. This creates a context for relating faith to ideologies that rules out the simplistic repetition of previous means of effectiveness and requires creative originality and flexibility. We now face the challenge to understand the mechanisms of evolution not only to make faith effective but simply to survive.

In this chapter, I propose to provide an analysis of Segundo's application of evolutionary insights and conceptuality for two reasons. First, insofar as Segundo's use of an evolutionary framework provides the required scope and profundity required to clarify the kind of interests and problems that characterize contemporary human existence, it thereby provides what, for Segundo, is the third fundamental precondition for his method. Second, though Segundo explicitly rejects the necessity or even usefulness of metaphysical inquiry for interpreting the significance of Jesus, his very own appeal to "transcendent data" demonstrates the need for some wider and cosmic framework in which to understand and ground that significance. I will explore whether an evolutionary perspective serves to provide just that framework and, perhaps, even a metaphysics, for Segundo.

Entropy and Negentropy

The evolutionary key which Segundo uses to bring Jesus forward two thousand years is, in large part, borrowed from Pierre Teilhard de Chardin. To be sure, the evolutionary outlook which Segundo adopts is less optimistic, one-sided, and accumulative than Teilhard's, but is nonetheless a dialectical process involving two contradictory forces that are essential and complementary, each in its own way -- *entropy* and *negentropy*, borrowing the scientific terms from thermodynamics. The first of these, *entropy*, is a universal negative tendency recognized in the realm of physical science as a continual degradation and diffusion of energy in terms of its utilization (the amount of energy always remains constant though the amount of usable energy does not). In the realm of spiritual or psychological energy, entropy is the force towards egotism, sin, and bondage. It is the line of least resistance, identified culturally with "mass" behavior. Even though the supply of energy remains constant, there are rich and complex concentrations and syntheses of energy that surface at every level (physical nature, the individual, society, etc.) which are profound and transformative even though they are relatively scarce. These phenomena, described as "negentropy," are spiritually represented as the force towards love, grace, and life and are "minority" phenomena.

All of life is characterized by the dialectical rhythm between entropy, on the one hand, and negentropy, on the other; between easy, degraded, and cheap energy which culturally is the path of simplism and immediatism, on the one hand, and the rare instances of genius and complexity, on the other. Both of these forces coexist from the very beginning of the universe, though each on its own plane, and each is necessary and important for the other. Thus, for example, Einstein's discovery may be considered a stroke of genius and, so, an example of negentropy; but that discovery could never have made the broad impact that it has made in our own day were it not made available in a more accessible form in less complex expressions (for example, in high school textbooks -- an example of entropy). Entropy should not be viewed as an entirely negative feature, and its necessary role in the whole balance of things cannot be underestimated. In Segundo's view, even sin, though it is a "missing of the mark" and evil, is, on another level, not absolutely bad because as entropy it is essential to the structure of human existence.[42]

Understanding the relationship between faith and ideologies in the context of the reality of entropy and negentropy is essential, for Segundo. Severe problems arise when we attempt to translate our values directly into practice while somehow avoiding the circuitous route of time, chance, and entropy. This path of inflexibility is eventually counterproductive to the values themselves. By the same token, any attempt to implement faith apart from ideologies turns out to be ideological in the worst sense of the word. Thus, entropy and negentropy must be kept in equilibrium, even though they apply to two different levels--negentropy on the level of values and entropy on the level of means. This asymmetry between the two yields a more complicated dialectic, says Segundo, than what is found in Hegel or Marx, precisely because this dialectic occurs on two different levels. If, however, negentropy and entropy are evaluated on the same level in terms of common criteria, they seem to oppose each other as good and evil.

This evolutionary dialectic also helps us interpret our human experience in terms of culture. Here, entropy and negentropy are translated into Segundo's interesting distinction between "masses" and "minorities." "Masses," as Segundo uses the term, does not refer to one social class of people as opposed to another.[43] "Mass" human beings are to be found in all social strata. In fact, the

---

[42]As examples from scripture, Segundo cites the use of the term "world" in John and the use of the term "flesh" in Paul. Both represent the negative tendencies in reality to close human beings off to freedom and truth and yet both are the indispensable *locus* for the effective realization of love and liberty (Segundo, 1964c: 77). Segundo writes,

> Without the "no" of the majority, the world would be constituted by monads inaccessible to every love which would utilize the materials of the world. Human beings would open themselves only towards their interior. Their flesh, with its windows of the senses, would in reality be no more than a type of transcendental illusion (76-77).

[43]It is clear from Segundo's chapter in his dissertation on Berdyaev (1963a) entitled "Eschatology and Sin" that this concept of the "masses" and "mass" behavior is stimulated by Berdyaev's own use of the terms. For Berdyaev, as Segundo points out, "mass" is a historical force that depersonalizes and diverts human beings away from the prophetic and creative while fastening itself to external and superficial features of human conduct. The masses, as Segundo says,

> are not precisely the popular masses, but the multitude which views things by their most extrinsic side, the most superficial, and also the most easily

word refers to persons only in a secondary sense and, instead, refers primarily to a "pattern of conduct" (1983b: II: 385) characterized by the kinds of people who allow themselves to follow the crowd or to be led by psychological or social manipulations with ease. In this way, "mass" conduct is simply entropy, but on a cultural level. Two qualities are especially characteristic of "mass" behavior -- simplicity and immediacy. In trying to solve problems or achieve some goal, mass behavior is marked by its pursuit of simple answers and direct solutions regardless of how complicated the problem might be. It is also marked by its pursuit of quick and immediate courses of action in the place of complex and long-range ones.

Mass behavior is not an entirely negative concept since it serves as the basis for continuity within groups and is essential for law and order. Christianity, however, proposes long-range, complex, and mediate solutions that run contrary to mass demands. In short, the demands of Christianity are "minority" demands. This results in the following problem: Christianity is a minoritarian phenomenon but claims historical universality. How can a phenomenon meet the conditions of historical universality but not be mass?

Segundo works out his understanding of history within this dialectic of masses and minorities, apart from which one might be led to the idea of an elitist or aristocratic Christianity. It is clear that history would fail to have anything like the continuity that it does have apart from the collective behavior of mass humanity. Nevertheless, the forces that bring into existence progress, development, and liberation are always a creative minority who, through the development of institutions and other mediations, bring the masses along. Segundo believes that Christianity should not fear that the institutional nature required to achieve its goals will dilute or do away with its essentially minoritarian character. There must, however, be a constant interplay of masses and minorities that keeps each one "honest," so to speak. This, for Segundo, is the essential and irreversible character of history.

On the ecclesiastical level, there is the same dialectical tension only now between the church, which is a minority community, and all of humanity which that church serves. That tension must be preserved and not lost or there would be no need for the church, its only purpose being to serve humanity. The church, on the one hand, has to develop human institutions and mediations that enable it to exercise real freedom and love, but it would be anti-Christian to dilute or waver with regard to liberty and love in order to achieve a mass adherence to Christianity. Thus, the victory of the church is measured not in quantitative terms but in functional terms with regard to its ability to advance human freedom in the world.

---

discerned (181).
Segundo also identifies various physical metaphors used by Berdyaev to denote this mass force such as gravity, entropy, or quantity (as opposed to quality).

Ironically, then, entropy is necessary in order to achieve and preserve any degree of negentropy in the world. It is no wonder, then, that Segundo takes exception to Teilhard's essentially "linear" view of the evolutionary process and, specifically, of negentropy in that process. As Segundo points out, Teilhard's "Omega point" -- the final victory of negentropy over entropy -- denies the integration of entropy with negentropy and is finally inconsistent with the way that even Jesus lived out his life. A christology that views Jesus as basically continuing only one of the lines of evolution -- "negentropy" -- is without basis or efficacy. Thus, the evolutionary quality *par excellence* is flexibility, or balance, between what one intends to do and the energy mechanisms with which and the objective reality within which one's projects are carried out.

Segundo's application of evolutionary insights to human social reality and specifically to the relationship between faith and ideologies is especially relevant for his fundamental interest in the task of the re-creation of Latin American culture in the wake of the serious destruction of his continent's social ecology. For example, Segundo uses the notion of genetic inheritance in biological evolution as an analogy to illustrate the energy savings achieved through anthropological faith. Just as each new biological organism does not have to "start from scratch," so to speak, in responding to its environment since the bulk of its responses are "pre-coded" into its very being, so a faith can provide energy savings on the level of cultural transformation. This it can do through the vehicle of referential witnesses who, as we have seen, provide each of us with images of the satisfactions yielded by interpreting ourselves and reality one way rather than another and by living in accordance with that interpretation rather than some other. Through referential witnesses--and the "transcendent data" to which they appeal-- each of us is able to adopt a meaning-world on the basis of factors that we could never ourselves experience. In addition, these data have roots in some more or less remote past--i.e., "tradition"--so that a meaning-system is more than simply *proposed*; it is, in a real way, *imposed*.

The importance of the relationship between faith and culture in terms of "tradition," for Segundo, is significant at this point. For Segundo, faith is "an anthropological dimension linking the human being to the past and present society" (1982: I: 391). Tradition serves the positive function of fulfilling the needs of human beings in structuring a world of meaning and values and thereby freeing up human energy and imagination for the important task of implementing faith in effective and creative ways. As Segundo says,

> Tradition is that which every society consciously assigns to heredity within the equation by which we reserve energy for those mental operations which seem more useful and important to us taking into account our context and its challenges (I: 391-392).

These other "mental operations" are precisely what Segundo has in mind when he speaks of "ideologies." In other words, the faith that is testified to us by referential witnesses within a tradition, when communicated meaningfully and adopted seriously, frees up the human being to spend energy more economically in the more challenging process of making faith "effective" in our own particular situation. Thus, just as entropy keeps the accomplishments of negentropy within certain energy limits on the level of thermodynamics, so also ideologies, on the cultural level, force faith to effectively realize itself within a certain economy of energy.

Evolutionary Epistemology

Fundamental to our being able to meet the challenge that evolutionary insights offer us is our ability to begin to think in a new way. What Segundo calls for is nothing less than a new epistemology and, so, a new hermeneutic, that corresponds to evolutionary reality and by which we can interpret the significance of Jesus. The novelty of evolutionary thinking and our relatively inadequate knowledge of its mechanisms make that task especially difficult but nonetheless necessary.

The place to start in developing this evolutionary epistemology, according to Segundo, is with Teilhard's insight that there is no separation to be made between "biological" evolution and "universal" evolution and that a formal analogy can be recognized at every level along with a fundamental unity of process. This, of course, means projecting or retrojecting the mechanisms operative in human beings onto reality, a process ostensibly rejected by many scientists who prefer to understand nature as "objective" rather than "projective." Analogy, argues Segundo, makes possible our moving from the fact of evolution to a corresponding epistemology as exemplified by Teilhard de Chardin who was able to convert his scientific discoveries into "a system of images, concepts, and symbols of value applicable to humanity and to the universe" (1970f: 155). Thus, analogy, says Segundo, is our "heuristic instrument par excellence" (1982: II: 843).[44]

This continuity between the levels of reality and within the patterns of universal history is the basis for Segundo's adoption of the following fundamental principle from Teilhard:

---

[44]Though Segundo recognizes the role of analogy in Teilhard, his own usage originates from his reading of Gregory Bateson. Bateson argues that "analogy" is not to be set aside as "unscientific" and points out, for example,

> that the types of mental operation which are useful in analyzing one field may be equally useful in another--that the framework (the *eidos*) of science, rather than the framework of Nature, is the same in all fields (Bateson: 74; Cf. Segundo, 1982: II: 838).

In the world, nothing could ever burst forth as final across the different thresholds successively traversed by evolution (however critical they be) which has not already existed in an obscure and primordial way. . . . Everything, in some extremely attenuated version of itself, has existed from the very first . . . (1959: 71, 78).

This, of course, does not mean that we find the "same thing" only smaller at a lower level or further back in evolution. What we find is a formal rather than a material analogy, not in the "pinpoint" occurrence but in the "process" and in the "relations" that produce the occurrence.

Another of the basic mechanisms by which evolution operates is "chance." While Segundo wants to emphasize the necessary role of chance, he does not believe that chance alone can account for everything, not even on the inorganic level. Thermodynamics with its law of entropy teaches us that only mind, information, or intelligence can keep a system from constantly ending up in equilibrium, not chance alone. It would be logically impossible for chance to move the universe toward ever increasing complexity given the very definition of chance. Chance would have to produce the same constant effect over millions of years. But, against all odds, things have gone toward order -- even and especially the replication and conservation of the results of chance itself. We see that purposiveness is inextricably mixed in with chance, "uses chance, and little by little takes charge of it, without ever annulling it" (Segundo, 1982: II: 869). As Segundo points out, the very notion of chance is anthropomorphic and, in fact, the biosphere "appears much more chancy than does the world of inert matter" (II: 859). The point here, once again, is that negentropy is already present even in the primordial stages of evolution:

While descending, and even bypassing the line that separates the inorganic from the biosphere, we find an unmistakable primordial form of the human and so we have to project concepts such as "information," "mind," and "performance" onto the most basic processes of matter. While ascending, it becomes clear to us that the notions of the primordial that seem to be the most objective have no meaning if not related to human purposes and, thus, with the notion of "order" (II: 865-866).

One final component of Segundo's evolutionary epistemology must be mentioned. The Darwinian postulate of "natural selection" and "survival of the fittest" led to epistemological premises exclusive of all purposive explanations for the evolution of species. Following Gregory Bateson's suggestion, Segundo wants to replace the Darwinian account with the epistemology of the lesser known, yet slightly earlier, Alfred Wallace. For Wallace, nature is much like a huge, natural circuit that selects based on the ability of organisms to integrate into its network of relationship and reciprocity rather than sheer "fitness" in terms of survival.

This account is more satisfying and explanatory than Darwin's, according to Segundo, because it refuses to reduce evolution to a convergence of genetic chance with environmental pressure. If chance alone, after all, were supposed to account for evolution, we might at least expect to see species move down the evolutionary tree. Wallace's hypothesis allows for the presence of another "internal" factor that is not chance -- negentropy, or purposiveness, that "'takes advantage of' every pressure in order to interconnect more species in a dynamically balanced circuit" (II: 881).

All the above pieces taken together constitute the basis of a new epistemology, for Segundo, which he refers to as not so much a scientific discovery as a "metadiscovery: a discovery about discoveries" (II: 866).

> They do not supply a knowledge about things but rather, primarily a knowledge about the science of things, that is to say, about how to structure science itself, its hypotheses, and its methods of investigation (II: 866).

The importance of this evolutionary epistemology for christological reflection should now begin to become obvious, and so I turn directly to this application of it.

Jesus and Evolution

Segundo's aim in using an evolutionary epistemology is to show "that something situated in history, such as Jesus and his project, 'recapitulates' -- in the strongest sense of the term, 'gives meaning to' -- the universe" (II: 885). Segundo lays out two steps that are necessary in order to show this:

> The first will consist in situating the central historical data that we possess about Jesus in the context of the global process that we are studying. The second will consist in extrapolating that concrete historical event previously situated, as a transcendent datum, in terms of universal reality (II: 886).

In fulfilling the first step, Segundo provides an interpretation of Jesus and his project in terms of the evolutionary conceptuality we have just examined. We find Jesus challenging the existing order in Israelite society with a substitute order, the kingdom of God. This new order demands the full integration of the marginalized and exploited into the human "circuit," and Jesus, in calling for this "step forward along the road of negentropy" (II: 888), is deemed to be "subversive" and an "agitator." Jesus demands relationships based on mutuality that respect others as integrating "centers" themselves rather than mere instruments; he challenges his hearers to integrate even their enemies into their own circuit (II:

889). In crafting the means to express his values, to give his message a hearing, and to arouse passion in both his followers and his detractors, Jesus exhibits the evolutionary qualities of creativity, flexibility, and originality. Those means, however, were effective in specific situations and contexts not necessarily applicable in other contexts, as Paul himself found out when he tried to convey the significance of Jesus to areas that were more culturally integrated into the Roman Empire (II: 814). Thus, for Segundo, we see a Jesus whose life and message situate him in the process of universal evolution by combining entropy and negentropy as creatively and flexibly as possible.

Segundo's second step is a bit more difficult than the first in that Jesus and his project must now become a "transcendent datum"; in other words, "the product of history is alleged to be the origin of history" (II: 890-891). As difficult as this task is, Segundo is confident that it is at least easier, thanks to our evolutionary epistemology, than when Christianity first formulated the issue at Chalcedon. As Segundo notes, "the primary effect of his divinization, then, was the de-historiciza-tion of Jesus" (II: 891). Evolutionary language, however, is capable of doing justice to "the universal dimensions of Jesus' significance without sacrificing his history" (II: 819).

But Segundo is clear that Jesus, as transcendent datum, or as recapitulator of the whole universe, is not so because he is absolutized and raised to an ahistorical level above time and conflict. What we must recognize, says Segundo, is that the statements "Jesus is human" and "Jesus is God" are not on the same logical level.

> The *higher* level of language is an affirmation about the *lower*, a metamessage about the historical Jesus. To say that the human being, Jesus, is God, then, is not to turn him into a demigod, an "apparent" human being, one who is "above" the conflicts and problems of history. By the same token, the *higher* level is not a mere exclamation of admiration or a mere mark of my feelings. Its function in anthropological faith is to *elevate* the concrete values perceived in the history of Jesus to the category of absolute, and to wager that to them the entire reality of the universe submits in a personal way (II: 892).

By taking Teilhard's principle that nothing in the world could ever appear that does not already appear in some obscure and primordial way, Segundo opens up a path for understanding Jesus as more than a mere pinpoint occurrence in the whole evolutionary process and yet not an abstract generality either.

> If Teilhard's principle is reasonable or correct, it is there that we shall see the historical Jesus linked up and related with all that has been and will be occurring in the evolutionary process. So ought also to be the case, by the

same token, with any person whose meaningfulness holds interest for us from the past (II: 854).

Segundo claims that it is the Apostle Paul who, perhaps more than anyone else, opens us up to this "formal" dimension of the meaning of Jesus throughout history without, at the same time, turning Jesus into an abstract generality.   Paul, obviously without the benefit of evolutionary insights, interprets the significance of Jesus in terms of an analysis of human nature that emphasizes the struggle of life over death, grace over sin, spirit over law.

> Paul seems to situate human existence on two planes: one characterized by its visibility and the other by its invisible accomplishment of what will finally be "manifested." The first is characterized by the greater distance between intention and realization, that is to say, *Sin*. The second, on the contrary, is characterized by a narrowing of that distance that, to a certain degree, brings our intentions closer to our own actions. This latter is characterized by life in the spirit, that is to say, the invisibility of *Faith* (II: 561).

Christ, viewed in this context, reaffirms and makes explicit a transcendent datum already present in humanity, namely, the victory of faith over sin and, thus, the possibility of living a life of freedom that is effective insofar as the gap between human intention and human action is reduced (II: 551). But just as Paul, in order to interpret the significance of Jesus, utilized a process of anthropological generalization characterized by the conflict between humanizing and dehumanizing forces within the human being and in this way was able to bridge the gap between the historical Jesus and the specific socio-cultural problematic of his own day, so today, Segundo believes, the interpretation of Jesus in evolutionary categories allows us to link the history of one particular individual with the fundamental process of the universe, not, to be sure, in some abstract way, but in a way that is relevant for our own urgent concerns to transform culture.

Thus, for example, we understand that, from an evolutionary perspective, negentropy cannot take the quick, linear course of evolution without destroying itself. Time must be integrated into its circuit along with chance and evil, and faith must always be expressed in terms of ideologies. Segundo recognizes the temptation to deny entropy in Jesus and attribute to him the "maximum negentropy" (II: 921), especially insofar as he is understood as a transcendent datum. Because Jesus was a human being, however, and because it was precisely his evolutionary flexibility that grounds our understanding of him as holding the place in history that he does, we yet detect in him necessary elements of entropy, such as his nationalism or the way he provoked his enemies and inspired others to do likewise. Segundo says,

Jesus' overcoming of Sin is as invisible as his victory over Death will be: an object of faith rather than of verifiable experience. Only when the final reality is presented to faith with the resurrection, will the whole transcendent datum of Jesus' victory over Sin fit into it. Not to deny history but to make it clear that he overcomes Sin insofar as his freedom never agrees, in bad faith, to be in complicity with an entropy greater than that required for the efficacy of his history project (II: 933).

But while the transcendent datum of Jesus' victory over sin is not verifiable by ordinary experience (as is the case with all transcendent data), the elements of entropy that we experience are all around us quite visible. The wager of faith, however, is

that *in the end* the values which surfaced in the historical project of Jesus will dominate all of reality. That the "ought-to-be" contained in them will turn out to be (II: 944).

In summary, then, the importance of an evolutionary perspective for interpreting the significance of Jesus, for Segundo, takes two forms: (1) it provides a framework for understanding the unique ability of Jesus perfectly to harmonize the lines of entropy and negentropy in his own being and for understanding the effective, creative, and flexible praxis in and through which Jesus expressed his own faith, and (2) it can demonstrate how a particular event, such as the historical life and death of Jesus of Nazareth, can be of universal significance without, at the same time, pretending that this kind of significance moves us closer to ideological neutrality. Any such attempt, as Segundo says,

is mistaken and deluded when it sacrifices every concrete realization to a vaunted higher one, condemning their means as partial, and waiting until one encounters one that will be a faithful copy of Jesus' own faith. Because the faith of Jesus himself was incarnated . . . in a limited, imperfect ideology vis-á-vis the criteria he himself taught. That is the price and meaning of the incarnation (II: 933-934).

If we fail to understand the dialectic at work in Jesus' own life, then in our own lives, "entropy will become uncontrollable and will become an intrinsic factor of death" (II: 934).

Christology and Metaphysics: Considerations with regard to Method

Segundo views metaphysics, as he does religion, as belonging to the realm of ideology rather than to the realm of faith. At one point, for example, he talks about a "conservative" metaphysics - one that "undermines the very foundation for any historical efficacy dependent on human beings" (I: 224). In general, Segundo is suspicious of metaphysics because it attempts "to achieve a conceptual unity where an irreducible plurality exists" (I: 91). Segundo writes,

> all the definitions of God we find in dictionaries are metaphysical ones and . . . form the basis of the misunderstanding which prevents us from detecting, among other things, nothing less than one of the founts of atheism (I: 91).

Segundo especially rules out the use of metaphysics in the communication of values, such as we examined in Chapter 3. As Segundo says,

> There is no value in revisiting [metaphysics] to talk about God when we possess an equally symbolic language that has already been articulated by Christian revelation. Indeed that language has been reformulated in a thousand different ways and even contradicted in a thousand different ways by the actions of those claiming to be Christian (I: 91-92).

Here again, Segundo's criticism of David Tracy is highly instructive in discerning Segundo's understanding of metaphysics. As we saw, Tracy identifies a "fundamental faith" at the limits of all ordinary human experience that is universal and the basis for all acting and believing whatsoever. Tracy identifies this dimension as a "religious" dimension and goes on to show how, for the Christian religion, "God" is the word used to designate the ground of this faith. For Tracy, it is only insofar as religious assertions about God as the condition of possibility for our fundamental faith are metaphysical assertions that these assertions can be said to have cognitive content. Segundo, however, objects to this procedure and views religion as properly belonging to the realm of "instruments," or "ideologies," which can be employed for any and every class of values.

At this point, it may be helpful for us to explore Segundo's assessment of the prospects of a "transcendental christology," such as is developed by Karl Rahner. Segundo identifies much of what he himself offers by way of inquiry into the structure of human existence as an example of the same process used by Rahner in developing a "transcendental anthropology" that will provide the necessary preconditions for christology (II: 59). As important as such preconditions are for christology, however, "studying the conditions under which talk about Christ is made possible does not thereby tell us anything about Christ" (II: 60). As Segundo says, the most salient characteristic of all transcendental thought or investigation, logically enough, is its *emptiness* with regard to those concrete phenomena about whose preconditions it is investigating (II: 59).

This "emptiness," as Segundo confirms, is not to be equated with "uselessness." This is so because apart from such transcendental investigation there can be no bridge between human interests and desires "as such" and the historical concreteness of Jesus of Nazareth.

Ultimately, however, Rahner's transcendental method fails because it purports to do much more than to tell us that faith is inevitable, but to provide us with criteria for distinguishing between an authentic and an inauthentic faith. Segundo criticizes both Bultmann and Rahner at this point:

> A transcendental anthropology *seems* full of concreteness and life with its expressions descriptive of human existence. In reality, however, such expressions refer to *categories* or "existentials." Terms as seemingly concrete as "fallenness," "being toward death," or "indebted being" in Heidegger, or the "hope of an absolute saviour" in Rahner, however, are only abstractions and are open to concrete human attitudes that are not only different from each other, but many times opposed to each other. Moreover, in our own particular case here, they are just as capable of opening as of closing access to Jesus (II: 61-62).

This basic criticism ties back to what we saw as the motivation behind Segundo referring to his method as an "anti-christology." Segundo, while not necessarily rejecting a scientific method of interpreting the significance of Jesus, does reject any attempt to interpret Jesus "free of subjectivisms and ideologies" in terms of "certain and universal criteria" (II: 63). Segundo sees in the method of Tracy, as well as Rahner, a confusion between form and content. The limiting experience of which Tracy speaks can only provide us the "form" of the basic trust that is the precondition of our existing or understanding but can never tell us anything about God. The structure of our basic anthropological faith is neutral, believes Segundo, as to the content of that faith.

PART II

A CRITICAL APPRAISAL OF
SEGUNDO'S CHRISTOLOGY

CHAPTER 6

FAITH, METAPHYSICS, AND PRAXIS

This study attempts to contribute to the ongoing discussion of the contemporary significance of Jesus and the method by which that significance is best interpreted by a theology which today seeks to be theoretically and practically credible and at the same time appropriate to the witness of faith. If the preceding part of the study has accomplished its purpose, it has made Segundo's own proposal for such a method clear and it has indicated how Segundo himself believes the significance of Jesus is best interpreted. I have tried to show that, for Segundo, the dimensions of faith and ideologies provide the basic anthropological context for interpreting the significance of anything or anyone whatsoever, most especially, Jesus of Nazareth. On the basis of this fundamental dual structure, we are able, first, to link up with those who have gone before us, especially the original historical witnesses to Jesus, and to discern the significance which Jesus held for them in their own process of coming to faith and of implementing that faith. Thus, the fact that we have no "uninterpreted" Jesus is not an obstacle to understanding the significance of Jesus, but rather a prerequisite. Then, on the basis of how Jesus responded to and impacted the projects and interests of his interpreters, we may infer how Jesus might impact ours. In this way, as I have pointed out, Segundo believes our own affirmations as to the significance of Jesus can justifiably claim to be appropriate to the original witness of faith. I have further shown that, both with respect to interpreting the significance of Jesus and subsequently living our own lives in response to that significance, Segundo believes that utmost attention must be paid to the mechanisms of evolution, the most important of which is the tension between the dialectical forces of entropy and negentropy, disintegration and novelty. Our own existence, according to Segundo, is a daily struggle to structure and implement our own particular world of meaning and values within this tension in terms of an ever new and liberating praxis, and it is this struggle that provides the fundamental context for interpreting the significance of Jesus. This is why I suggest that Segundo's christology is best understood as a christology of "effective faith." I have shown that the evolutionary framework proposed by Segundo provides a way of conceptualizing and communicating the significance of Jesus as a "recapitulator" of the universe in that Jesus' own person is a supreme example of the processes at work in the universe and of the authentic response by a human being to those processes in terms of living out an "effective faith."

Segundo's statement of the problem facing any christology which desires to interpret the significance of Jesus in a meaningful and relevant way today holds enormous potential, it seems to me. But in spite of the creative contribution which Segundo makes to our understanding of the nature, method, and urgency of christology, finally, I must judge his own proposal as not entirely adequate or effective given the criteria which Segundo himself intends to meet.

In this chapter, I wish to evaluate Segundo's analysis of the praxic aspect of the christological question and the method which he proposes for interpreting the significance of Jesus in terms of the structure of our own faith and ideologies. As my own appraisal will make clear, however, this question is hardly separable from the metaphysical aspect of that question and, accordingly, that aspect will also be considered in this chapter. Thus, for the reader who may be expecting a precise symmetry between the previous three chapters which served as an exposition of Segundo's christological method and the following three chapters which serve as my own appraisal of that method, though there is a certain amount of symmetry, the metaphysical and praxic aspects of the christological question seem to me to be such that they are finally not so much two questions but rather two inseparable dimensions of one question. In Chapter 7, I will evaluate Segundo's understanding of the historical aspect of the christological question and the method which he proposes for understanding who Jesus is historically and for establishing the appropriateness of claims regarding the significance of Jesus. Finally, in Chapter 8, I will evaluate Segundo's employment of an evolutionary framework and conceptuality with regard to its usefulness for interpreting the significance of Jesus in terms of a unified conception of reality as a whole.

Choosing Faith

In *Nuestra idea de Dios*, Segundo states that anthropology is something of a privileged *locus theologicus*--"the one and only place where God and the human being encounter one other" (1983b: 110). In Part 1 of this study, I have shown the consequences of this belief for Segundo's own christological method and how the structure of human existence is the fundamental starting point both for discovering who Jesus is and for bringing him forward 2,000 years. Segundo's method, in this respect, fits more or less squarely within a contemporary trend followed by many theologians such as Karl Rahner, Wolfhart Pannenberg, David Tracy, Schubert Ogden, and others, each of whom begins his theological reflection with a fundamental anthropology and holds that it is only insofar as we first disclose the most basic and universal dimensions of human existence that we can then interpret the content of the Christian witness of faith in any meaningful and relevant way.[45]   Viewed in this light, Segundo is but carrying out the implications of Vatican II, and especially its document, *Gaudium et Spes*, with its openness to the "whole human family" and not simply the "sons of the church" (Flannery: 904). In fact, Segundo generally exhibits what Franklin Gamwell calls "the modern commitment" or, alternatively, "the humanistic commitment," which Gamwell summarizes as:

> the increasing affirmation that our understandings of reality and ourselves in relation to it cannot be validated or redeemed by appeals to some authoritative expression or tradition or institution.   In other words, our understandings can be validated or redeemed only by appeal in some sense to human experience and reason as such (1990: 3-4).

But as surely as Segundo does see himself within a context that seeks to interpret Christian faith in a way that is both relevant and credible to the common experience of human beings simply as such, whether religious or not, Segundo is primarily interested in the structure of human existence as a starting point for theology in order to reverse and overturn--or better, to "liberate"--what he sees as the ahistorical method of classical, academic theology which begins with orthodoxy or divine revelation and then turns to its practical application in history and in society.   Segundo wants to construct for theology a method that, as I have pointed out, "is more interested in *being liberating* than in *talking about liberation*" (1975b: 13) and that, therefore, is situated solely within the historical, political, and social realm of existence.

As similar as Segundo's procedure is to that of other contemporary theologians, then, his project of transforming theology into a critical social force by means of revolutionizing its method is significantly different from these others, precisely with regard to this common anthropological starting point.   This difference is of utmost importance for this study and swirls around a constellation of key concepts including "faith," "religion," "metaphysics," and "God."

The uniqueness of Segundo's view of faith is primarily a product of his analysis of how human beings come to faith.   Segundo makes it clear that persons come to adopt a particular meaning-world or scale of values as their own on a "wager" based on the testimony of "referential witnesses."   Segundo does allow for "transcendent data" as a kind of objective criteria by which one chooses a particular faith and so the "wagering" he has in mind is not totally capricious.   Yet

---

[45]Indeed, when it comes to specifically christological reflection, the formal structure of Segundo's approach is especially similar to that of Schubert Ogden. Both begin their critical reflection on the significance of Jesus by beginning with an analysis of human existence precisely in terms of a fundamental faith that grounds all that we say or do (Cf. Segundo, 1982: I: 19ff; Ogden, 1982: 30ff).

these transcendent data enter in at the "limits" of our experience and their truth is neither directly verifiable or falsifiable; thus, in the end, even acceptance of transcendent data require a wager. As Segundo says,

> When I speak of "transcendent data," I am talking about something which is relevant for human beings precisely because the latter are operating continually in a "limit-situation." In other words, they get beyond the limits surrounding them through a kind of wager (1982: I: 192).

This idea of "wagering" is essential for Segundo and, taken along with his notion that our faith can only be validated "eschatologically,"[46] places human beings in a situation characterized by tremendous challenges in terms of implementing their meaning-world in relevant and effective ways. Because there can be no direct empirical verification of the validity of faith, there are no easy solutions, no magical formulas, and no pre-established and repeatable courses of action upon which we may fall back. Faith is dynamic and requires creativity, flexibility, and, most of all, a heightened sensitivity to what will work best in this or that circumstance.

The question to be asked of Segundo at this point, however, is whether his notion of "wagering" is really consistent with human experience or whether, perhaps, human beings do not rely on a more fundamental perception of the way things in general are both for the adoption of a faith and even for the implementation of that faith. Even granting that human beings do not simply begin with a conception of ultimate reality and then pull down out of it a ready-made value-system complete with a collection of precise implications for praxis, and granting that human beings are always confronted with real risks that give faith a wager-like quality in the face of numerous unpredictable circumstances in life, doesn't their world-view--or as Clifford Geertz puts it, "the picture they have of the way things in sheer actuality are, their most comprehensive ideas of order" (79)--have much more to do with how they come to faith than Segundo allows? Furthermore, granting that such a world-view does not and could not provide any kind of "empirical" validation for one's faith, doesn't human faith generally require some sort of objective validation on the basis of which it is understood to be more

---

[46]For example, in the case of christology, Segundo claims that the self-validation of faith is "eschatological" precisely in view of the resurrection of Jesus, the transcendent datum which exhibits just that characteristic of eschatological verification:

> Here the eschatology is the resurrection of Jesus that unveils the future and allows us to see the victory of life and of the human cause already present in the midst of a life apparently subjected to death; a victory that will appear in its total scope and reality at the end of history (1982: II: 20).

than merely arbitrary because it is the "authentic" possibility of our own existence?

One might argue, of course, that in Segundo's own account of how human beings come to faith, "transcendent data" serve as re-presentations[47] of just such a general conception of reality, as Segundo seems to indicate when, for example, he claims that they are data relating to the "sum-total" of what a human being can experience, or an individual's experiences "taken as a whole" (1982: I: 38). But when we examine closely what Segundo says about transcendent data, we find several obstacles to understanding them in this way. In the first place, these data never really point beyond the plane of personal and social relationships and are inextricably tied to the sheer testimony of the referential witnesses who provide them. Segundo affirms as much when he claims that faith "cannot have has its object reality, in other words, the whole complex of circumstances, things, and persons"; rather, "its object can only be specific persons" (I: 48). At one point, Segundo does speak of transcendent data, after having been accepted solely for their own worth on the basis of the testimony of human witnesses who guarantee them, as being subsequently "existentially 'verified' insofar as they fit in logically and coherently with the other data that the human being perceives and with the values it desires to realize" (II: 955). But there is nothing to suggest and too much else to deny that, for Segundo, these "other data" are anything other than the contingent or fragmentary features of our existence with which faith must daily wrestle. Furthermore, though Segundo claims that in appealing to transcendent data, human beings are convinced that "reality is on their side," it is clear that what is meant by "reality" here is, as Segundo says, "some *ultimate instance* of reality," understood in an eschatological sense (I: 192). Thus, for Segundo, human beings understand reality to be on their side in the sense that someday, ultimately, they will see that one particular way of acting rather than another will prove to be the most satisfying. Segundo incorporates language here such as "at the end of history" (II: 20). But, apart from the issue of what such a phrase could

---

[47]My use of the word "re-present" throughout this study is little more than an appropriation of Schubert Ogden's insight that what is everywhere and always manifested by God to human beings in the events of nature and history as God's "original revelation" may, on the basis of some particular objectification of it, be re-presented or re-expressed in the form of some "special revelation" (such as Christianity) which is constituted precisely as such by that re-presentation. Thus, for example, Ogden says,

> Consequently, insofar as the God who is presented to us in all our experience and understanding is also re-presented to us through explicit concepts and symbols, we are confronted with a special revelation that may indeed claim to be decisive for our existence (1986: 40; Cf. 1961: 156).

possibly mean given Segundo's own evolutionary understanding of history, to claim that some future experience or experiences will validate our faith as authentic is quite different from claiming that experience as a whole or as such serves to thus authorize our faith. In the final analysis, transcendent data do not re-present those features of reality or of our experience which are always the case and with which we have to do no matter what else is the case, but rather serve to communicate possibilities of future satisfactions that are beyond any experience and which require a corresponding leap of faith. Therefore, transcendent data can provide no sort of objective basis in reality for meaning and values short of the guarantees that certain human witnesses (even a tradition of such witnesses) can provide as to how things will turn out in the end.

One might further argue, however, that Segundo's entire attempt to translate evolutionary insights into an "evolutionary epistemology" serves to provide a general view of reality, if not a somewhat formidable example of metaphysics. But Segundo argues explicitly against the usefulness of the latter in this context and, as I shall demonstrate more fully in Chapter 8 of this study, he employs this evolutionary framework for quite different purposes than to provide a comprehensive world-view that could ground or authorize faith as our authentic possibility. Nonetheless, even the utilization of this evolutionary framework to provide the coordinates by which we may locate Jesus as the referential witness *par excellence* requires incorporating a general view of nature, self, and world, and Segundo can hardly avoid at least an implicit metaphysics in his christology, despite his claims to the contrary.

One key to evaluating Segundo's reliance on the wager-like quality of faith and his corresponding rejection of the usefulness of a world-view or metaphysics is to be found in exploring his appeal to the realm of "limit-experiences" which serves as the basis for his notion of "transcendent data." These limit experiences are, for Segundo, the impossibility which every human being faces in deciding what path in life will be the most satisfying on the basis of their own personal experience.

Segundo, as I have shown, prefers to draw the primary distinction between his own view of faith and that of David Tracy in terms of the "content"--or, better, "object"--of faith itself. Segundo sees Tracy's notion of faith as so general and indeterminate as to be uncritical and irrelevant for the task of cultural transformation today. Then, too, to Segundo's mind, Tracy's view ends up making religion a universal dimension of human existence and placing a higher premium on whether one has interpreted their limit-experience correctly in terms of the concept "God" than on the actual values one chooses. In other words, as experience has taught us again and again, though human beings may name the limits of their experience similarly by reference to God or by using explicitly religious language, they may still manage to adopt value-structures that are quite at odds not only with one another but with the values which Jesus himself proclaimed. Segundo, to the contrary, thinks that because faith is predicated upon one's trust in persons, rather than upon an abstract conception of order and value, the radical line of demarcation is between values chosen rather than between whether one is a believer or a non-believer (which, of course, undergirds his confidence that it is possible to present a "Jesus for atheists").

But though Segundo is fond of drawing the contrast between himself and Tracy in this way (viz., a general faith in the worthwhileness of existence versus faith in persons and in the particular scales of value and systems of meaning to which those persons bear witness), I would submit that the more decisive contrast between the two occurs even deeper at the level of how "limit-experiences" are themselves understood, even prior to whether these experiences should or should not be properly referred to as "religious." A great deal, it seems to me, hinges upon whether we conceive of this realm of "limit-experience," with Tracy, as the basic horizon and ground of our common human experience (93) or, with Segundo, as the edge, or "jumping off point," of our experience. In other words, we might ask whether the limits of our experience are most adequately conceived of as the ground, basis, or possibility of any experience whatsoever or, rather, that point where, when all is said and done, we must "transcend"[48] experience, and leap beyond it?

I think a good case can be made for the former rather than the latter not only on the basis of its more appealing theoretical grounds (in that the limits to our experience, though not verifiable empirically, must yet be true of and, indeed, exhibited by all of our experience whatsoever), but also on the basis of its practical grounds in terms of pointing up not only the significance of our praxis (that what we do is of permanent and ineradicable worth), but also the validity of that faith which praxis must itself embody if it is to be understood as our "authentic" praxis. Thus, given this alternative to Segundo's understanding of the "limit" involved in our experience, I find much more convincing the line of thought pursued by David Tracy and Stephen Toulmin (whom Tracy follows at this point) that the "limit" question in science is not, for example, that point where we must simply give up on or move beyond what science can itself discover by virtue of its own empirical methods. Rather, the answer to such a question is the necessary basis for being able to do science at all, the very conditions of possibility for scientific inquiry. So also, the "limit" question in morality is not that point where we must admit that we have no basis either in experience or reason for our moral decisions and must thus move beyond the limits of moral argument. Rather, an answer to this "limit" question is the ground and confidence as to why we should be moral at all (Cf. Toulmin: 204ff; Tracy: 91ff).

---

[48]Segundo consistently uses the word "transcend" in the sense of extending beyond some limit. The idea of transcendence as logical priority or as inclusiveness doesn't seem to enter his thinking, or if it does, it is rejected as vague, indeterminate, or empty with regard to values and meaning.

The real problem for Segundo's analysis of faith, then, and one that seriously hinders his ability to carry through with consistency the task of christology which he himself outlines is that it lacks any objective criteria by which that faith could be validated as either authentic or inauthentic. Faith, instead, shows up only in the "gaps" of our life:

> to say society here is to say *faith*. In effect, what are we to call a universal, unfailing tendency to fill the gaps of our experience with the borrowed experience of others? (1982: I: 19).

It is extremely difficult to see how reliance on particular "referential witnesses" (even Jesus) for one's meaning-world or value-system could ever be other than arbitrary apart from some metaphysical grounding of this existential dimension called "faith." Indeed, it is even difficult to understand just what is the significant nature of this personal witness apart from some general world-view which is presupposed by that witness. Nowhere is this deficiency in Segundo's thought more obvious than when Segundo attempts to ground how one "scales" one's values. This scaling, as I have shown, is based on how one perceives what "ought to be." But surely this requires a basis or fundamental vision both of what can be and of what is. Thus, even the faith *of* Jesus can never simply evoke in us an understanding of our praxis as authentic apart from a particular understanding of ultimate reality that serves to validate the meaning we give to our existence.

In the end, I fail to see how Segundo's wholesale rejection of the role of metaphysics for analyzing our human situation can place his notion of how we come to faith on anything but shaky grounds. For example, he claims that a particular meaning-world is adopted on the basis not of individual experiences but "experience as a whole" and yet he rules out metaphysics as having a role in the adoption or communication of faith. But what could "experience as a whole" possibly refer to if not that totality of reality which metaphysics has as its task to conceptualize? What is a "meaning-world" if not an overall idea of how things in general are and, consequently, our understanding of ourselves in relation to this totality? What do phrases like reality "in the ultimate instance" or "at the end of history" (II: 20) mean apart from some metaphysical conceptuality? In the end, even though Segundo may be able to give some meaning to the notion of anthropological faith, he can neither argue for its validity nor press for its urgency apart from some basis in how things are understood to be in the case of reality itself.

As I hope to show both in this and in my final chapter, there is an understanding of metaphysics which is of more than a little significance to the question of values and that meets Segundo's fundamental criticism of Tracy (leaving aside whether that criticism is fair or not), namely, that the distinction between those who have and who have not correctly interpreted or "named" their limit experience takes precedence over the actual values chosen. I would argue that it is precisely the function of what Segundo calls "religious faith" to explicate or "name" that basic faith which is the authentic possibility of every human existence simply as such and that this process of "naming," while always reflective and never constitutive of that possibility, yet provides the means of validating that faith and pressing for its urgency in such a way as not to detract from or take precedence over the actual values chosen but, on the contrary, to show that one particular scale of values as opposed to another is the most liberating given the meaning which ultimate reality is taken to hold for us.

The Language of Faith

In Chapter 1, I introduced Segundo's distinction between "gospel" and christology" and there suggested that keeping some such distinction clearly in mind would be essential for developing an adequate and effective christological method. I also mentioned that this distinction is especially important with regard to the relationship between theology and praxis. I now wish to show how this is so in terms of Segundo's own method and it is here that I find the work of Clodovis Boff, in *Theology and Praxis: Epistemological Foundations*, to be particularly helpful. Boff, not unlike Segundo or Ogden, distinguishes between two types of discourse--"religious" and "theological." The difference between the two he states as follows:

> Religious discourse--the human response to the word of faith is "defracted" into a multiplicity of discursive practices: kerygma, catechesis, homily, prophecy, testimony, magisterial teaching, hymnology, ritual, and so on. Religious discourse is situated just at the intersection of the word of faith with theology. It is the word of faith on the way to becoming theology. . .
>
> Theology arises when the *ratio fidei* already present in various degrees in religious discourse, becomes systematic, methodical, disciplined. This is the difference between theological reason and religious reason . . . . theology is distinguished from religious discourse by the *mode* of cognition of the same content--that is, by its method (110).

What distinguishes religious discourse from theology, according to Boff, is not its vocabulary but its grammar (125), not the former's "lack" of reason, but rather the *degree* and *mode* of the use of reason by each. As Boff says,

> discursive practices of a religious nature are governed by rules no less than is theological practice. The only difference here is that their rules, unlike those of theology, constitute a *regularity* rather than a *legality*. The rules of simple religious discourse are as it were buried within the discourse itself, so that the one enunciating the discourse does not advert to them.

By contrast, the rules of theology are explicitly laid down, positively established, and critically controlled (111).[49]

One of the primary distinctions to be drawn between the two types of discourse, in Boff's view, is the relationship of each to *praxis*.

> The varieties of religious discourse . . . are all concerned with *direct practice*. They express life as actually experienced, and are developed with a view to the solution of concrete problems. Accordingly, they set in motion a type of language that corresponds to life experience, and to practice. . . . Theological practice, on the other hand, has no immediate objective in life experience. It is not built in direct function of a practice. Its immediate objective is the cognition of that of which faith is the experience and simple consciousness: God's salvation (111).

Thus, to Boff's mind, we have a more "performative" and "self-involving" type of language when we come to religious discourse while theology is more "indicative" and seeks "consistency, precision, and semantic constancy." Religious discourse is a language in, by, and for faith and praxis while theology is the interpretation and criticism of that prior discourse.

This principle, elaborated so concisely by Boff, is of critical importance for this study and for evaluating Segundo's christological reflection. We find, on the one hand, that there is a fundamental sense in which we may talk about the priority of praxis over theory in that praxis is the "point of departure" of theology; in other words, as Boff says, "praxis prepares the agenda, the repertory of questions, that theology is to address" (200). On the other hand, however, this does not and cannot mean that praxis is the fundamental determination or verification of theology. On the contrary, theology must be able to maintain a critical distance from that discourse which is born in praxis and with a view to praxis in order to assess the validity and pertinence of that discourse. As Boff says, "in theology we no longer have the believer speaking, praying, or giving witness--we have the theoretician reasoning, discoursing, criticizing" (127).

Segundo, as I have shown, maintains a relationship both of complementarity and autonomy between theology and praxis. He believes that, while theology must ever sharpen its hermeneutic preunderstanding by coming back again and again to the praxis in which faith is born and implemented, theology does not merely "arise" from praxis, and orthopraxis is not the main criterion

---

[49]Cf. Charles Wood's way of putting the matter:

Theology as such is not witness, not even of a refined and sophisticated sort. It is rather an attempt to bring witness to reflection, and to ask about its validity -- its faithfulness, its truth, its aptness to its circumstances (24).

for evaluating theology. With regard to such a view, I think Segundo would find himself in full agreement with Boff. The question, however, is whether Segundo is prepared consistently to develop and accept the implications of this relationship in his own method.

Segundo does not always distinguish with sufficient clarity when he is talking about the discourse of faith and when he is talking about the discourse of theology and, because of this, the dimension of praxis in the christological question, far from being heightened or even exaggerated, is instead diminished. All too often, the lines become blurred between the two levels of discourse so that Segundo's criticisms of "academic" theology are often the result of an unfair comparison between the more "iconic" language of faith and the more "digital" language of theology. Segundo, for example, proposes that iconic language such as poetry is often the most adequate to communicate the satisfactions linked with a particular value-system, and that scripture, if it is to be understood correctly, must be recognized as an example of the language of witness expressed in the form of testimonies, images, and actions and then interpreted as such. Segundo argues that the inexactitude of the premises of faith is what gives humans the "room," or flexibility, to create their own unique and effective way of fleshing out the meaning-world they adopt and keeps us from being "bound" to one singular mode of expression (ideology). But while Segundo is undoubtedly correct in such an assessment, the criteria thus employed for evaluating this imprecise language of faith on the basis of its own peculiar structure as the language of witness all too often become the same criteria Segundo employs for assessing both the language and the method of theological discourse, resulting in a lack of what Boff would call "criticity" (126) on the part of the latter. Segundo, for example, quotes Hans Küng as saying "Theology can never be content to be graciously tolerated within a field where conclusions are notably inexact and lacking in binding force, as if 'religious truth' were similar to 'poetic truth'" (Küng, 1976: 87). Segundo responds by claiming that Küng's statement "proves again how theology has unwittingly been moving farther and farther away from the eminently poetic fonts of its knowledge; the Bible, patristics, and the church tradition of the saints and mystics" (1982: II: 54).

The problem here is more than merely verbal "slippage" on Segundo's part but is the fruit of Segundo's understanding of faith as not simply pre-rational or pre-critical but fundamentally anti-rational and anti-critical, immune to any assessment of its validity by reason. Faith, as Segundo says, is "self-validating" with respect to reason (I: 119) and based on premises that are beyond "proofs," whether for or against it:

> [Faith], rationally speaking, is a-rational and a-scientific, however human and necessary it may be judged. That is why we cannot assault the meaning-structure of anyone by brandishing in front of them some demonstrable "falsehood" (I: 120).

That is not to say that faith is therefore closed, fixed, and unchanging; it can, after all, be deepened and modified by a process of conversion initiated by contact with certain "transcendent data."   But even these data and the premises which communicate them are beyond the control of reason and science.

What Segundo means here by "a-rational" or "a-scientific," to be sure, is our inability to subject faith to any kind of empirical verification or falsification. He gives the following example:

> What if, for example, we could demonstrate in a scientific way, that a particular structure of values is *unrealizable*--inasmuch as reason and science can come into play here. Even that would not mean that we had proved "faith" false, since it would still be possible to value failure by claiming that reality is not what it ought to be. Practically all martyrs, religious or not, have preferred to maintain their meaning-structure over against the concrete unviability of their projects (I: 120).

From the above it is clear that the arena of verification and falsification which Segundo has in mind, as well as the understanding of "reality" with which he works, is our daily historical existence made up of an ever-changing variety of contingent features which may or may not be what they ought to be--in other words, the empirical "facts" which we have to take into account in leading our lives--and to the extent that this is the reality which Segundo has in mind, he is surely right--faith is not and cannot be validated by the contingent features of our existence.[50]   Of course, empirical facts are certainly taken into account by each human being, and if a critical mass of facts begins to contradict our own structure of meaning, we may experience a crisis of faith or begin to call our faith into question; but faith, as Segundo says, is the way we interpret facts or "punctuate" a series of events and is, therefore, something we bring to our reality rather than something we deduce from it.

Given this understanding of the structure of faith, it is no wonder that theology as critical reflection on faith becomes a virtually impossible task for Segundo and that we often find him making the claim for his theology that it is not theology at all. But if Segundo's theology is not theology *per se*, that is not simply or primarily because it does not presuppose or explicitly advocate for any particular theism; rather, it is because a fundamental contradiction obtains between theology conceived of as the employment of critical reason in the evaluation of

---

[50]It should be mentioned that Segundo's thought at this point is heavily motivated not only by the rejection of any kind of empiricism that attempts experimentally to verify or falsify faith on the level of science, but also, by the rejection of a rigid literalism that tries to prove the validity of faith by "sticking to the letter of the Bible" (II: 21).

the truth-claims of faith, on the one hand, and faith, understood as beyond the reaches of such critical reason, on the other. The real culprit here, it seems to me, is Segundo's use of Gregory Bateson's distinction between "iconic" and "digital" language, and not the simple use of it alone, but the lack of a clear reflection on the way such different types of language are related to the different dimensions of human experience which they reflect.

While it is true that there is a range of human experience that is subject to empirical verification or falsification and that may, therefore, be expressed "digitally" (such as, for example, whether it is night or day), it is not at all clear that the dimension of human experience which deals with meaning and values--the dimension of faith--and which does not admit of such empirical verification or falsification is, therefore, non-digital, beyond the scope of reason, and adequately evaluated and communicated only by an iconic language consisting of metaphor, poetry, or images. On the contrary, though the language of witness may function at its best in precisely the kind of iconic or symbolic ways Segundo suggests, when it comes to a reflective understanding of the claims of that witness, it is difficult to see how they can purport to be meaningful in any cognitive way, let alone true, apart from our giving some rational account of the kind of experience that could possibly serve to verify those claims, thereby establishing their ability to refer. This does not mean, however, that the claims of faith must therefore be subject to *empirical* verification or falsification. Rather, if such claims have to do with the very meaning-structure on which our entire existence is premised, as Segundo admits, then it is our entire existence which finally must confirm those claims. But is there a language that can adequately give expression to claims which are existentially true though not factually true or empirically verifiable? I would argue that there is such a language and that the significance of Jesus cannot be interpreted critically apart from such language.

Charles Hartshorne makes the point that the real issue with empirical knowledge is not so much the question of its verifiability as the question of its falsifiability. He says,

> The crucial test of empirical generalizations is not that this or that obser-
> vation agrees with them but that deliberate and carefully designed obser-
> vational attempts to falsify them fail to do so. The negative test is the
> decisive one. Crackpots tell you how experience supports their claims;
> they do not tell you what conceivable experiences would show the claim
> to be false (1989: 177).

Hartshorne gives three examples of knowledge--mathematics, formal logic, and metaphysics--all of which make assertions that no conceivable experience can falsify and which, therefore, are to be considered non-empirical knowledge. There is a great difference, however, between the first two in this list and the third. Schubert Ogden puts the matter this way:

there is evidently a whole class of assertions that intend, as merely mathematical and logical assertions hardly do, to assert something about existence, and thus are existential assertions, but nevertheless are not factual. I refer to the class of strictly *metaphysical* assertions, the chief defining characteristic of which is that, while they assert something to be existentially the case, they neither are nor could be factually falsifiable (1977: 320-321).

Ogden goes on to give an example of a metaphysical statement, "The universe exists." In accordance with Hartshorne's observation mentioned above, we can say that this statement is non-empirical or non-factual in that there are no conceivable conditions for its falsification, and yet, at the same time, it clearly makes an assertion about what is existentially the case. According to both Ogden and Hartshorne, simply because metaphysical statements are not factual does not mean that they are not meaningful and true. As Ogden says, "every fact, even every conceivable fact, does and must verify them, and no fact, not even a conceivable fact, could ever falsify them" (321).

The logic involved in the metaphysical assertions described by Ogden is evidently just the kind of logic required by the language of faith insofar as it intends to say anything that is cognitively meaningful and true. But it is precisely metaphysical assertions which Segundo rules out for either the communication or evaluation of the language of faith, not merely on the level of witness, but also on the level of reflection. Even transcendent data, though they are often communicated digitally, cannot, as Segundo says, be "experimentally verified" (1982: I: 170).

But if what Ogden says about metaphysical assertions is true, then not only can the language of faith be confirmed by experience, it must be confirmed by every conceivable experience and falsified by no conceivable experience. Segundo does not account for such language and, in essence, reduces the realm of experience to the realm of the strictly empirical. Because of this, Segundo's analysis of human existence is not sufficiently comprehensive, in my judgment, to ground the meaningful communication of meaning and values, not to mention the validation of that meaning and those values.

Of course, Segundo does, as I have mentioned, advocate the practice of what he calls "existential validation" and, in this respect, his argument takes much the same form as that of Dorothee Soelle. Soelle, in her response to Schubert Ogden's *Faith and Freedom*, addresses Ogden's claim that liberation theologians tend to "obscure any distinction between theology and witness" (1979a: 33-34). According to Soelle, rather than obscuring the two, liberation theologians insist that the language of testimony, prayer, and confession *is* the proper theological language and that "They feel no need to transcend this type of God talk by systematization into a doctrinal and/or metaphysical language" (10). Soelle goes on to argue as follows:

If praxis and faith are seen as essential, and theory and theology are seen as handmaidens of faith without any value in themselves separate from these, then this distinction concerning modes of language loses relevance (11).

Instead, concepts of God must be evaluated by a "functional criterion," by which she means that they must be tested to see whether they are liberating or oppressive. As Soelle says,

We have no interest in a metaphysical truth claim about God's being in itself. Truth in the understanding of liberation theologians is essentially "concrete": any metaphysical or revelational doctrine of God makes truth abstract (11).

Soelle asks, instead, if an "existential interpretation" is possible; in other words, if there is a possible "third way between a theoretical objective talk that excludes passion, self-expression, and the call to struggle, and a merely personal immediate talk which excludes rationality and objectivity?" (11) To find such a language, Soelle looks to the "existential interpretation" of Heidegger and Bultmann and claims that this language "is 'existential' in the sense that it is committed, impassioned, and praxis-oriented" but that it "is 'interpretative' in the sense that it is reflective, reasonable, and theory-oriented" (11). How "interpretative" this kind of language can actually be, however, is a matter of question in Soelle and, indeed, in Bultmann if, by that word, we mean not only the reflective or rational character of existential language, but also its ability to express what is actually the case, objectively. Bultmann's existentialist interpretation does, to be sure, have its own "objective" referent, but there is yet room, it seems to me, for a more fully developed ontology, along the lines of a neo-classical metaphysics such as Charles Hartshorne's, that could amplify the sense in which existential language mediates to us what is actually the case with existence apart from the kind of "objectivism" provided either by mythology or classical ontology.[51]

As in the case of Soelle, so also with Segundo, it is a strictly functional criterion by which theological language must be measured. Thus, in virtually every case where Segundo calls for an "existential language" to communicate the dimension of human meaning and values or where he calls for an "existential validation" to judge that same realm of meaning and values, the existential criteria of validation thus suggested are reduced to a kind of ethical or performative criteria whereby one's faith is validated to the extent that one's way of acting or living is transformed (I: 189). But such criteria, as employed by Segundo, though they address the ethical implications of our faith, can never really judge the

---

[51]Cf. Ogden's criticism of Bultmann at this point (1961: 151ff).

cognitive content of that faith insofar as they lack any metaphysical component that could take into account reality itself--the totality of existence on which our faith, and therefore our praxis, is grounded. That, of course, is because reality, in Segundo's opinion, is "neutral" vis-á-vis the values we choose, a question which I will more fully consider in Chapter 8 of this study.

The result of Segundo's conceptuality at this point, then, is that the language of faith is really not existential language at all in that, rather than actually *asserting* something to be the case existentially, it instead expresses a kind of intention or attitude toward life and is thus reduced merely to the ethical component of that language quite apart from its metaphysical presuppositions. But far from giving the dimension of praxis that is presupposed in the question of faith its due importance, Segundo's method reduces that dimension to something arbitrary and non-binding--hardly expressing the kind of claim implied in the witness of the martyrs who maintain their particular faith against all types of adversity.

Of course, all of the above is not to claim that every claim which faith makes is therefore a metaphysical assertion. Indeed, there are a whole host of factual assertions to which the witness of faith attests, not the least of which, as Ogden points out, are "our creation by God and our redemption by him" (1977: 321). What the above does point out, however, is that the language of faith, while not univocal, implies existential claims which, by their very nature, function metaphysically to refer beyond the contingent features of our daily existence which we must take into account in order effectively to implement our faith, to the ultimate reality with which every existence must concern itself and which stands as the necessary presupposition of all that we think or do. Thus, for instance, if we return to Segundo's example of martyrs who prefer to maintain their meaning-structure, even when it becomes unviable within the concrete conditions of their life, we may ask how it is that these martyrs are able to maintain their faith in such conditions. Is it simply by virtue of a "wager" that the path testified to by a particular "referential witness," or "tradition" of referential witnesses, will turn out to be the most satisfying in life, even though one can never know that personally for oneself or ahead of time? Or is it not rather also and even more fundamentally due to a fundamental confidence that, though the contingent features of our existence may or may not lend themselves to maintaining such a meaning-structure, yet our understanding of reality itself--that is, our most general understanding of ourselves in relation to the whole in which we exist--is taken as not only permitting but empowering and authorizing us to live in accordance with one particular meaning-structure and not another? If so, then even though faith must undoubtedly be said to be beyond empirical control, that is far from saying that it is beyond the control of experience or reason or that it is simply "self-validating." Thus, though I would not want to diminish what Segundo so eloquently describes as the "wager," or "risk" of faith, I think that we must so understand the adventure of faith as to include the more fundamental risk that the reality upon which we ground not only our structure of meaning and value but also, inevitably, our entire praxis, is such as to permit our claiming that one particular meaning-structure and its implications for praxis will, indeed, be the most satisfying and authentic possibility in life.

Faith and Christology:
Chalcedon as a Case in Point

In Part I of this study, I tried to demonstrate that the reason for Segundo's extensive treatment of how we come to faith and the kind of language that is appropriate to the witness of faith is to clarify the role of faith in adequately interpreting the significance of Jesus of Nazareth. On the one hand, then, christology becomes the proving ground for Segundo's analysis of faith and, on the other hand, Segundo's method of analyzing faith is taken to be the appropriate method for christological reflection. Because of this, I think it would be helpful to take one particular christological example--namely, Segundo's treatment of the Chalcedonian definition--in order to determine thereby just how adequately and effectively Segundo's method serves as a tool for critically interpreting the significance of Jesus. Chalcedon is an especially fruitful case in point for evaluating Segundo's method because it provides us an opportunity to appraise not only how he himself critically interprets the significance of Jesus in dialogue with an historical expression of that significance that has been normative for the Christian tradition for centuries, but also because the issue of christological language--especially, the role of metaphysics in that language--surfaces explicitly in that dialogue.

In the first place, Segundo claims that Chalcedon, in order to answer the question of Jesus' significance, inherited a "theological" approach that can be found in the post-paschal writings of the New Testament and that is characteristic of the christological reflection of the first four centuries. That is not to say that before the resurrection people were not concerned with the relationship of Jesus to deity; only that after the resurrection that question responded to different interests than before. This is especially the case with the early conciliar creeds and definitions whose interests, as Segundo says, were "to establish--in a 'digital' way--the dogmatic statement which, by the fifth century, would be considered normative for all later christological thinking" (1982: II: 629). Segundo claims that the pre-paschal Jesus did not appeal to his own divine status or relationship with deity but instead interpreted his message and even his thaumaturgical power as signs of the establishment of the kingdom of God. Jesus explicitly rejected the approach of those who wished to establish his divinity first in order to decide whether or not they should follow him and was concerned that the language of faith move in the right direction. These two questions--the question of the historical project of establishing the kingdom of God and the question of the relationship of Jesus to God--must, says Segundo, be understood as questions on two different logical levels (II: 630) with the former having a logical priority over the other. To mix these two logical types has negative consequences:

> the testimony grounding faith is effective to the same extent in which it is *human*, in other words, insofar as it can demonstrate a suitable road to happiness. God himself cannot stir up faith in any other way. . . . Since we can grant our faith only to a witness who has an impact on us and offers us a way to happiness, every *mixing* of divine or superhuman characteristics in that witness, far from strengthening our faith, will sooner or later eliminate it completely (II: 634).

Segundo realizes that the cross and resurrection of Jesus were bound to shift the language of faith from one logical level regarding the historical question about the kingdom to another logical level regarding the theological question about Jesus' divine character. Thus, as Segundo says, "the message *of* Jesus became a message *about* Jesus" (II: 637), or as Bultmann says, the *what* of Jesus' message is replaced by the *that* of Jesus' message. Bultmann puts the issue this way:

> Such a summons to decision for or against his person implies a christology, although not, of course, either as speculation about a heavenly being or as the construction of a so-called messianic consciousness. In fact, this christology cannot be a matter of theoretical observation at all but only of explicating the answer of decision for him, of obedience to his word, of obedience which lets one's situation be disclosed as new through him. This christology becomes explicit in the early community to the extent that it confesses that Jesus has been made Messiah by God and as such will come. From this it is clear that the community understands Jesus' word--and that means not its timeless content of ideas, but his having spoken it and their having been addressed by it--as the decisive act of God. But this is also to say that their transmission of Jesus' proclamation could not consist in a simple reproduction of his ideas. Instead, the proclaimer had to become the one proclaimed. The *that* of his proclamation is precisely what is decisive (1982: 5-6).

For Bultmann, this necessary shift from *what* to *that* is what makes possible our being both confronted by Jesus' message as decisive for our existence and also called to decision on that basis. Segundo, too, understands the importance of this shift as opening up the way we are to understand Jesus' message as significant (expressed, for example, in the titles of Jesus, such as "Messiah," "Word," "Alpha and Omega," etc.), but is much more concerned that what is truly of significance about Jesus usually gets erased completely or at best diluted by such a shift. The problem is that the shift from *what* to *that* is not always taken account of properly nor is it always made in a well-balanced way. Therefore, rather than understanding the second question, that is, the theological question as to Jesus' divine character, as a "*meta-message*: a message about the message, about how to understand it, about the level (cognitive and operational at the same time) that this faith attains" (1982: II: 636), the levels instead become confused and the first question as to the historical project of bringing about the kingdom of God is virtually erased by the second. This is especially the case, for example, in Peter's sermon on the day of Pentecost where Jesus' death is attributed to prior design by God, the historical project of Jesus is forgotten, and any reference to the kingdom is omitted. Segundo's response to this sermon points up what he takes to be the crux of the matter:

> In effect, this reply *mixes* two designs of a different logical level in the real life of Jesus: the one that Jesus consciously and deliberately shoulders, and the one that God has for Jesus and for other human beings whether they are aware of it or not. Then, the very logical conclusion is drawn that the second design is, in the final analysis, the more valid and significant one, if not the only authentic one. But, as we have seen, far from making any contribution to anthropological faith in Jesus Christ, it instead places his life and message on the plane of ideology (as a magical instrument of salvation), or makes them irrelevant for those who look to Jesus for the meaning they might give to their human existence (II: 639-640).

Thus, according to Segundo, the difference between the preaching of Jesus and the preaching of Peter is *not* the difference between *message* and *meta-message*; rather,

> That message is no longer concerned with knowing whether people's values fit in with those of the kingdom, however initially and gradually, but rather with whether they do or do not recognize Jesus as the Messiah of Israel. The first could require months or years as well as concrete manifestations. The second is acknowledged in a matter of minutes (II: 641).

Segundo has a great appreciation for the early councils, especially Chalcedon, insofar as they are more consciously careful to keep the two "languages" or "logical levels" about Jesus distinct. Even though they obviously bear the marks of their age in terms of the conceptuality they employ, they maintain a balance that is often ignored by contemporary christologies which are rather uniform in attacking these ancient expressions, feeling they have surpassed them. As Segundo says,

The great value of the solutions they gave to the christological controversies of the first few centuries, especially the formulations of Chalcedon, lay in their healthy and tenacious effort, which had to be conscious in some obscure way, not to let one of the pertinent questions about Jesus become mixed in with the other as if it were on the same plane and shared the same meaning-*content* about Christ. In other words, they struggled for centuries to maintain the distinction of logical levels with regard to Jesus, and thereby the richness and originality of his anthropological testimony (II: 641).

Segundo's distinction here between "message" and "meta-message" is helpful, it seems to me, in facilitating our understanding of how the symbols and concepts used to assert the significance of Jesus' message by both the New Testament as well as the later councils and creeds ultimately function as a "meta-message"--as an indication of how we are to understand Jesus and his message, namely, as decisive or, as Segundo says, of "absolute" significance for human existence--and this, despite their wide variety and their more or less adequate attempts metaphysically to identify who Jesus is in relation to God. *That* these symbols and concepts function as a meta-message and *how* they function as a meta-message, however, are two different matters and, with regard to the latter, Segundo's argument, it seems to me, departs from the course taken by both the New Testament and later councils in a way that will lead him inevitably to a dead end.

If, for example, we take the statement "Jesus is God" settled at Nicea and presupposed by Chalcedon, and if we interpret that statement with Segundo as a "meta-message" about Jesus, then it would appear that two ways of understanding just *how* that statement functions as a meta-message open themselves up to us. The first way of understanding that statement is that it serves as an expression of the belief by the earliest witnesses of Jesus that in their historical encounter with him, they have been confronted with, as Ogden says, the "decisive re-presentation of ultimate reality" and, therefore, "the authentic understanding of one's existence in relation to this ultimate reality" (1982: 129). The second way of understanding the statement "Jesus is God," however, and the way characteristically pursued by Segundo, is that this statement functions as a way of qualifying a particular human faith (that of Jesus) as "absolutely" significant for us. Thus, the values implied in and called for by Jesus' own historical project of bringing about the kingdom of God are "absolutized" and the reference to God serves to connote that absolute quality. I think the difference between these two ways of understanding the statement "Jesus is God" can best be demonstrated by looking a little more closely at Chalcedon itself.

Even though Chalcedon simply presupposed the dogma of Nicea and Constantinople that, as Richard Norris says, "there is in Christ only one 'thing' and that this 'thing' is precisely the eternal Son of God" (1966: 75), actually declaring that dogma in terms of language was not easy. One had to maintain several elements simultaneously: first, that the qualities predicated of Jesus (growing up, suffering, dying, etc.) were truly human predicates and not only apparently so; second, that the subject of all these verbs was the Son of God; and third, that there could be no mixing of the divine and the human to the point of ending up with two subjects in the one person Jesus. The real issue for Chalcedon, then, was how to talk about the divinity of Jesus, not in terms of *whether* Jesus was divine, to be sure, since that had already been decided, but rather *how* one could properly talk about that divinity given the other factors that one had to maintain.

To Segundo's mind, there were only two possible approaches to such "talk" about the divinity of Jesus--either (a) by way of metaphysics or (b) by way of the actual history of Jesus and its place within a tradition of historical witnesses. Since there could be no mixing of the human and divine, the second route would seem to be closed. However, Segundo believes that the vehicle of the *communicatio idiomatum*--the communication of properties--if understood properly as a linguistic communication, predicates historical, human qualities of God but does so grammatically, not metaphysically, thus avoiding the kind of mix that would yield two subjects in one person. Rather than asserting two subjects in Jesus, the one divine and the other human, Chalcedon solves the problem by asserting a divine subject with human predicates. Furthermore, this linguistic road travels only one direction. As Segundo points out, the *communicatio idiomatum* did not predicate impassibility, for example, of the human Jesus in order to give him a unique metaphysical status. It did, however, apply to God the predicate of, for example, anthropological faith, not, of course, in order to make God a human, but rather, in order to qualify the particular anthropological faith found in Jesus as "absolute." Thus, Chalcedon rejects an approach that starts with the religious or the metaphysical significance of Jesus and only subsequently moves to Jesus' anthropological significance. Rather, it begins with the historical encounter of Jesus, and claims thereby to give content to the meaning of divine nature. Segundo concludes:

> *all theological* language, without being impoverished thereby or diminished in the least bit, has to be, at the same time and for the same reason, *anthropological*--not because of the unconscionable audacity of human beings but because of the incommensurable audacity of God (1982: II: 656).

For Segundo, then, how the concept God functions in the statement "Jesus is God," is to claim that the *what* of Jesus (his anthropological significance, i.e., his structure of meaning and values) is "absolutely" significant. In other words, the predication runs only one direction. The concept of God is empty and it is the "attitudes" of Jesus (II: 645) that give it content. We might ask, how do we then keep the statement "Jesus is God" from becoming a mere tautology, "Jesus is Jesus"? Segundo anticipates this question and responds that

> *in this type of language*, the concept God, rather than being something that *anyone* could know in its essence and that, *moreover*, would possess and impose certain value-judgments, is, in the first place at least, the predicate connoting the *absolute* character of a specific value associated with an equally specific line of conduct (II: 645-646).

This "absolute character" of Jesus' message is something, says Segundo, that can confront every human being, whether they are religious or atheists because it does not depend on some prior metaphysical belief in God but solely on an anthropological faith in a witness.

Here, it seems to me, we are faced with the enormous problem of clarifying just how the significance of Jesus can be understood as either decisive or absolute on the grounds merely of his historical witness. Though we may well want to agree with Segundo that the metaphysical claims entailed in the Chalcedonian definition ask too much by way of consent on the part of contemporary human beings, we must still ask what could possibly give to the "meta-message" (that is, the claim as to how we are to understand Jesus and his message) its "absolute" character, whatever shape or form that meta-message takes? In other words, if it is not some metaphysical belief about Jesus' divine nature that gives to his message a certain urgency and decisiveness for human existence, than what does give it those qualities?

Segundo entertains this very question of why Jesus should be trusted as a witness over against any other witnesses and claims that there is "something more" operating here than just the sheer attraction of Jesus' historical witness. There are not, he says, as many "gods" as there are value-systems and we do not, therefore, have to adopt blindly an anthropological faith, wagering that in the end, eschatologically, this faith will be revealed as the correct one. According to Segundo, this would be sheer "fideism" (II: 649). What is required in order to warrant the kind of significance which is claimed for Jesus--that "something more" that could ground our meaning-world and absolutize it--is not anything that reason or science could produce or control, however, but is rather a tradition of "transcendent data." Thus, even though Jesus' kingdom-building project appears historically as a failure, his followers "comprehend" that he is more than that by interpreting his life in terms of a particular tradition, or process of "learning to learn," and by connecting that process with particular transcendent data about human existence. Here, I think, Segundo *moves close* to correcting an impression which one picks up throughout his entire christology, namely, that it is the sheer impressiveness of Jesus' witness, his own actualization of authentic faith, that renders his life and message decisive for our existence.[52] Segundo states that the "transcendent data" which give a unique and definitive meaning to Jesus' witness can never be the result of a mere observation of Jesus' life.

> Thus, neither simple contemplation of the sequence of events marking the life of Jesus (including among them the "apparitions" of the risen one) nor the sole attraction to the value that dominates his life, love unto death, is enough to lead us to a reasonable conclusion that we are faced with the transcendent datum by very name: i.e., that Jesus is God or, if preferred, that the ultimate reality was manifested to us in him (II: 650).

We will recall that it is precisely the above two elements, *transcendent data* and *tradition* that, for Segundo, turn faith into "religious" faith. According to Segundo, however, this faith is still open to atheists and its character as "religious" should not be taken to presuppose any kind of metaphysical beliefs.

> I do not consider this faith to be "religious" because it *talks about God*, i.e., because it employs a universal and metaphysical concept of a transcendent being. It is not religious by virtue of its content, but rather because it attains a degree or quality of irreversibility in its adhesion that, in terms of language, creates a God, an Absolute, and definitively entrusts the whole existence to it (II: 651-652).

Segundo, then, concludes that if Chalcedon is problematic, that is not fundamentally due to an internal flaw or even primarily a case of its outdated conceptuality, but rather a case of forgetting *all* of what Chalcedon said. Even though Chalcedon could not be other than dependent upon a metaphysics that tried to talk about Jesus in terms of words like "nature" and "substance," the doctrine of the *communicatio idiomatum*, when interpreted as a grammatical solution to the christological problem, talks about deity in a way that actually runs counter to the metaphysics of a fixed, unchanging, divine nature, in that God is made the subject of historical experiences and becomes his own nature in history. According to Segundo, then, what we find when we come to Chalcedon is a grammar that is not entirely consistent with its metaphysics. The real accomplishment of Chalcedon, however, was precisely its grammatical solution, not its metaphysical conceptuality; unfortunately, subsequent christology has been rather unanimous in preoccupying itself with metaphysical solutions to the christological problem at the expense of that grammar.

---

[52]I say *"moves close"*, because, finally, I must conclude that Segundo's overarching method wars against this understanding and inevitably defeats it.

I find Segundo's interpretation of Chalcedon at this point to be particularly sound and insightful at several points. Segundo's general interpretation of Chalcedon in terms of its grammar is confirmed by the work of Richard Norris who says of Chalcedon:

> What makes its *Definition* intelligible is not its advocacy of a particular theory of the Incarnation, but its tacit insistence on the subject-attribute paradigm as a Christological model. . . . in fact what the Council offers is not a philosophical explanation of the structure of the Person of Christ, but a Christological *grammar*, which is based in the last resort on the logical form of traditional confessional statements about Christ (1966: 76).

Norris insists that the Chalcedonian definition becomes intelligible only when it is understood as "a definition of the normative form of any statement about Christ" rather than as a metaphysical or psychological account of the constitution of Christ's person, and he goes on to say, "The *Definition* is not talking about Jesus; it is talking about Christian language about Jesus" (78). Furthermore, the logic of this language is a subject-attribute logic that, confirming Segundo's thesis, starts with a divine subject (the Word) and predicates of that subject the experiences of human existence. Norris concludes that the rule of christological language which Chalcedon provides is that Jesus is one subject who must be spoken of as God and, at the same time, as a human being.

> To give an account of Jesus, then, one must talk in two ways simultaneously. One must account for all that he is and does by reference to the Logos of God, that is, one must identify him as God acting in our midst. At the same time, however, one must account for him as a human being in the ordinary sense of that term. Both accounts are necessary. One cannot understand Jesus correctly by taking either account independently, even while recognizing that they really are different accounts (Norris, 1980: 31)

As astute as Segundo's analysis evidently is in recognizing the fundamental value of Chalcedon for interpreting the significance of Jesus, however, it is not at all clear why one should understand Chalcedon's application of human predicates to a divine subject as a way of absolutizing the faith or values of Jesus. Indeed, this path seems completely to reverse the direction of Chalcedon's logic at this point. Segundo himself insists that Chalcedon is careful not to apply classical divine qualities (such as impassibility, aseity, etc.) to the human Jesus and yet is that not precisely, at least in terms of logic, what Segundo's approach does? I would argue that, on the contrary, the logic of Chalcedon supports our interpreting a statement such as "Jesus is God" as a "meta-message" in the sense that the meaning of ultimate reality for one's own faith and ideologies has been discovered in the limited historical encounter with Jesus of Nazareth.

This, however, by no means implies that we must approach the significance of Jesus "from above" or by an analysis of his unique metaphysical or psychological constitution and, in essence, Segundo pushes us into a false dilemma at this point. He claims that Jesus rejected any attempt by people first to determine his divinity and then, on the basis of that determination, to proceed to adopt the values associated with the historical project of the kingdom. True enough, but, for Segundo, the only other option available is that Jesus is considered humanly significant as a witness and that, on the basis of a tradition of transcendent data to which he himself as well as his original interpreters appealed, his values are professed to be "absolute"--a profession expressed in christological titles such as "Messiah" or "Lord," or in statements such as "Jesus is God." But is there not a third option which, beginning with an historical starting point, to be sure, understands Jesus as the decisive re-presentation of ultimate reality, not on the basis either of his own divine physiology or on the basis of his own historical achievement of living a heroic life of love unto death, but rather because, on the basis of the historical encounter with him by the earliest witnesses, the conclusion is reached that Jesus "recapitulates," or "sums up" that which is implicit in every structure of meaning which we human beings give to our existence, including both our notion of what is ultimately real and our understanding of ourselves in relation to what is ultimately real along with the implications of that understanding for praxis.[53] Thus, even though the interpretation of the significance of Jesus obviously requires that we start "from below," that is from the historical encounter of Jesus by his original witnesses, it nonetheless requires reflection upon both the metaphysical as well as the praxic dimensions of that significance. It is my contention, however, that neither the metaphysical nor the praxic dimension of Jesus' significance is given full justice by Segundo's method, precisely because he reverses the logic of the fundamental christological assertion.

---

[53]Without defending Norman Pittenger's christology, which, in general, is closer to Segundo's than to the option for which I advocate, I yet find the following statement by Pittenger to be quite to the point for my purposes here:

> For us, the uniqueness of Jesus can only be seen in his specialty, his supreme and decisive expression of that which God always and everywhere is "up to" in his world. Here a suggestion made recently in a lecture by Professor Moule of Cambridge will help. Professor Moule has noted that there are *two* kinds of uniqueness: one of exclusion and one of inclusion. Jesus is not unique, then, because of him and of him only can it be said that God is operative there; he is unique by inclusion, in that he includes, takes up into himself, and gives point to all that God is doing, has done, and will do (1971a: 214).

Segundo's analysis, for example, becomes severely strained in his handling of the contradiction which he detects in the Chalcedonian definition between, on the one hand, the application of human predicates to a divine subject and, on the other hand, the classical metaphysical notion of God as unchanging and impassible. On the basis of this contradiction, Segundo proceeds to reject metaphysics as a whole for the task of christology because the only kind of language that can talk about God as an experiencing, becoming subject is a metaphorical or symbolic language. This "iconic" language of poetry that can express God as angry, sad, changing, demanding, or giving, claims Segundo, is a more adequate language than metaphysics for christological reflection. In fact, Segundo says:

> The language of metaphysics which presents God as the "unmoved mover" is nothing more than bad poetry from start to finish. It is false poetry: false for presenting as descriptive language what is not that, and also false for not observing the elementary laws of logical language (1982: II: 662).

In Segundo's opinion, there are simply some kinds of human experiences that cannot be expressed in digital language--namely, the kind that "can usher us into the 'divine' significance of Jesus of Nazareth" (II: 662). The kind of grammar presupposed in the *communicatio idiomatum* can never be literal, digital language; rather, the communication "between history and the dimensions of the human being on the one hand and the way of expressing oneself about the divine on the other" (II: 668) requires strictly iconic language. If Chalcedon failed in any area, it was a failure to recognize this and to attempt, rather, to purify its digital language and wipe out any iconic language.

As sympathetic as I am with Segundo's rejection of the classical metaphysics presupposed by Chalcedon and as convinced as I am that not all forms of metaphysics (for example, a neo-classical or "process" metaphysics) conceive of God in such a way as to rule out the real difference that history makes to God, finally, the fundamental christological issue at this point, it seems to me, is not how God can be conceived, whether digitally or iconically, as an experiencing, becoming, historical subject (as important as that issue may be in other contexts). That would be to take the symbols and concepts of christology literally rather than, as Segundo suggests, as a "meta-message" about how to understand the life and message of Jesus. Rather, the fundamental issue is how we are to understand Jesus' life and message as a "recapitulation" or "re-presentation" of what is always and everywhere the case.

In evaluating Segundo's entire argument above, I think we must conclude, first of all, that there are elements in Segundo's thought and method that are profound in their implications for interpreting the significance of Jesus. However we judge the kind of "Christian atheism" for which Segundo seems to have such an affinity, the possibility of living out a Christian faith without believing in the God of classical metaphysics is just as truly confirmed by those who, while rejecting the notion of God as classically formulated, are just as adamant that there yet remains a more satisfactory conceptuality by which the notion of God may be adequately expressed. So also, Segundo's two concepts--tradition and transcendent data--point out, in a very penetrating way, the need for some existential warrant for understanding Jesus' significance as decisive apart from either appealing to Jesus' own personal values and faith, on the one hand, or interpreting Jesus as an incarnation of deity so as to imbue his message with divine authority, on the other.

I am forced to conclude, however, that the existential warrant for which Segundo's own probing analysis cries out is not effectively delivered and is, in fact, negated by his own christological method. This is true, in the first place, because, throughout his christology and built into the very fabric of his method is an insistence that the very human qualities of Jesus--his character, his evolutionary flexibility, his values, his faith, etc. are the basis of his significance for human existence. This premise is the foundation stone not only for Segundo's quest for the historical Jesus but is also the methodological "alpha and omega" of Segundo's interpretation of Jesus within an evolutionary perspective. It is true that Segundo states explicitly that what can be said about Jesus' faith can never be the condition of recognizing the transcendent data that render his significance as decisive for human existence (II: 650), but Segundo is just as clear that it is precisely what can be said about Jesus' own personal faith that is of ultimate significance for us (II: 803). If this seems like an impossible contradiction, that is because Segundo's own methodological presuppositions, especially with regard to the role of metaphysics in christology, do not enable him to bridge the gap between the historical encounter with Jesus and the claims for the decisive significance of Jesus which that encounter yielded. Segundo is surely right that, on the one hand, the real achievement of Chalcedon was to provide a grammatical rather than a metaphysical solution to the problem of the divine and the human in Jesus and he is undoubtedly correct in his claim that, on the other hand, Chalcedon's dependence on classical metaphysics is bad grammar. The problem is that, apart from some recourse to metaphysical language, Segundo does not really have any adequate existential grammar with which to replace this bad grammar (not that metaphysical language in and of itself is sufficient to constitute a language that can communicate existential meaning). Segundo's "transcendent data," because they finally stop short of re-presenting the meaning of ultimate reality for us (and, therefore, fail to function metaphysically to that extent), can never really provide the existential warrant for taking Jesus as decisively significant for human existence. The best Segundo can do, it seems to me, is to suspend beside each other the historical encounter with Jesus, on the one hand, and the claims to the decisive significance of that encounter, on the other.

Faith and Ideologies

The implementation of faith in terms of ideologies is, for Segundo, that which gives his method of interpreting the significance of Jesus its purpose and urgency. Just as faith must meaningfully structure itself in terms of concrete, historical mediations, apart from which it is dead, so Jesus will be virtually uninteresting to contemporary human beings unless his significance can be interpreted in such a way as to connect up with and give meaning to this universal and necessary process of faith expressing itself in terms of ideologies.

As I have noted, "ideologies," for Segundo, are determined by considerations completely *other than* (though not necessarily *opposed to*) faith. In other words, it is reality itself (taken in the sense of the contingent "hard facts" of our daily living) with which we must come to grips in order to select the appropriate ideologies. Segundo wants to challenge Christians to avoid being "always right but never heard" and this means taking the risk of purchasing effectiveness even at the high price of violence or other negative values.

Because of this significant difference between how a faith is chosen, on the one hand, and how ideologies are chosen, on the other, there is an obvious and necessary independence between the two that, as articulated by Segundo, yields an almost constant dilemma between either paying a high price for the effectiveness of faith (often to the point of contradicting the values being expressed) or, simply, a dead faith. As Segundo puts the matter,

> the greatest of the problems associated with freedom is that, in order to realize values, we must "learn" methods which in themselves are independent of those same values. . . . whereas our scale of values depends entirely on ourselves, judgment about our "methods" depends on factors that escape us (I: 21).

Faith, in and of itself, of course, does not dispense ideologies, even though a tradition of faith can provide an important vehicle for us to "learn how to learn" to implement our faith in terms of ideologies. Thus, the obvious and crucial question arises: what is the relationship of faith to ideologies, if any? In other words, even if we agree with Segundo that faith is "not a universal, atemporal, body of content summing up revelation" (1975b: 140), what real difference does faith make to our concrete participation in the historical project of human liberation; indeed, how can we finally say with Segundo that "love is the *final* goal of this social morality" (1983b: II: 465)? James H. Olthuis, in his critique of Segundo, puts the question this way:

> But how do we decide what is orthopraxis? Segundo clearly holds that right action is action that humanizes and liberates. "There are no universal truths in the process of liberation; the only truth is liberation itself"

[Segundo, 1975b: 135]. But is the situation actually as clear-cut and simple as this statement suggests? Surely it is possible to distinguish what is liberating from what is reactionary, what is loving from what is sinful, what is humanizing from what is dehumanizing only when we are guided by some quintessential notion of what it means to be liberating, loving, and humanizing. It would seem axiomatic that we are able to decide what is and what is not truly human only when we know the universal truth content of "truly human attitudes" (Olthuis: 86).

Obviously, this problem of the relationship between faith and ideologies becomes especially acute in the case of those ideologies that utilize violence or that employ other evils in order to correct an evil. Segundo attempts to resolve the issue by taking two opposites, love and egotism, and by asking where violence is to be situated with respect to each. He answers,

> I think that any phenomenological analysis can demonstrate with ease that violence pertains to *both of these opposed tendencies*, a sort of no man's land between the two. Egotism is no more violent than love, just as love is no less violent than egotism (1975b: 179).

What Segundo wants to avoid, it is clear, is the idea that there is one set of means which are the exclusive property of love and another set of means which belong exclusively to egotism. Yet Segundo does admit that while instruments such as violence, money, sex, or power are essentially neutral, "they do possess an inner mechanism of their own" and that it is not only possible but easy for human beings to "become enslaved to those inner mechanisms" (180). Simply as human beings, we are all subject to a certain "economy of energy" which calls on us prudently to distribute the limited store of energy at our disposal if love is to be effective. Thus we necessarily put some people at arm's length (a form of violence) in order thereby to love others.

The importance of this understanding for christology, according to Segundo, is that, though Jesus is often presented as one who was above and beyond any "economy of energy," a careful exegesis of the gospels reveals, on the contrary, a man who was just as subject to the "law of the limitations of human capabilities" as the rest of us. As examples, Segundo cites Jesus' failure to exhibit concern for John the Baptist after his arrest, the restriction Jesus placed on his ministry, confining himself and his disciples only to Israel and elsewhere exhibiting blatant signs of Jewish nationalism (Cf. Mark 7:27), and the way Jesus broke off dialogue with the Pharisees, casting insults at them. As Segundo says,

> Only an idealistic oversimplification of Jesus' real attitudes can present him as a human being dedicated to love without limits, without resistance, without violence (187).

Here, I believe, the real contours of the problematic relationship between faith and ideologies become bold and conspicuous. Faith and ideologies finally have no inherent or immediate connection apart from the sheer necessity of their mutual co-existence, for Segundo. Even the "inner mechanisms" of certain means, while acknowledged by Segundo, are brushed aside quickly in his analysis with no further contemplation as to their importance for understanding the faith-ideologies relationship. Of course, just as problematic is Segundo's characteristic application of the relevance of the faith-ideologies dialectic for christology in terms of Jesus' own personal attitudes and actions which, both positively and negatively, provide an "example" not only of the important quality of expressing one's faith ideologically, but of the necessary "economy of energy" which we must all take into account in so doing. Thus, Jesus' significance is empty by way of providing any real meaning-content in terms of ultimate values that could guide our historical praxis (such as "love," or even "liberation," for example); rather, the significance of Jesus is purely formal as an example of one who did what all of us must do, namely, exercise our freedom within a particular economy of energy. When Segundo says that "*efficacious* love is the only demand imposed by Jesus for all time" (1983b: II: 474), he is pointing precisely to this very principle--Jesus does not teach us primarily about love, but about effectiveness (Segundo, 1982: II: 119; Cf. Ching: 25ff). Ironically, we find here in Segundo's understanding of the relevance of the relationship of faith and ideologies for interpreting the signif-icance of Jesus the very logic that Segundo bemoans in Peter's Pentecost sermon--namely, that the "what" of Jesus (his significance for our understanding of who we are called to be and the implications of that understanding for concrete, historical praxis) ends up being replaced by the "that" of Jesus (his having merely implemented his own understanding of who he was called to be in terms of a concrete, historical praxis).

It seems to me that, here again, the lack of a metaphysical dimension to Segundo's analysis of faith yields disastrous results, in this case, for understanding the relationship between faith and ideologies. Rather than trade in on his own evolutionary perspective at this point (the potential of which I will discuss more fully in Chapter 8), Segundo prefers to analyze the relationship between ends and means through the lens of a typically Marxist causality. Of course, Marxism does offer Segundo some very useful resources in clarifying how ideologies influence a faith--as Segundo points out, our own praxis can often "checkmate" a faith through its ideological critique "to the extent that faith is incoherent; it can unmask 'bad faith'" (I: 273). But as undoubtedly useful as Marxist analysis is in this respect, its notion of historical causality is, perhaps, one of its most dubious features, as is demonstrated almost daily by world events. Of course, Segundo does take a critical stance toward the deterministic materialism of Marxism (not necessarily of Marx himself who typically comes off having been misinterpreted by others), insisting that the term "mode of production," for example, "is much less materialist than is usually assumed by both its detractors and, even at times, its advocates" (I: 221). Segundo believes that Marx is usually misinterpreted as not taking into account the "human relations" that obtain in and through work and that, therefore, provide a good deal of the "spiritual" element in production or causality. As Segundo says,

> The concrete is complex. It is material and spiritual, even for historical materialism--at least for that of its founders (I: 222).

Segundo instead contends that the necessary and determining relationship between mode of production and ideology in Marxist materialism is not "immediate," thus cutting off creativity on the part of the human spirit, but rather operates "in the last instance, which is to say, it is open to a relative autonomy" (I: 222).

Segundo points out that the portion of the Marxist camp who are most impatient about bringing revolution are often the same ones who stress an extreme deterministic relationship between the economic structure and the ideological superstructures, depriving the latter of any autonomy. In Segundo's opinion, this "cleaves the *praxic* bridge between impatience and deeds" (I: 223).

> It is as if, in order to give greater efficacy to a hammer, one would attempt to strip away all autonomy from the arm that uses it, claiming that the arm is determined in the first instance by the very instrument it is using (I: 223).

Instead, Segundo recognizes that there must be "an *absolute* that can order all that relativity within a praxis" (I: 228). As Segundo says,

> we cannot bring structure to action without something unconditioned that subjects everything else to unity. That unconditioned need not be God or a metaphysical entity, but it has to be a value (I: 228).

Just how that value functions as an "absolute," however, apart from simply saying that it must, formally, is something Segundo does not seem to be able to account for and, again, it is, finally, this vacuum in the relationship between faith and ideologies that deteriorates from within the urgency and meaning of a faith-inspired praxis.

Conclusions with regard to Method

By way of conclusion I would like to consider a question that, in several ways, ties together the foregoing discussion and brings its implications to a head with regard to the praxic and metaphysical dimensions of the christological question. That question, raised by several interpreters of Segundo (Hewitt, 1990: 5; McCann, 1981a: 143; Cf. Bertram; Olthuis: 86ff), is whether or not Segundo's christological method, by ridding Jesus of any theological significance, finally turns theology into little more than a critical social theory and, consequently, whether or not Segundo is more of a social theorist than a theologian. Marsha Hewitt puts the question this way:

> It can be reasonably argued, that in Segundo's hands, liberation theology reveals itself as containing the seeds of its own negation *as theology*, which is inevitable when politics becomes an ontological category, and when history is posited as the sole locus of human freedom. What Segundo does in his later methodological work, whether he intends it or not, is to expose those seeds of theological self-negation within liberation theology and push them very near to their logical conclusion. I will stress once more that the "antichristology" of Segundo's treatment of the historical, human Jesus is an illustration of Segundo's methodology applied to the gospels. In my view, it logically follows that if religious faith as such has any place in the historical project for social change, it can only be as an inspirational force within each individual's own beliefs. If Christianity is to be a force for changing society, then it is in the form of a critical, public ideology that offers a credible alternative to the existing ideological constructs already present in Latin America. It is my view that these are the logical conclusions implicit in Segundo's later work. Segundo openly states that strictly formal, inactive faith in God or Christ is ultimately irrelevant in itself, for the project at hand: liberation from all forms of alienation (1990: 14).

Hewitt's assessment of Segundo is, in large part, an accurate representation of a definite problematic in his christological method, even if, as I believe, Segundo does not intend it this way.[54] As I see it, that problematic, as spelled out by Hewitt, has two interrelated components, and it is virtually impossible to treat them separately. The first problematic tendency in Segundo's method is that faith actually becomes irrelevant to liberating praxis and is relegated to a merely "inspirational" role in the private life of each believer. This tendency, I believe, would never arise were there a closer and more immediate relationship between

---

[54]Hewitt's book-length dialogue with Segundo is a useful analysis of the role of critical social theory in the latter's work, though what she takes as the inevitable results of Segundo's method are far removed, it seems to me, from Segundo's own intentions. It is rather clear from reading Hewitt's book, however, that she does not assess the results of his work as entirely negative and, in fact, if what she claims is true with regard to the consequences of Segundo's method, then it is apparent that Hewitt would probably be more in fundamental agreement with those consequences than would Segundo!

faith and ideologies. Though faith is always embodied in ideologies, makes no sense apart from ideologies, and relativizes every particular ideology insofar as it [faith] is "absolute" (1975b: 201), faith, at the same time, provides no normative truth content for directing daily life (192-193) or criteria by which one can determine appropriate ideologies. As Segundo says, "If someone were to ask me what I have gained from my encounter of faith, as a clear-cut, absolute truth that can validly give orientation to my concrete life, then my honest answer should be: nothing" (124). While I'm not sure what sense it makes, and therefore how true it is, to say that, for Segundo, "politics becomes an ontological category," it does seem to me that Hewitt has put her finger on the real difficulty with Segundo's conception of faith--namely, its irrelevance to human praxis apart from a metaphysical, if not explicitly theological, grounding.

The second problematic tendency which surfaces in Hewitt's question is closely related to the first, namely, that Segundo's theology, insofar as its fundamental goal is to change the world, must become social theory and ideology-critique, thereby rendering its own theological concepts *qua* theological as equally irrelevant to liberating praxis. As Hewitt asks,

> One is left wondering if, with Segundo, theology *qua* theology has come to its historical conclusion. What possible place *sui generis*, can theological concepts have in a world where the meaning of all human purpose and activity is understood in the light of the ultimate goal of human liberation in history? (1990: 14)

There can be little doubt, I think, as to Hewitt's correctness in identifying the fundamental motive of Segundo's christology and, indeed, of his entire theological endeavor as the historical, social, and political transformation ("liberation") of culture. This "pre-theological" commitment is essential for understanding Segundo's method and, as I have already shown, it is this prior commitment that makes of theology a "second step" and rules out the possibility of there being any "autonomous, impartial, academic theology" (Segundo, 1975b: 18). Theology, as a second step, best serves this commitment to liberation as an ideology-critique not only of society but of itself in order to expose how ideologies hide the true nature of oppression and injustice and to show how Christianity itself has functioned ideologically as just such a distorter of the truth in favor of the *status quo*. The question remains, however, whether theology, insofar as it is engaged in just that task, must thereby rid Jesus of any "theological" significance, interpreting him instead in terms of the latter's solely "human" significance (by which Segundo means, clearly, his political and ethical significance, i.e., the values that Jesus himself embodied and implemented ideologically in terms of what was appropriate to his own context).

In answering this question, we must first remind ourselves, I think, that even though Segundo often uses "ideology" in a neutral sense that reflects more directly the realm of praxis (i.e., the pre-theological realm), there is obviously a sense in which "ideology" refers to a theoretical activity, defined by Clodovis Boff as "error occurring under the appearance of truth" (42). Segundo does not always distinguish carefully between these two senses of the word "ideology" and this allows him to slip back and forth between a view of ideology as an interpretation of reality tied to particular interests and practices, on the one hand, and a view of ideology as sheer implementation of faith, on the other. Of course, what Segundo is driving at is that any and every implementation of faith is tied to particular interests and practices and, to that extent, Segundo is surely correct. Indeed, that is precisely what, as Segundo points out, the tools of modern social sciences and Marxist philosophy have taught us so well:

> What cognition now finds before it is a realist hypothesis: the world is the way it is because a real someone is interested in it being that way. And once philosophy (or cognition) is applied to the praxis of changing that objective world, dialectic shows us how that *practical* process is set in motion (1982: I: 234).

But because Segundo allows himself to slip back and forth between these two meanings of the word "ideology," he also ends up with no real method or criteria for judging the value or truth of ideology, since ideology is "neutral" and serves as no more than a means to an end. In fact, the only real "errors" an ideology can commit are (a) ineffectiveness and (b) absolutizing itself when it is, in actuality, only relative. In this way, though Segundo can show how every faith is expressed ideologically (in terms of being tied to particular interests and practices), he can also avoid passing judgment on any ideology apart from what I consider to be his one and only moral criterion --"the end justifies the means" (1975b: 194).

Here, however, the insight of Clodovis Boff is helpful in understanding one of the problems with Segundo's approach:

> to affirm without qualification that the notion of "ideology" refers to any idea whose function is the justification of a practice of an interest simply gives us no information. Surely every idea will have some relationship to determinate interests or practices. To my mind, the real question is: *what* interests? *Cui prodest*? Is the interest legitimate or not? Now we are dealing with the relationship between knowledge and (ethico-political) function. Here the designation "ideological" connotes the "unjustifiable"-- not the simply unjustifiable, however, but the *unjustifiable in the guise of the justifiable*. We are dealing with the immoral in the guise of the moral (42).

But how can one determine what is or is not justifiable apart from some moral criterion or criteria, or, perhaps, some norm that can adjudicate in the matter?

That norm need not be an external heteronomous authority standing outside and above our existence, but it must be comprehensive and inclusive of our existence. In the end, it seems to me, Segundo's analysis of faith and ideologies lacks just the theoretical foundation that the practical urgency of cultural transformation requires.

To return to Hewitt's question, then, I would argue that if Segundo dissolves theology into social theory or ideology-critique, as she and others claim, it is not because for him the focus of theology is no longer God or even God's relationship to humanity and human history. Though I would want to argue that the concept of God is of considerably more value than Segundo allows for expressing our notion of what is ultimately real, the "historical" direction in which Segundo points theology is not, it seems to me, the real difficulty with his method and is, in fact, the only legitimate direction which I take it that an adequate theology can travel today. Thus, to suggest, as Hewitt does, that Segundo's positing of history "as the sole locus of human freedom" pushes theology to the brink of its own negation as theology or that theological concepts no longer have a place "in a world where the meaning of all human purpose and activity is understood in the light of the ultimate goal of human liberation in history," seems to me to misread the fundamental problem with Segundo's method. As I see it, the more basic problem is not that affirming a thoroughly historical context for understanding the meaning and value of human praxis yields fundamentally anti-theological results, but rather, especially with regard to christological method, that the necessarily historical context in which we find ourselves can hardly provide, in and of itself, any indication of why our praxis is to be taken as authentic and of more than merely passing or trivial significance apart from clarifying the relation of that praxis to the understanding of ourselves that is warranted by what we believe to be ultimately real.

If Segundo cannot conceive of any essential role for this latter, necessarily metaphysical, dimension of relating faith to ideologies, but rather, as Hewitt says, "must negate theology to whatever extent that it posits an absolute, unchanging and universal truth in order to relativize theology within historical contextuality" (1990: 50), then perhaps we are indeed forced to agree with Hewitt's conclusion that, for Segundo, "theology is subsumed by critical social theory" (50).

CHAPTER 7

FAITH AND HISTORY

Historical Understanding

I have tried to show that, for Segundo, the significance of Jesus is a thoroughly historical and humanistic significance, rooted in a view of human existence that completely rejects any distinction between a religious and a secular sphere of reality. Segundo's approach is "anti-christological" in that it first detects a split between history and christology and then goes on to opt for the former rather than the latter as the starting point for interpreting the message of Jesus. By rejecting christology in favor of history, Segundo is not thereby saying that he would rather start with the "historical Jesus" than with the "Christ of faith," if that is understood to mean that he would rather avoid the interests and needs of those doing the interpretation in favor of a more historical and, therefore, objective and scientific approach. This would be a grave misunderstanding of the way Segundo conceives of the word "historical." For Segundo, the historical is not opposed to the subjective or ideological but rather to the metaphysical, absolute, and universal. Christology is ahistorical in that, by its very definition, it attempts to grasp "something of universal validity" about the individual named Jesus of Nazareth with the result that the transcendent in our experience takes on a kind of reality of its own, independent of history, and serves as the divine starting point for the interpretation of the significance of Jesus. The problem, therefore, is that christology, by its very nature, wants to talk about a *logia* about a person, but, in Segundo's mind, this is plainly contradictory. Rather, as Segundo says,

> God can only be revealed in connection with values that are humanly significant, and those values have to be manifested historically on one or more of the planes where the human being places the meaning of its life and the possibility of happiness. There is not, then, strictly speaking, a revelation of God that does not take its course through preferences and concrete realizations on the plane of interpersonal relations, education, societal life, economics, and politics (1982: II: 124).

For Segundo, the proper approach to interpreting the significance of Jesus is, on the contrary, one that begins with the historical encounter of Jesus of Nazareth rather than with God or ultimate reality. This means that we must begin with the ideologies through which Jesus conveyed his own values and meaning-world and by virtue of which he was able to relate in a credible way to the particular interests and needs of his own historical epoch. Then, and only then, can we reinterpret Jesus' message to our own or to subsequent historical situations through new and appropriate ideologies that themselves make credible contact with the needs and interests of our day.

A tremendous problem surfaces at this point, however, with regard to Segundo's distinction between a "historical" approach to the significance of Jesus and a "christological" approach to that significance. Segundo rejects "christology" because it entails the impossible contradiction -- "*logia* about a person," but this view, it seems to me, is inconsistent with the implications of Segundo's own understanding of the kind of question that christology answers, namely, not just who Jesus is in himself, historically, but who Jesus is in his significance for "our understanding and the fulfillment of the human being" (II: 26). Segundo, because he believes that christology, as a science, requires a kind of "objectification or reification" which would falsify the encounter with the person of Jesus, opts instead for what he believes is the only other choice, namely, a "historical portrait" of Jesus that bases itself on a reconstruction of the faith of Jesus and, especially, the ideologies that served as the vehicle for that faith. Thus, imitating Segundo's strict use of word etymologies, we might say that Segundo rejects christo*logy* in favor of christo*graphy*.

What Segundo does not always appear willing to remember when he turns to the historical dimension of the christological question is his own claim that the only way of talking about Jesus so as to "open a path for us to consider him as a witness to a more humane and liberated human life" (II: 29) or, really, to talk about any historical figures in order to understand not simply who they were in themselves, but also their meaning for us here and now, is to speak of them existentially (II: 55ff). Thus, one must make a distinction between a *logia* about the historical person as he or she actually was (which certainly cannot rise above mere description) and a *logia* about the existential significance of that person.

The thought of Rudolf Bultmann is especially helpful at this point in clarifying just how we come to know historical phenomena. Bultmann is sympathetic to the kind of misgivings expressed by Segundo about a scientific methodology when it comes to trying to understand the significance of a historical phenomenon. Bultmann writes,

> Because science seeks to know phenomena, it makes them the objects of thinking, it "objectifies" them. Scientific thinking thereby disengages itself from immediate encounter with the phenomena and assumes a certain distance over against them - as subjects to objects (1984: 131).

Bultmann questions, however, whether the way of "objectifying thinking" really is the way that leads to knowledge of the essence of phenomena, especially historical phenomena. Instead, there is a way of thinking and talking that is not objectifying, says Bultmann, "insofar as there is a perceiving that does not take place in the distance of disinterestedness, in the passivity of mere receptiveness, but in which the interested activity of the person, of existence, is controlling" (139).

This way of approaching historical phenomena relies upon an existential relation to history which is the basic presupposition for understanding it. According to Bultmann,

> This does not mean that understanding history is "subjective" in the sense that it depends on the personal preference of the historian and thereby loses all objective significance. On the contrary, it means that history can be understood precisely in its objective content only by a subject who is existentially concerned and alive. It means that the scheme of subject and object that has validity for natural science is not valid for historical under-standing (150).

Furthermore, this kind of historical understanding does not have to "avoid individual or singular facts," as Segundo fears a "christology" must, but, rather, makes of facts of the past real historical phenomena in that they now are meaningful for a historical subject who understands them. As Bultmann cautions, however, this does not mean that historical phenomena are "ambiguous" but only that they are "complex and many-sided." The historical subject does not attach meaning to them by arbitrary preference, but rather "they acquire a meaning for anyone who is bound together with them in historical life" (84).

Segundo's own method is, in many respects, not averse to this kind of existential-historical approach and the influence of Bultmann is apparent throughout his work. For example, Segundo would definitely not want to exclude the interests of the one who encounters Jesus in understanding who Jesus is as a historical phenomenon. To the contrary, Segundo explicitly states that we cannot uncover the significance of an interesting historical person or event apart from some interpretive scheme that originates within our own present reality and is retrojected back into the past (1982: II: 798). However, what Bultmann under-stands as the "preunderstanding" with which any historical subject approaches a historical phenomenon -- namely, "a way of asking questions (that) grows out of an interest that is grounded in the life of the questioner" (1984: 73) -- too often becomes, in the hands of Segundo, a preference or bias that, according to him, comes with the territory. Segundo remarks that approaching the message of Jesus with self-interested prejudices is "inevitable" and that "it is better that the word of God resound to prejudiced ears and, in accordance with the biblical imagery, possibly be suffocated . . . than that efforts be made to sterilize it beforehand" (1982: II: 56-57; Cf. 1975b: 11ff).

Ironically, Segundo's method at this point unintentionally pushes faith into a privatized and interior realm that is far removed, it seems to me, from the public, political, historical world that Segundo seeks to impact. This it does by washing away or bypassing any element of the interpretation of Jesus' significance either by Jesus or his original followers that reflects their religious needs or a wider, and perhaps even metaphysical, outlook in favor of reconstructing the most reliable historical "data" about the "prepaschal," real human being, Jesus of Nazareth. As Segundo says,

> The historical portrait of Jesus--and even of future christologies--must be based on those facts or events which are more certain and then proceed from that nucleus. And that which logically seems more certain . . . is what was attributed to Jesus *without reference* to his passion, death, and resurrection (II: 72).

Segundo here contradicts his otherwise solidly existential approach to historical understanding in favor of a kind of empirical approach to the synoptic gospels, which, as he admits, are hardly unbiased sources. But even though, as Segundo says, "we have no document that is neutral or 'historical,' in the sense which we give that term today," he yet goes on to claim that "it is obvious that the documents which come closest to such characteristics are the three gospels called *synoptics*: Mark, Matthew, and Luke" (II: 69). I will have more to say on the crucial issue as to why Segundo is willing to go this route, given the enormous difficulties with the sources at our disposal for such a purpose and given Segundo's otherwise intense desire to move away from who Jesus was in himself to who Jesus is "for us," but at this point I would at least suggest that it has primarily to do with his more fundamental suspicion of any religious or metaphysical framework creeping in by which we would interpret the significance of Jesus and thus nullify the truly historical and political significance of Jesus for basic, human, anthropological faith. But, then, this approach simply begs rather than answers the questions as to *why* a historical approach should confine itself to the political ideologies rather than also to the religious or metaphysical ideologies through which Jesus' significance was expressed and, instead, reveals the strong anti-religious influence of Marx on his thought even where he attempts to break with Marx--namely, in recognizing that religion may itself become a powerful and potentially liberating ideology. Here again, however, we see that the historical, for Segundo, is fundamentally opposed to the metaphysical and so the only legitimate historical approach to Jesus via his own ideologies and those of his interpreters is one that seeks to shed any and all religious or metaphysical interpretation of the significance of Jesus.

I must admit, of course, that Segundo's rejection of a "christological" approach to interpreting the significance of Jesus is not entirely unjustified, and his own christological concerns at this point are consistent with a widespread dissatisfaction in contemporary christology, generally, with a "christology from above." If we say, however, that, on the one hand, historical knowledge has an objective pole in that it requires that we have some general understanding not only of what it means to exist as a human being but of the broader reality that grounds and gives meaning to the life of the historical subject, then we must conclude that Segundo's historical objectivity falls well short of such an understanding and becomes, rather, a highly questionable attempt merely to describe "what happened." On the other hand, if we say that historical knowledge also has a subjective pole in that one is moved to ask about historical phenomena not from individual preference but out of history itself, that is, the historical life of the individual, then, too, I think we must admit that, Segundo cannot finally show why Jesus would be interesting to anyone apart from either proximity or private bias, thus reducing historical subjectivity to an uncritical prejudice.

The Historical Jesus

The result of Segundo's preoccupation with the historical as opposed to the christological, or even theological, is his application of the faith-ideologies dialectic to a study of the historical Jesus and the political meaning of Jesus' message. As I have already indicated, this means that the pre-paschal, "historical" Jesus is carefully distinguished, both theologically and exegetically, from the postpaschal, resurrected Christ of christology which is itself a particular ideology-complex that has evolved over the centuries. Segundo wishes to sift out the explicitly religious significance of Jesus that has accumulated over the years in order to move us toward understanding Jesus as a witness to a particular structure of meaning and values that places a primary importance on human liberation in a material and historical sense. Segundo believes that his analysis of the relationship between faith and ideologies makes possible and, indeed, necessitates a christological method that places the limited, historical existence of Jesus and our own concrete projects and interests in a "hermeneutic circle." Because history continually poses new challenges to any faith, we *must*, as Segundo says, "go back and explore more deeply the meaning already discovered, so that it may become significant and effective in the new context" (II: 611). Because no faith is ever inseparable from its ideological expression in terms of new and concrete forms, we *can* travel back "through" the projects and interests of Jesus' interpreters to that original faith of Jesus himself. Thus, as I noted in my examination of Segundo's quest for the "historical Jesus," this quest is understood by Segundo to be historically possible (though Segundo lacks consistency here) and theologically necessary. Putting aside for the moment the historical possibility of this task, one must certainly inquire as to the kind of historical, theological, and anthropological presuppositions that undergird Segundo's thought and lead him to believe that a reconstruction of the historical Jesus is important or necessary.

There are two problems in this regard to which I would like to draw attention. The first problem goes back to the very task of christology which, as I attempted to show, is, for Segundo, the task of critically interpreting the significance of Jesus for us. Segundo shows how that significance is appropriated by human faith and incorporated into the way a human being values and, inevitably, how a human being implements those values in life in terms of ideologies. In the last chapter, I suggested that Segundo's analysis of faith, however, was deficient with respect to any kind of metaphysical aspect that would ground our choice of a particular scale of values and that would allow us to evaluate a meaning-world as either authentic or inauthentic. Instead, that choice became the rather arbitrary one of relying on "referential witnesses" who offer to us a particular meaning-world as both satisfying and fulfilling. Even to the degree that Jesus becomes a "transcendent datum" for our faith, that is because he lives out his life with an exceptional "evolutionary flexibility" that assigns him a place in universal evolutionary history.

Jesus, then, is significant for Segundo primarily as a referential witness, albeit an incredibly important one, in whom we trust and whose particular meaning-world we adopt as our own rather than as one who, quite apart from his own conscious adoption and implementation of faith, was so experienced by people that they found themselves confronted with and, in turn, bore witness to, what they took to be the most decisive re-presentation of what is, always has been, and always will be the case with every human existence, namely, the authentic possibility of faith. For Segundo, Jesus is a historical example of liberating faith, "a witness to a more humane and liberated human life" (II: 29). As Segundo affirms, if every human being structures a world of meaning *as if* they knew ahead of time what would be the most satisfying way of living, and if it is "referential witnesses" who present us with the most fulfilling ways to live that existence and so structure our lives, then

> Jesus of Nazareth is undoubtedly one of those witnesses, framed in one tradition that precedes him and enables us to understand him, and in another that follows him and enables us to translate and update him for our circumstances. Indeed he is one of the most important witnesses that humanity can point to over the past two thousand years (II: 40).

My question at this point, however, is whether the christologies of the New Testament would be satisfied with such a minimal claim for the significance of Jesus. As Schubert Ogden says with regard to the New Testament writers:

> in their understanding, Jesus is not merely one authority among others, even the primary such authority; rather, he is the primal *source* of all authority made fully explicit, and hence not *an* authority at all in the same literal sense of the word (1982: 79).

Segundo, however, though he recognizes that it is not Jesus in himself that christology wants to talk about, but Jesus insofar as he is significant for us, insists on identifying the "historical Jesus," much like the revisionary christologies to which I drew attention in Chapter 1, as the subject of the christological assertion and thus turning Jesus into one more historical witness to a liberating and humane life. The method of christology, consequently, becomes the route of uncovering just how Jesus actually was this witness and in what that witness consists (what Jesus actually said or what Jesus actually did). This, of course, leads us back to the third problematic in the revisionary consensus, summarized by Ogden as follows:

> According to the position typically taken by revisionary christologies, Jesus can be truthfully said to be Christ, or any of the other things that the christology of witness has appropriately asserted or implied him to be, if, but only if, he himself, as a human person, perfectly actualized the possibility of authentic self-understanding (65).

One can readily see how close is the relationship between this third point and the second point (identifying the subject of the christological assertion as the historical Jesus) in what Ogden sees as a consensus in revisionary christology. Really, both points rise or fall together; one can hardly justify the claim that Jesus is the Christ because he actualized this or that faith if one cannot even justify the possibility and necessity of identifying the subject of the christological assertion as the historical Jesus. At any rate, what ultimately becomes of Jesus in the hands of Segundo's "anti-christology" is that, in order to avoid interpreting the significance of Jesus by ascribing to him some special metaphysical status, he is instead treated as what Bultmann calls a "hero." Bultmann's warning is instructive and apropos at this point.

> This view of Jesus in terms of his character as a hero is utterly opposed to his own understanding of human existence; for man as a character has his center in himself, and the hero stands on his own feet, this being his greatness as a man, which is here regarded from an esthetic point of view. Jesus, by contrast, sees man in his relation to God, as standing under God's claim (1982: 3).

Apart from the more theological reasons for challenging Segundo's project of reconstructing the "historical Jesus," we must also, I think, call into serious question the very possibility, historically, of this same project given the kinds of sources from which one would have to reconstruct that Jesus. It is frankly difficult to know what to make of Segundo's method at this point. It is clear that Segundo recognizes the nature of the documents that are available to us for this task and admits that it is useless to attempt to arrive at a Jesus that is interpreted by no one. What is not clear, however, is whether Segundo is prepared to accept the full implications of this fact in the development of his own method. Despite what Segundo *says* about the sources with which christology must work, what Segundo actually *does* with those sources is to approach them on the basis of an operational distinction between Jesus as he actually was and Jesus as he is represented as being by his original witnesses. Given this contradiction, then, between what Segundo admits about the nature of the sources of christology and the method which he actually pursues, one can only characterize his attitude toward the kind of biblical scholarship which attests to the virtual impossibility of reconstructing a historically accurate picture of Jesus as mere "lipservice." Segundo tries to deflect some of the responsibility for taking into account the nature of the sources by offering the disclaimer, "My effort here is not one of biblical exegesis . . . I shall base my comments on the historical and exegetical data that seem more certain to me without burdening the reader with disquisitions and proofs that are alien to the aim of this book" (1982: II: 104). But ultimately, his method is so dependent on the exegetical work which he takes such pains to deliver that it is difficult to see how the data which he claims to be "more certain" can play the central role they do play without a clearer and more consistent assessment of the criteria by which they are considered to be certain.

Because of this failure to consider with full seriousness the implications of the nature of the christological sources at our disposal, the bold lines of Segundo's christological task begin to blur and fade as he moves through the process of uncovering the historical Jesus. Though his "anti-christological" method is billed as a hermeneutical approach, the purpose of which is to employ several interpretive "keys" to unlock the significance of Jesus for various circumstances and contexts, Segundo quickly finds himself attempting to prove the empirical-historical truthfulness of what he designates as "Jesus' *own* key," and, in so doing, produces a new mythology of Jesus that presents itself as literal truth -- a mythology not now in a religious or supernatural sense, but in a political and ideological sense. I am inclined to agree with the judgement of Marsha A. Hewitt, in her review of Segundo's *The Historical Jesus of the Synoptics,*

> Now it is one thing to engage in a hermeneutical analysis of the gospels to demonstrate their contemporary relevance in a particular context. But Segundo goes much further, claiming that his political hermeneutical reading of the gospels corresponds to the literal facts, which betrays the presence of a positivist, empirical thrust in Segundo's thinking, which tends to reduce history to historiography (1989: 50).

Christological Hermeneutics

Segundo is undoubtedly correct in his assessment that theology has classically worked in a one-way rather than a circular movement, starting from a deposit of divine truths and then applying those truths to our actual circumstances. Segundo's clarification of the role of the human subject in the process of interpretation is especially useful in helping us all to see how our own interests and agendas influence how we understand the message of scripture. Segundo, for example, shows how the distinction which Marx draws between "science" and "ideology," where the former is taken as completely objective and value-free, is misleading (Segundo, 1982: I: 124ff).

But as important as is the role of the human subject and his or her interests and practices in the hermeneutical process, Segundo's own view of the scripture which is to be interpreted is somewhat contradictory and difficult to nail down. On the one hand, we must recall the distinction he makes between "proto-learning" and "deutero-learning." There, Segundo emphasizes that the Bible is not a stockpile of finished answers to all of life's questions and that people who resort to the Bible as a finished "deposit" for all their questions of value and meaning are like children who retreat to the infantile security of their parents. As Segundo says,

> They avoid the healthy risk of interpreting Jesus anew in the face of equally new problems. In the face of those new problems the words of Jesus, if taken literally, betray his Spirit. Regarding them as something magically endowed with truth, people end up offering inhuman solutions in Jesus' name (II: 16).

Segundo advocates, instead, a view of the Bible as a record of the process of learning to learn and, thus, Segundo can say that "it is necessary for us to keep going back and writing gospels" (II: 16). John and Paul, for example, comprise the vast majority of scriptural resources on which Segundo reflects. These writings, as Segundo says, provide "the first phenomenology of Christian existence" (1964a: 8)[55] and are something of a model for how real human beings had to deal with their own historical situation in expressing Christian faith.

On the other hand, however, for Segundo, scripture is still normative and the primary source to which the theologian returns in order to interpret human experience. But, more often than not, that normativity takes on a rather uncritical character and becomes the place to which we turn in order to respond to specific situations with the "mentality" of Jesus and one could make the argument that in actual method, as distinct from methodology, Segundo's own appeal to scripture,

---

[55]Segundo borrows this phrase from Rudolf Bultmann.

especially in his quest for "the historical Jesus of the synoptics," tends to approach scripture as a "deposit." The problem here, as Elisabeth Schüssler-Fiorenza points out, is that, while Segundo's hermeneutic circle represents a helpful leap beyond methods which attempt an objective, unbiased approach to scriptural texts, it yet fails really to extend its suspicion to scripture itself. As Schüssler-Fiorenza says,

> [Segundo] does not take into account the fact that not only the content of Scripture, but also this second-level learning process can be distorted
> . . . . Segundo's model does not allow for a critical theological evaluation of biblical ideologies as "false consciousness" (101).

This criticism is not without basis, in my opinion. Segundo, as I have pointed out, claims that what makes Jesus interesting to us is the gap between interpretation and interpreter, which allows us "to derive and to infer" from what Jesus decided with regard to other matters at other times how he might respond to our projects today. But this begs the question of the relationship of Jesus' very interpreters, whoever they were, to Jesus himself. They also had to derive and infer from Jesus' message and responses his views on matters about which they wrote.

In Schüssler-Fiorenza's mind, liberation theologians in general accept the neo-orthodox hermeneutic that all scriptural traditions are meaningful and true and therefore claim our obedience. Liberation theology in general, then, fails to judge whether a text is appropriate and helpful to the struggle of the oppressed for liberation and too often comes off close to "proof-texting." As Schüssler-Fiorenza says, what is needed is "to bring a critical evaluation to bear upon the biblical texts and upon the process of interpretation within Scripture and tradition" and to "reflect on the fact that the process of interpretation of Scripture is not necessarily liberative" (101-102).

Just this difficulty with Segundo's hermeneutic method makes the issue of whether, or to what extent, Jesus was "political" all the more problematic in Segundo's christology. Segundo, as I have noted, puts into practice the christological method that he advocates by undertaking three examples of the kinds of successive historical readings which he claims are required by an adequate christological hermeneutic circle. Because of Segundo's rather uncritical approach to scripture, as explained above, the first reading, that of the synoptic gospels, is placed on a different level from the other two insofar as they are considered "derivative" and "inferential," basing their interpretations of the significance of Jesus on the prior significance of Jesus for his apostolic witnesses. Because Matthew, Mark, and Luke are the closest thing we have to "historical" documents (in the more objective, scientific sense of the word) they are the most trustworthy or "certain" for Segundo's development of an historical portrait of Jesus. Even within the synoptics, however, Segundo utilizes criteria to distinguish what is even "more certain" still. So, for example, he relies, first, upon the distinction between what is "postpaschal" and what is "prepaschal" in the synoptic narratives so that "what seems more certain, on the basis of the evangelical testimony itself, is what was attributed to Jesus *without reference* to his passion, death, and resurrection" (1982: II: 72). The second criterion rests on the recognition that the writers of the gospels often interpreted their account of Jesus' significance in terms of an ecclesiastical context and with respect to ecclesiastical problems. Thus, we must distinguish between what is "pre-ecclesial" and "post-ecclesial" in the gospel records. The third criterion for determining the historical reliability of the gospel narratives, according to Segundo, is the "literary criterion," or group of criteria with regard to form, transmission, genre, and language.

So far as it goes, I do not find Segundo's method of searching the synoptic gospels for the earliest and most original testimony about Jesus to be that divergent from some of the better New Testament scholarship now available. Indeed, as Willi Marxsen suggests, it is possible, by means of literary criticism to determine "with considerable certainty" those layers of tradition about Jesus which show no influence of the events of the crucifixion or Easter (1976: 146). Marxsen calls this material the "Jesus kerygma" as opposed to the "Christ kerygma" but insists that we must yet remember that

> the purpose of the Jesus kerygma is not to present a historically accurate account of Jesus' words and deeds and to hand them on with historical fidelity. It is rather, to proclaim anew Jesus' words and deeds (precisely as *his* words and deeds) to each subsequent generation (146).

The real difference between Segundo and Marxsen at this point, however, is that, while Segundo insists that this core of pre-paschal data portrays the "historical Jesus," Marxsen claims that, even here, "Jesus is never to be reached except together with the people who told about him" and that "this is no longer the 'historical Jesus'" (1989: 47). The possibility that the difference between Marxsen's approach and Segundo's approach is merely semantic is a real one, in my opinion. As adamant as Segundo is in trying to reconstruct "the historical Jesus," he is just as adamant that a Jesus apart from interpretation does not exist. But though *some* of the difference may be semantic, certainly not *all* of it is. A Jesus apart from his interpreters may not exist, but that does not preclude Segundo, oddly enough, from reconstructing the "historical Jesus" precisely *through* his interpreters by de-ideologizing their accounts of him. But, whereas Bultmann's method of demythologizing, as Schubert Ogden points out, demands the equally important process of existentialist interpretation, I am not at all certain that Segundo's method of de-ideologizing results in a parallel process of "political interpretation" (Cf. Ogden, 1982: 94ff). To be sure, the Jesus now reached by

Segundo through the ideologies of his original followers is "political."[56] But that kind of empirical-historical judgment is far different (and more dubious), it seems to me, than the interpretation of Jesus' political significance for us, which is not only more appropriate to the historical materials at our disposal but more urgent for our own praxis.

Conclusions with regard to Method

Segundo's analysis of faith and ideologies provides, to a certain degree, a framework within which a revisionary christology can avoid the kind of problems to which both it as well as traditional christologies have been prone. There is, after all, a sense in which the claims of christology about who Jesus is are not beyond the control of empirical-historical inquiry and Segundo's insistence that we begin with "the historical encounter with Jesus" rather than with assertions as to his metaphysical status or divine "nature" seems, on the whole, the only legitimate approach. Willi Marxsen makes a persuasive case, for example, that no responsible christology can proceed along the traditional lines of a christology "from above." As Marxsen says, traditional christology tends to reverse the way the witness to Christ itself comes to be.

> What others have formulated as a *consequence* of their faith may not be made into the *basis* of faith for those who come later. People entrusted themselves to the acting Jesus of Nazareth (a human being!). In connection with the experience of thus entrusting themselves (that is, with faith), they were able to qualify his activity and, on the basis of the activity thus qualified, also to qualify him as the one who enacted it. But since what they experienced in faith was so overwhelming, they were not able (as a consequence of their faith) to qualify highly enough the one who had aroused this faith short of claiming, finally, that "in him God has encountered us." Thus "Jesus (subject) is God (predicate)," is a christologically possible assertion.
>
> But if we take assertions that arose as a consequence of faith and reverse them, christology from below becomes christology from above. And with this, we go beyond the limit to the possibility of christological assertions, because we treat a statement that is only ever possible as a derivative one, as if it were primary (1989: 52).

---

[56]For Segundo, the most historically reliable piece of data that we possess about Jesus, confirmed even by non-Christian historical witnesses, is that "Jesus of Nazareth died, after having been condemned by the Roman authorities, as a *political agitator* (1982: II: 106).

Even the resurrection of Jesus is treated by both Marxsen and Segundo alike as a test-case of how christological assertions are made. Thus, if we look carefully at how the assertion that God raised Jesus from the dead originated, there is no way of getting around its basis in some experience or, in other words, "from below." As Marxsen says, "talk about the resurrection of Jesus is always a derivative assertion" and, further, "it is a 'mortal sin' of theological work to take assertions that have arisen in one direction and to argue with them in the opposite direction (54).

In many ways, what Segundo says about method is not fundamentally opposed to the way Marxsen "asks historically about Jesus" rather than "asks for the historical Jesus" (47). Segundo insists that as long as we avoid the ideological-historical process of how Jesus came to be significant, remaining content with who Jesus *was in himself*, we will fail to take up with the required creativity and flexibility the task of constructing our own world and making important decisions which require new and appropriate solutions. Instead we will always be looking over our shoulder at some fixed "deposit" of answers to see "what Jesus did." But here we find a clear example of the contradiction between what Segundo says about method and the method which Segundo actually employs. Methodologically, Segundo makes a distinction between the apostolic witness and the Jesus to whom the apostles bear witness, but in terms of actual method, Segundo makes no functional distinction between a "referential witness" and the source of that witness and treats Jesus himself as one of the former. So also, methodologically, Segundo understand his historical inquiry not as a reconstruction of Jesus as he actually was (that quantity being historically impossible to uncover given the kinds of documents with which we must work), but as a reconstruction of the earliest Christian witness. In practice, however, Segundo undertakes a painstaking excavation of the synoptic gospels in order to uncover the world of meaning and values to which Jesus himself bore witness, i.e., the faith of Jesus himself. Thus, even though the "historical Jesus" about which Segundo *talks* is essentially the Jesus which his original followers understood him to be insofar as he was existentially meaningful for their lives, the "historical Jesus" which Segundo *actually reconstructs* is hardly different from the kind of portraits which have now become commonplace in the method of many theologians who still believe that presenting Jesus "as he was" is both possible and necessary for christology.

CHAPTER 8

EVOLUTION AND "EFFECTIVE FAITH"

In the previous two chapters, I have tried to express my agreement with Segundo in his insistence that the question of the significance of Jesus can hardly be asked or answered independently of the question of who we are and of the historical praxis by which we both create ourselves and transform our reality. I have nonetheless insisted that the way Segundo both asks and answers the question of the significance of Jesus is yet far removed from the New Testament's claim that the significance of Jesus for us is, in some sense, an ultimate significance. Even if that ultimate significance cannot be expressed apart from an inquiry into the historically-relative conditioning factors that go into who we are, it would certainly seem to be fundamental to such inquiry, and so I have argued that one of the primary weaknesses in Segundo's attempt to offer a method for interpreting the significance of Jesus for today is that it consistently fails to take into account the logically prior question of the ultimate reality that gives meaning to our existence and consequently grounds our praxis as worthwhile and of more than passing significance. I have tried to show that at virtually every turn in Segundo's christology, the role of metaphysics is extremely problematic and that his own characteristic manner of rejecting all metaphysics on the basis of a preponderance of "bad" metaphysics with which especially christology is plagued, though somewhat understandable, is finally unjustified.

It is my belief that, though Segundo is determined in his typically strict adherence to the demands of reason and logic in theological argument, a more explicit and careful development of conceptual categories, which are none other than properly metaphysical, is required to give his argument the practical force and theoretical clarity he desires. I would add that this criticism is no minor cosmetic adjustment on the face of Segundo's method but strikes to the heart of his fundamental effort to interpret a "Jesus for atheists." Segundo's belief that the question of God is not logically prior to the question of the significance of Jesus and that anyone should be able to comprehend that significance quite apart from any prerequisite theistic system is integral to his entire endeavor and constitutive of his method as a whole.

In reading Segundo, nonetheless, one cannot help but be impressed with the centrality of his reliance on an evolutionary perspective, gained in large part from Teilhard de Chardin, in which virtually every aspect of creation, history, and existence is interpreted. As Segundo says,

this evolutionary outlook is not the "content" of the Christian message . .
. . this outlook is *the key* to Christianity. In other words, we might say
that from that angle one ought to view the whole Christian message--and
particularly the relationship between sin and redemption.

From within this key, all the elements fall into place. From the
beginning, the entire universe is thrusted toward a liberation grounded on
truth in praxis. From the very beginning the universe shows proclivity towards easy and conservative solutions (1983b: II: 407).

But if this evolutionary outlook provides the hermeneutical key by which we can
best understand the Christian message insofar as it is precisely the process and
mechanisms of evolution that constitute the certain, universal, and unfailing
features of the reality in which we find ourselves, then perhaps this evolutionary
worldview does provide for Segundo just the kind of metaphysical framework,
even if implicitly, required for conceptualizing the "existential warrant" which
Segundo himself recognizes that any appeal to the decisive or absolute significance of Jesus requires. The purpose of this chapter is primarily to explore just
this possibility. Before moving, however, to a specific appraisal of the potential
of Segundo's evolutionary perspective for christology, I would first like to offer
a summary appraisal of Segundo's understanding of metaphysics with regard,
specifically, to judgments of value. In the final analysis, I think that it is the
alleged neutrality of metaphysics toward judgments of value that ultimately causes
Segundo and other liberation theologians to steer away from employing metaphysics in their theologies in more than a merely implicit fashion.

Metaphysics and Value

I have already pointed out that, for Segundo, metaphysics, like religion, is
to be placed under the umbrella of ideology rather than under the umbrella of
faith. Metaphysics, as Segundo rightly points out, can be and has been used
ideologically to support virtually any and every class of values. But perhaps the
most serious problem with metaphysics, to Segundo's mind, is that it attempts "to
achieve a conceptual unity where an irreducible plurality exists" and "this unity
of content does not at all dovetail with concrete experience" (1982: I: 91).

But even if we admit that faith is not simply metaphysics and that
Segundo's reservations with regard to metaphysics are in some sense justifiable,
if not justified, I contend that the real problem with metaphysics, for Segundo, is
to be found in his own understanding of metaphysics. Segundo, as I have
attempted to show, consistently identifies the metaphysical with the non-experien-
tial. But even though this distortion does pass and has passed for metaphysics,
it by no means is the only or the best understanding of metaphysics.

Metaphysics, as David Griffin says, "does not deal with alleged entities
that lie beyond all possible experience, nor with theory as opposed to practice, but

rather with the elements involved in all practice" (1981: 185). Thus, it is quite incorrect to understand metaphysics, at least in the Whiteheadian sense that provides the framework for process thinkers like Hartshorne, Ogden, or Griffin, as making no appeal to experience. On the contrary, because metaphysical traits necessarily characterize all existence, any and every experience must exhibit those characteristics. What distinguishes metaphysics, however, from other disciplines which take experience as their starting point is its search for strict generality or universality. No possible experience could fail to exhibit a metaphysical trait, and thus every experience either actual or conceivable must exemplify that trait. Of course, even though metaphysical statements are true of all experience and denied by none, that is not the same as saying that they can be verified or falsified empirically. Here lies the crucial distinction -- between the word "empirical" and the word "experiential."

But if metaphysics, by its very nature, is "the study which evaluates the *a priori* statements about existence" (Hartshorne, 1970: 19), isn't virtually any state of affairs compatible with a metaphysical claim, rendering metaphysical claims neutral with regard to values? As Segundo says,

> We could go further here and say that this neutrality is in reality resistance. For when we use a mechanism of reality to serve some value, we are extracting it away from its own proper dynamism (which knows nothing of this or any other value). So then, the great problems of our civilization can be summed up in one: i.e., What is the best and most economical way possible to combine the meaning of existence with the know-how to manipulate reality? (1982: I: 41)

Theodore Walker, a black liberation theologian, makes a similar point to that of Segundo:

> The status of a strictly metaphysical assertion, taken alone, or only in combination with other strictly metaphysical assertions, is a matter about which black theology and most other theologies of liberation have shown little interest, and this is so for the best of reasons. The obvious reason is that strictly metaphysical assertions are, in regards to ethics, singularly uninteresting (248).

Walker goes on to reason that this is true, since, if a metaphysical statement is affirmed by every actual and conceivable fact and falsified by no actual or conceivable fact, then no state of affairs either actual or possible could contradict it. The difference, however, between Segundo and Walker at this point is worth mentioning. Walker is careful to point out that it is only "strictly metaphysical assertions, taken alone, or only in combination with other strictly metaphysical assertions" that are "singularly uninteresting." Walker then borrows a classic statement by Charles Hartshorne from *Creative Synthesis and Philosophic Method*,

> Philosophy has two primary responsibilities: to clarify the nonempirical principles and to use them, together with relevant empirical facts, to illuminate value problems of personal and social life (1983: xiv).

Far from being uninteresting or unnecessary, the nonempirical principles of which Hartshorne speaks are of the utmost importance with regard to the values we adopt for ourselves. Walker recognizes this and goes on to supply the "relevant empirical facts," i.e., the reality of oppression in the world, that would allow him, as both a theologian and social ethicist, "to illuminate value problems of personal and social life."

Franklin Gamwell also offers insight into the relationship between metaphysics and ethics, utilizing Hartshorne's understanding of metaphysics to show how ethical claims require a metaphysical principle for their justification. Gamwell begins with Hartshorne's distinction between local (non-metaphysical) and cosmic (metaphysical) variables, the term "variable" being used to identify "a trait or characteristic in terms of which two or more realities can be compared" (Gamwell, 1984: 125). Local variables, for Hartshorne, would be "those which are or might be exemplified in some but not all conceivable realities, so that only some realities can be compared in terms of them," while cosmic or metaphysical variables are "those of which every conceivable reality is an instance, such that all possible realities may be compared in terms of them" (Gamwell, 1984: 125).

According to Gamwell, in order for human activity to be comprehensively evaluated, one must utilize a moral principle that is a specification of a cosmic variable. One might hold, as Gamwell claims that John Dewey does, that because value is peculiarly human, the variable by which human alternatives is to be judged is local to human existence. That would be true, so the argument goes, because it is only human action that is considered good or bad and nonhuman activity or experience does not admit of such an evaluation. Gamwell points out the inconsistency in this view, however, in that the very comparison between human existence and nonhuman existence requires a variable that is inclusive of both and that is not merely local to human existence. Furthermore, since any conceivable reality can become a constituent of human alternatives *as conceivable*, these alternatives, as Gamwell says,

> must exemplify characteristics in terms of which they can be evaluated. In short, the wider evaluative variable must be one exhibited by all conceivable realities. But precisely this is the definition of a cosmic or metaphysical variable (128).

Thus, according to Gamwell,

all possible realities may be evaluated as better or worse, and value must be understood as a characteristic inscribed, as it were, in the foundations of the universe (128).

For a process metaphysics such as Hartshorne's, that cosmic variable is the principle of creative synthesis.

Gamwell's line of reasoning clarifies, even if it also qualifies, the assertion commonly made that facts cannot imply values or that "is" does not entail "ought." In the narrower sense in which we might use the word "is" -- namely, to refer to the local characteristics or contingent features of reality -- it is true that no moral claim can be derived, and certainly Segundo would be correct in rejecting any kind of easy alliance between ethics and social reality or the "correspondence" theory of truth that is contained therein. As Gamwell says, "The fact that certain actual or possible realities exhibit certain local characteristics rather than others never entails any moral conclusions. . . . science cannot build a bridge to value" (129). However, this does not mean that "ought" can never be derived from "is" when "is" is understood in a broader, or metaphysical sense. Moral claims are not, therefore, independent of statements about the necessary features of reality. Rather, "because moral claims depend upon a metaphysical variable, a metaphysical statement about reality, as specified to human activity, does imply a moral claim" (129).

All this is not to say, however, that any metaphysical system will do in this regard, and Segundo's misgivings about metaphysics are not entirely misplaced. Indeed, it is precisely because metaphysical systems are hardly "neutral" to the struggle for human liberation that they lend themselves either negatively or positively to that struggle and, to that extent, function "ideologically" in an unavoidable way. Just as moral claims depend on a metaphysical variable, so also, whether consciously or unconsciously, all systems of metaphysics reflect the historical praxis out of which they arise. Thus, as Enrique Dussel has pointed out, "all theoretical exercise has its own autonomy, but only a *relative* autonomy" (1985: 181). A passage from Aristotle's *Politics* demonstrates this clearly:

> But it is nature's intention also to erect a physical difference between the body of the freeman and that of the slave, giving the latter strength for the menial duties of life, but making the former upright in carriage and (though useless for physical labour) useful for the various purposes of civic life--a life which tends, as it develops, to be divided into military service and the occupations of peace. . . . It is thus clear that, just as some are by nature free, so others are by nature slaves, and for these latter the condition of slavery is both beneficial and just (13-14).

It is clear from this passage that the difference in history and society between the slave and the free person becomes grounded in, or perhaps projected onto, the very fabric of reality. More recently, this same Aristotelian metaphysical view, guided by the idea that every instance of reality has its own undeniable *telos* toward which it "ought" to aim, has been used more than once to keep certain groups (women, for example) in their alleged place in order that they might fulfill their own particular *telos*.

Nevertheless, despite the ideological relationship of metaphysics to praxis, it seems to me that, on the basis of the above discussion, one must finally admit that risk does not mean impossibility and, that, an inquiry into the metaphysical ground of value and meaning is indispensable in terms of both communicating and evaluating one's faith. There is, I believe, an understanding of metaphysics and, furthermore, of God, quite unlike that of classical metaphysics which warrants more than merely its rejection. Ogden sums up the situation thus:

> But just this points up the limitation of the wholesale denunciation of metaphysics that are the stock in trade in certain theological quarters. The conventional view that one's only choices are either to accept some traditional metaphysics or else reject metaphysics altogether is the result of selective perception and is utterly misleading as to the philosophical options which are presently available (1963: 95).

Metaphysics and Evolution

One of the qualities of a metaphysical system, as just mentioned, is its ability to express meaningfully and coherently the universal and unfailing features of reality itself. Given this understanding of metaphysics, the question naturally arises whether Segundo's employment of a Teilhardian evolutionary worldview in his christology functions as just such a metaphysics? The question itself might not even so much as surface were it not for the strange coincidence that, on the one hand, metaphysics is explicitly of such little value for Segundo and, yet, on the other hand, Teilhard's evolutionary scheme is. One is tempted to reduce the whole problem to a linguistic one. Either Segundo's use of Teilhard is not really metaphysical or Segundo's rejection of metaphysics is merely verbal. Certainly the process metaphysics of thinkers such as Hartshorne, Ogden, and Gamwell, cited above, trade heavily on insights that can only be characterized as "evolutionary"; indeed, as Norman Pittenger says, "the central conviction of American process-thought is that the evolutionary perspective must be taken with utmost seriousness (1971b: 25).

Part of the difficulty here may be that, quite apart from determining how an evolutionary worldview functions in Segundo's thought, it is difficult enough to ascertain how it functions for Teilhard de Chardin himself. Teilhard's work, as Ian G. Barbour notes, can be understood in a variety of ways: "as evolutionary science, as poetry and mysticism, as natural theology, and as Christian theology" (1971: 324). But certainly, the writings of Teilhard also reflect an impressive example of process metaphysics (Cf. Barbour: 1971; Teilhard, 1968: 54-60), even if, as Barbour indicates, that metaphysics is more or less "undeveloped." However we understand Teilhard, nonetheless, what I find most ironic about Segundo's reliance on him is that the primary values which Segundo places on Teilhard's evolutionary perspective are precisely those contributions by Teilhard which lend themselves most clearly to the description of a "conceptual unity" that, as I pointed out previously, Segundo criticizes so emphatically--namely, its ability to communicate the redundancies in universal history, trace out the lines of a unitary process with analogy on every level, account for the dynamic of entropy and negentropy that characterizes literally every experience, and then assign Christ a place in the whole process as "recapitulator" of the universe. In essence, Segundo rejects metaphysics for the very reasons that he is drawn to what he calls an "evolutionary epistemology" -- namely, its ability to make sense not only out of individual historical experiences, but of experience as a whole and at every level.

Perhaps the most appropriate way to understand Teilhard's writings, claims Barbour, is as an example of a "theology of nature."

> Some interpreters take *The Phenomenon of Man* to be a form of natural theology, an argument from evolution to the existence of God. I have suggested that it can more appropriately be viewed as a synthesis of scientific ideas with religious ideas derived from Christian tradition and experience (1990: 27).

In this case, it is precisely the religious tradition based on religious experience and historical revelation that becomes the starting point for Teilhard and traditional doctrines are reformulated appropriately in the light of current science. But if Teilhard's writings tend to draw on science and religion as relatively independent sources, as Barbour indicates, there is also a real sense in which he draws on a more common set of conceptual, methodological, and metaphysical assumptions that are shared by the ideas of science and the ideas of religion, which do not necessarily preclude us from calling his a "theology of nature," but which do indicate that the theological doctrines which he espouses (and to which Segundo subscribes in much the same fashion) are a clear example of complementary "models" within what Barbour calls a "paradigm" (1990: 41-58).

A "paradigm," as Barbour uses the word, is different from either a "myth" or a "model" and represents one of three scientific viewpoints that can clarify the precise nature of religious language.[57] A "myth," for example, is a story or

---

[57]Barbour's distinctions arise out of a comparison of the formal structure of the language used by both science and religion (1974, 1990) in defense of an attitude which he calls "critical realism":

stories that characterize what is the case with some aspect of the cosmic order or with the human being and are literally neither true nor false, usually fulfilling some important social function. A "model," on the other hand, is

> a symbolic representation of selected aspects of the behaviour of a complex system for particular purposes. It is an imaginative tool for ordering experience, rather than a description of the world. . . . Models in religion are also analogical. They are organizing images used to order and interpret patterns of experience in human life. . . . Ultimate models-- whether of a personal God or an impersonal cosmic process--direct attention to particular patterns in events and restructure the way one sees the world (1974: 6-7).

Just as models lead to theories, or beliefs, by which the data of our experience are ordered, so "paradigms," organize and give coherence to models. Thus, the shift to evolutionary thinking has led to a variety of models about creation and history that integrate the data of experience with the content of the Biblical witness within an overall appeal to what Barbour calls a "paradigm"--"a broad set of metaphysical and methodological assumptions" (1990: 54). So, for example, Teilhard speaks of evolution as long ago ceasing to be hypothesis and as now "a general condition of knowledge which henceforth all hypotheses must satisfy" (1965).

But if Teilhard's thought and Segundo's dependence upon it are understood as paradigm-dependent "models," then, while they do intend to talk about what is real, they often employ the religious language of imaginative metaphors and symbols which serve to express analogies. Barbour sums up the phenomenon of a "model" as follows:

> Religious models have additional functions without parallel in science, especially in expressing and evoking *distinctive attitudes*. We have said that religion is a way of life with practical as well as theoretical goals. The life-orienting and emotional power of religious models and their ability to affect value commitments should not be ignored. Models are crucial in the *personal transformation and reorientation* sought in most religious traditions. Some linguistic analysts and instrumentalists hold that religious language has only these noncognitive functions. I argue, in reply, that such noncognitive functions cannot stand alone because they

---

Against instrumentalism which sees both scientific theories and religious beliefs as human constructs useful for specific human purposes, I advocate a critical realism holding that both communities make cognitive claims about realities beyond the human world (1990: 16).

presuppose *cognitive beliefs.* Religious traditions do endorse particular attitudes and ways of life, but they also make claims about reality (46).

Segundo, it seems to me, remains rather consistently at the level of "model" in his interpretation of the significance of Jesus.[58] That is not to say that what he has to say is meaningless or fictional or that his analysis of human experience is not illuminating. But even though Segundo is able to give a fresh, vigorous, and apt account of Jesus' meaning for us and even though the paradigm upon which he is dependent has conceptual, metaphysical, and methodological resources by which he can critically reflect on that meaning, yet because he interprets human experience consistently at the level of "model," his analysis of human experience and, indeed, of the significance of Jesus does not make full use of those resources in terms of a process of critical reflection and, therefore, can hardly make the kind of claim to validity or urgency required, it seems to me, by the contemporary struggle for human liberation on our planet. Therefore, I think we can say that what Segundo borrows from Teilhard is a "religious model." But insofar, as Barbour says, "the movement from stories to models to concepts and beliefs is a necessary part of the theological task of critical reflection" (47), I am not convinced that Segundo has fully completed that movement.

Jesus -- the "Transcendent Datum"

Nowhere is the employment of Teilhard's evolutionary perspective as a "model" more apparent than when we come to Segundo's interpretation of the significance of Jesus. One might expect that Segundo's use of evolutionary thought in interpreting Jesus might provide the kind of "ultimacy" or "decisiveness" for Jesus' life and message that we found to be virtually missing in his presentation of the "historical Jesus." Certainly Segundo does attempt some such movement but definitely not along the lines of a "transcendental christology" as in the case of Rahner nor along the lines of explicating Jesus' "decisive representation" of ultimate reality as in the case of Ogden. Instead, Segundo prefers to interpret Jesus within the evolutionary process of the universe, drawing an analogy between Jesus' own perfect flexibility and creativity in living an "effective faith," on the one hand, and the universal process of entropy and negentropy that characterizes evolutionary reality.

---

[58]Segundo, for example, justifies the use of analogy as a vehicle for moving from scientific discoveries to an epistemology that can discover value and meaning in the universe and communicate it to all humanity because of a "powerful desire for coherence" claimed by Teilhard as fundamental to all human beings (1970f: 156).

I have pointed out already, for example, that Segundo's starting point for interpreting the significance of Jesus is the universal anthropological process by which an individual orders his or her life in accordance with a faith -- a meaning-structure or value-structure -- based on the testimony of referential witnesses. There are times when Segundo treats Jesus as just such a witness (1982: I: 100, II: 29), though often it is his faith -- and his ability to make that faith effective in terms of ideologies -- that is witnessed to by others who become for us referential witnesses. The "evolutionary flexibility" maintained in Jesus by incorporating into his existence a necessary balance of both faith and ideologies, entropy and negentropy, gives him an important role in the process of universal evolution-- indeed, he "recapitulates" that process. But here again, even in the case of the word "recapitulate," which is used only a few times in *El hombre de hoy ante Jesús de Nazaret*, we find no explicitly metaphysical import, but rather, an analogical way of incorporating the significance of Jesus into Segundo's evolutionary model.

At some point, of course, Jesus and his mission are converted into a "transcendent datum" which now grounds meaning and value for others and provides the "ends" for which ideologies are the means as well as the "absolute value" to which all other values are subordinated. But how does "the historical Jesus" become a "transcendent datum"? Segundo asks the question this way:

> Why fall back precisely on Jesus of Nazareth as the central point of significance of that universal process, which continues after him? Why wager everything on him despite his limitations, which are evident in his concrete historical actualization, as adequate as it was within the parameters of evolution? In other words, why--with an anthropological faith--are we taking Jesus out of his specific historical situation and projecting him back to the beginning of the universe and, even more, forward toward its end? (II: 935-936)

Everything rides on this conversion of Jesus from historical example to "transcendent datum," and yet Segundo is able to offer very little by way of helping us to understand how this conversion can and does take place. Rather, it simply *can* take place in the parameters of an evolutionary "model." The real weakness with Segundo's method, at this point, shows up in the fact that he never really answers this question adequately, and, insofar as he does answer it, the conversion to transcendent datum takes place based on Jesus' more or less perfect actualization of faith so that Jesus is little more than an "example" or "witness" to faith. Here again, the metaphysical resources of an evolutionary paradigm could perhaps assist Segundo by providing a way of conceptualizing the sense in which Jesus can be said to "recapitulate" the universe or, as Ogden says, "decisively represent" ultimate reality.

Evolution and Praxis

As I indicated in Chapter 6, it is finally the question of praxis, understood by Segundo as cultural transformation, that gives theology, if not its justification, then at least its urgency. I also there expressed dissatisfaction with Segundo's statement of the relationship between faith and ideologies because of its lack of clarity in drawing out the internal connection between the two. Rather, as I pointed out, that relationship is simply the formal one characterized, first, by the need for faith to implement itself in terms of ideologies and, second, by the relativization of any and all ideological expressions by virtue of the absolutization of a process of learning to learn.

It seems to me, at this point, that Segundo would do better with an evolutionary model than a Marxist model when it comes to analyzing the relationship between faith and ideologies. For one thing, it may be that this relationship is not best expressed in terms of the kind of causality expressed by the terms "ends" and "means," but, rather, in terms of integration into the evolutionary circuit, i.e., in terms of the more "ecological" causality described by Segundo. Often, when Segundo undertakes social analysis, he does view reality in terms of the latter. For example, in examining the poverty of Latin American countries, Segundo rejects any simple, mechanical, or direct causes put forward by others such as demographic features, political instability, temperamental deficiencies, etc. and instead views the whole process of development in wealthy countries and underdevelopment in poor countries as an interdependent and rhythmic process where unbridled consumption on the part of one country sets up an unbalanced and destructive social ecology within which other countries suffer (Segundo, 1973e).

By more fully utilizing the insights of an evolutionary epistemology, we can perhaps see a broader context for understanding historical praxis and for determining the wider implications of various ideologies which intend to give expression to a faith. Evolution no doubt teaches us that entropic means must often be used for negentropic purposes, but evolution also teaches us to define effectiveness not in terms of sheer causality -- the production of certain ends by the use of particular means -- but rather as the successful integration of a variety of factors into an entire circuit. An evolutionary perspective also teaches us the relationship of the "within" or "purposiveness" of life to its results or effectiveness. Thus, the relationship between faith and ideologies may be more like that between an acorn and an oak tree than that between a hammer and driving a nail. As Mohandas K. Gandhi says,

> Your belief that there is no connection between the means and the end is a great mistake. Through that mistake even men who have been considered religious have committed grievous crimes. . . . The means may be likened to a seed, the end to a tree; and there is just that same inviolable

connection between the means and the end as there is between the seed and the tree (10).

Of course, Gandhi's comments are made from within a different religious tradition from that within which Segundo writes. Yet one could easily argue that there are just as ample conceptual and metaphysical resources in an evolutionary paradigm to motivate Segundo to move beyond a mechanical model of cause and effect to a more organic and processive one, as there are, say, in modern Vedantic Hinduism. Both paradigms offer a way of understanding the relationship of means to ends by appeal to the universe as a "circuit" where all phenomena are interconnected and dependent upon one another such that certain forms of mechanical causality are simply ruled out.

Conclusions with regard to Method

Segundo recognizes that one of the greatest dangers of theological method is that conditioning the method conditions the problematic. Segundo points out that the opposite danger is equally perilous--namely, "to call reality what is not reality but a misconceptualization of it, and so to bring to our theology cries of enthusiasm or despair rather than authentic questions that can be answered theologically" (1980: 179). In Segundo's mind, theological method must sail between two reefs:

> I believe that a good method demands a certain preliminary hermeneutics of reality, and here enters the "mediation" that, together with commitment --because without it it's extremely conceptualistic and ideal--contains hermeneutic principles of reality. That is, that the question is how to interpret reality: how to go from the newspaper to what lies beneath the reality that seems ephemeral, contingent; what is at stake beneath the events that are taking place? (179-180).

Really, it is this interpretation of reality that is the first step of the hermeneutic method and which allows and prods the theologian to question the witness of faith with depth and profundity. But, though Segundo's principle, as stated above, is quite valid, so far as it goes, I would still need to ask whether Segundo's method really interprets reality profoundly enough. In other words, is interpretation of the reality witnessed to by the daily newspaper, armed as fully as we could be with the tools of the socio-analytic sciences, in and of itself, really sufficient to ground our praxis as more than of merely passing significance? Do we not still require the interpretation of reality in its most general and unfailing features such as can only be mediated to theology by the theoretical tool of metaphysics?

To be fair to Segundo, his rejection of metaphysics is not quite as vehement and explicit as is possible. His is, at least in part, a reaction against an oppressive and heteronomous metaphysical doctrine of God and divinity that has led the church to subordinate virtually any historically functional and relative values to vertical, timeless values. This difficult situation, however, only points up the urgency of a method that can demonstrate, on the one hand, how it is that, only insofar as ultimate reality in itself has one structure rather than another, a particular faith expressed in terms of ideologies may be meaningfully said to be "authentic" and, on the other hand, how, as Ogden says, "it is only insofar as acting in one way rather than another is how one ought to act in relation to one's fellows that ultimate reality can have the meaning for us it is asserted to have in taking it to authorize one self-understanding ["faith"] rather than another as authentic" (1983: 35). Thus, while Segundo's proposed logic for communicating and evaluating statements about value need not be reduced to metaphysics, one may, with reasonable justification, claim that the communication of a particular value-structure necessarily utilizes statements that contain a metaphysical aspect which provides an objective mooring in reality for our praxis.

This corrective to Segundo's analysis of the kind of question that christology asks will enable him to provide more adequate criteria for critically interpreting the meaning-world which Segundo's New Testament "referential witnesses" (the apostles) offer as the authentic possibility of human existence gained from their historical encounter with the person of Jesus of Nazareth.

Segundo is quite convincing that evolution has become a *task* for human beings, not just a biological phenomenon. The sobering question that makes Segundo's project so very important is whether we will take up that task with ecological flexibility or whether through inflexibility we will push the world to a catastrophic end. My own belief is that taking up the task of making faith effective in our own evolutionary context will have to rest on more than a "wager" even if it can never rest on some kind of empirical proof. It is clear to me that Segundo is groping for something upon which faith can be grounded that is not a matter of empirical verification or falsification but that is somehow grounded in the reality of our experience. I am not at all sure that "transcendent data," if properly understood, are not just that conceptual tool needed to communicate that ground. As Segundo himself would admit, it is difficult for human beings to be inspired to praxis if they do not feel that reality is "on their side." I doubt, however, whether the kind of connection that Segundo draws between faith and reality is tight enough to ground a faith that expresses itself in liberating praxis. It is also not at all clear how Segundo's faith can really rise above the relativity of the "referential witness," and, surely, if values such as justice, liberation, solidarity, or human rights are to have the kind of universal claim on human beings that Segundo intends them to have, they will require some kind of mooring in reality as it "is" and not merely as it is wagered that it will be.

PART III

TOWARD AN ALTERNATIVE
LIBERATION CHRISTOLOGY

CHAPTER 9

JESUS AND EVOLUTION

In one way or another, Segundo does attempt to develop for christology a method for interpreting the significance of Jesus that is credible, appropriate, and effective. However, with regard to each of the tasks for which an adequate christology is responsible, he is not wholly successful. His insights into the praxic dimension of every human existence are profound but, because he fails to clarify the metaphysical dimension of existence, he cannot account for why the praxis of liberation should be understood as the "authentic" praxis for human beings today. He suggests an evolutionary perspective for understanding history and for interpreting the significance of Jesus for historical praxis but finally fails to use that key to fully unlock that significance. Furthermore, even though Segundo's research into the earliest stratum of Christian witness bears some fruit for christology, it is misidentified as "the historical Jesus" and, again, of very little use in understanding why it is that the earliest witnesses should take Jesus to be of "ultimate" importance, not to mention why we should also.

It is my belief that many of Segundo's anthropological, sociological, and epistemological resources and, especially, his evolutionary "key," if utilized more adequately and deepened by a more satisfactory account of the ultimate reality which grounds every human existence, could be employed more effectively to interpret critically the significance of Jesus. The more satisfactory account I have in mind, at this point, is a neo-classical or "process" philosophy along the lines developed by Alfred North Whitehead and Charles Hartshorne. Here we find, I believe, a philosophical resource that not only affirms the evolutionary character of reality, but does so in a way that overcomes some of the more obvious deficiencies of a Teilhardian perspective (such as its anthropocentrism or determinism, for example). To make full use of the resources offered both by Segundo and by process thought for the interpretation of the significance of Jesus, however, I can hardly see how we can avoid the threefold task of christology mentioned in Chapter 1--namely, the praxic, metaphysical, and historical dimensions of christological reflection--all of which taken together comprise an adequate christological method. In this final chapter, then, I will do little more than point out the general outlines of these tasks, their relevance for christology, and their relationship to one another within the overall perspective of an evolutionary world-view shared by Segundo and process thought. Though I do not hesitate to describe what follows as an "alternative" to Segundo's christological reflection, that should by no means be taken as an indication that Segundo's thought is, therefore, being set aside or rejected. By the same token, I do not think a process metaphysics can simply be engrafted onto Segundo's theological method as if that were all that were required to produce a credible, appropriate, and effective christological method.   Rather, I take it that Segundo's thought provides a significant proposal to be dialogued with and a host of profound challenges to be reckoned with in any contemporary reflection on christological method; indeed, that is the kind of approach that Segundo himself models with respect to other thinkers with whom he dialogues, and it is just this kind of approach that makes his own theological reflection so vigorous, dynamic, and challenging.

Christological Method

Segundo's anthropological starting point, it seems to me, can hardly be gainsaid as the place to begin for critically interpreting the significance of Jesus. That is true, of course, because the significance of Jesus is first and foremost a significance *for us* and not simply *in itself.* This situation could hardly be otherwise.   Apart from an inquiry into who we are and the structure of our existence by which anyone or anything becomes significant to us, it is difficult to comprehend how we can even begin to talk about the significance of Jesus.

Where, I think, Segundo makes his greatest contribution not only to the method of christology but to the method of theology in general is in identifying this existential structure as the dialectic of faith and ideologies. This dialectic serves as a methodological tool that enables us to correlate the message of the witness of faith and our own human existence in a way that is forceful and appealing on both theoretical and practical grounds.   In the first place, the dialectic of faith and ideologies employed as a methodological tool can help us to understand the structure of the witness of faith as one integral process whereby self, society, and world interrelate and influence one another, thereby forming the context for the interpretation of Jesus' meaning for us. We, therefore, approach that witness equipped with theoretical instruments that can determine the meaning and assess the validity of that witness *in and through*, but never *apart from*, the ideologies through which the message of that witness is expressed. In the second place, that same dialectic makes it possible to re-interpret the meaning of Jesus for our own existence in a way that does not simply acquire some "content" about Jesus and then "apply" that quantity of information to our moral beliefs and practices, but that, instead, mediates the significance of Jesus to an existence that is, at its very base, socio-political as well as individual; active as well as reflective.

But even if this dialectic of faith and ideologies provides a useful methodological tool insofar as it adequately reflects the structure of human meaning and praxis for which Jesus or anyone else is said to be significant, for just that reason I am more inclined to talk about this existential structure in terms of "faith and praxis" rather than "faith and ideologies." As I have already indicated, Segundo's neutral use of the word "ideology" has, on the one hand, the negative tendency of confusing the issue as to what course of action in a human life may be deemed justifiable or unjustifiable; authentic or inauthentic; humanizing or dehumanizing. On the other hand, however, it provides a positive and indispensable way of recognizing that all human meaning and self-understanding, simply as such, is intricately connected to particular interests and practices. Segundo's claim that faith must be expressed in terms of "ideologies," however, seems to me finally to destroy the validity and usefulness of both the "negative" and the "neutral" senses of the word "ideologies" and so I take it that the word "praxis" is a better word to place in dialectic with faith than the word "ideology." Just so, however, an adequate christological method can never be content that it has amply addressed the praxic dimension of the christological question apart from taking into account the ideological relationship of understanding to practice.

But if we grant that the task of christology is to interpret critically the significance of Jesus for human existence and if we grant, further, that it is only on the basis of an ethical analysis of human existence, employing the insights of the human and social sciences as well as the message of the biblical witness, that we can come to see that the dialectic of faith and praxis constitutes for us just that structure of human existence and, therefore, of how anyone or anything becomes significant to us, then we should have no difficulty in admitting that this is all the more true in the case of someone who is said to be of "ultimate" significance to us.

By "ultimate" here, I simply mean that the person in question serves to represent, as Segundo says, "the ultimate possibilities (or limits) of the universe and the human being" (1982: I: 97). But just this formulation implies that the ultimacy in question has, on the one hand, a metaphysical aspect, in that the ultimate possibilities of reality itself (Segundo lapses into more empirical language--"universe") are taken as permitting, empowering, and authorizing the human being to structure his or her life in terms of faith and praxis, just as, on the other hand, it has a praxic aspect, in that the ultimate possibilities of the human being--in terms of faith and praxis--are taken to be permitted, empowered, and authorized by reality itself.[59]

---

[59]My way of putting the matter is obviously indebted to Schubert Ogden's description of the structure of what he calls "the existential question." That question, says Ogden,

> can be described as the question about the meaning of ultimate reality for us, which asks at one and the same time about both ultimate reality and ourselves: both the ultimate reality that authorizes an authentic understanding of our own existence and the authentic self-understanding that is authorized by what is ultimately real (1982: 34).

An adequate christological method, then, if it is to interpret critically the significance of Jesus for human existence, understood as an "ultimate" significance, must at the very least explore not only the praxic dimension of that significance but also the metaphysical dimension of that significance. The metaphysical dimension of that significance, of course, presupposes a clarification of the "nonempirical principles," as they are referred to by Hartshorne. Apart from some such clarification, it seems to me, it is difficult to comprehend how the adoption, communication, and evaluation of faith could ever be more than arbitrary or ideological (in the negative sense of the word), and, while such a clarification can never remove the "wager-like" quality of faith, it can express the "ultimate possibilities" of reality and of our existence previously mentioned. In thus expressing these possibilities, however, christology is not simply reduced to metaphysics. Rather, what christology interprets is that which has been decisively re-presented in Jesus, namely, the meaning of ultimate reality "for us" (Ogden, 1982: 34). But when we talk about the meaning of ultimate reality "for us," here, inevitably we mean not only "for our faith" but "for our praxis."

Just as the metaphysical dimension of Jesus' significance, presupposes a clarification of transcendent data, so also the praxic dimension of that significance implies a clarification of the "value problems of personal and social life," as they are referred to by Hartshorne. This does not mean, however, that christology is simply reduced to ethics, either. Rather, what christology interprets as the meaning of ultimate reality for us, as that has been decisively re-presented in Jesus, illuminates these questions of value and allows us to consider a particular praxis as our "authentic" praxis. I should add here that the social and human sciences also fulfill a function for christology that is indispensable in effectively interpreting the praxic significance of Jesus--namely, to provide what Hartshorne calls the "relevant empirical facts," i.e., the socio-political context and structure of our praxis. Apart from the role of these sciences, it seems to me, any talk of praxis or of Jesus' significance for our lives will remain abstract and ineffective, and so it is no wonder that liberation theologians such as Segundo have typically defended a central role for them in theological method. Clodovis Boff explains how these sciences are to be incorporated into theological method:

> The sciences of the social enter into the theology of the political as a *constitutive part*. But they do so precisely at the level of the raw material of this theology, at the level of its *material object*--not at that of its proper pertinency, or formal object. Thus although the theology of the political must lend an attentive ear to the sciences of the social, in order to gather from them information necessary for its discourse, neither this attention nor this gathering may be taken for what they are *not*--theology in the formal sense of the term. The undeveloped insertion of sociological material into theology without the care to rework it in accordance with the formal object

of theology, so as to integrate it organically in an articulation of the whole, would be to betray both theology and the sciences of the social (31).

So far, all that I have said has not directly addressed the issue of how an adequate christological method goes about arguing for the faithfulness, or "appropriateness," of its claims about Jesus' significance. Obviously, this issue requires us to come to terms with the nature of the witness of faith to which such claims must be justified as appropriate. Here, as I have already indicated in Part II, I find both promise and difficulty in Segundo's method. Segundo, as I noted, takes up the necessary inquiry into how Jesus was historically understood by the earliest witnesses to him and, for this task, relies on the tools of historical-critical research. Then, too, Segundo also employs the tools of the social sciences, here again, to demonstrate how every testimony to the significance of Jesus is ideologically reflective of particular interests and practices on the part of the witness. After exposing those ideological expressions for what they are (deideologizing) Segundo's hermeneutic circle fails to move on to a productive political interpretation of Jesus' significance of Jesus. Rather, the earliest layer of testimony to Jesus is taken as "the historical Jesus" and, by treating this portrait as a core of empirical data, Segundo ends up contradicting his preference for the existential impact that Jesus made on his interpreters. In essence, once he has become enamored with the "political" character of the historical Jesus, he is "boxed in" to that political "key" (which, as he says, is "Jesus' own key") and, while he quite ably explores other ideologies about Jesus (for example, that of Paul and Ignatius Loyola), he is not finally able to fully account for the ultimacy or decisiveness which the synoptic witnesses attribute to Jesus.

But if we proceed on the basis of what only a fully developed historical inquiry into the witness of faith can justify--namely, that the earliest witnesses to Jesus take him as having a decisive meaning for their lives--then we will have to do more than the deideologizing which Segundo undertakes. Christology will have to interpret politically for our praxis the meaning of certain key transcendent data which Jesus' original witnesses take to be re-presented by him and which they, in turn, express ideologically. Then, and only then, will we have the grounds to speak about that which may be considered, because of what Jesus means for it, our "authentic" praxis.

The Evolutionary Significance of Jesus

By drawing on the resources of the various theoretical disciplines already mentioned (metaphysics, ethics, the social sciences, historical criticism of scripture, etc.) and by drawing on the biblical witness itself, I would now like to undertake a dialogue primarily with Segundo in order to develop some of the broad outlines of how I would propose to go about expressing the meaning of Jesus today.

First of all, it is clear, the specific context in which Segundo writes and to which he wishes his christological reflection to be relevant is the situation of a destroyed and destructive social ecology on the Latin American continent. On the surface of things, the political repression, perpetual social unrest, and structural violence that characterizes so much of Segundo's context may seem distant from and unimaginable to a North American context. But what Segundo describes as the deeper and more fundamental needs of cultural and anthropological transformation that give his christology a real urgency point to a situation of dehumanization and social injustice that is not foreign to North America:

> It would be infantile and extremely dangerous to maintain the kind of attitude of those who dream merely of a return to representative democracy, an end to repression, and the recovery of respect for those human rights which were in force in better times. There are much more fundamental things that have to be reconstructed. Otherwise the cycle desperation-subversion-repression will reappear again and will continue to sink its teeth deeper into a continent becoming increasingly sick. What is needed is a creative "wisdom" to reconstruct human beings and society from the roots of their relational base up (1982: I: 367-368).

Segundo's comments, I think, are not simply local to Uruguay or even Latin America but express what has become of paramount importance to every human existence today. This is especially true when we factor in what Segundo says about the delicate ecological balance (both social and environmental) which is required for just this task of reconstruction of the human being and society and when we factor in what Segundo says about the unavoidable intertwining of the individual and social dimensions of this task. What Segundo calls for, it seems to me, is a fundamental liberation at the very base and core of our personal and social existence, but not, for that reason, a liberation that is merely abstract or theoretical. Segundo claims that at the heart of human existence today is a fundamental desire for a liberation that attacks the cycle of oppression and dehumanization at its social and anthropological base rather than addressing itself simply to superficial issues. It is this liberation, it seems clear, with which any and all claims about the significance of Jesus must today reckon in order to demonstrate their "practical credibility."

I would suggest that Segundo's penetrating analysis of the contemporary longing for liberation points up the need for three existential qualities which can guide the task of human and social reconstruction--freedom, love, and creativity. Freedom, of course, is synonymous with the word "liberation," but, when viewed by Segundo within an evolutionary framework, freedom takes on a meaning that points beyond the various concrete struggles for political liberation in society to the only thing that can finally ground those struggles and give them lasting significance--namely, the freedom that comes from *faith*.[60]   This is true, for Segundo, because in an evolutionary model such as Teilhard's, all of creation, history, and human existence can be viewed as a dynamic of entropy and negentropy, or in terms of a delicate energy calculus where faith preserves and gives meaning to freedom. In society, for example, *legislation* is analogous to genetic inheritance on the biological level, while the *freedoms* which are permitted and even legislated in society as essential human rights play the role of "homeostatic mechanisms" (I: 377) that permit us to learn creativity through trial and error. Too little freedom stifles creativity. Too much freedom ("cheap energy") causes ecological destruction and imbalance, as exemplified by the United States where only 6% of the world's population consumes 40% of the world's production.

Faith provides a kind of "energy savings" for the human being. That does not mean that faith is a deposit of ready-made solutions for human and cultural reconstruction, but rather that faith mediates "transcendent data" about the possibilities and limits of reality[61] and the human being to our praxis. Faith gives us the freedom to be creative. By communicating to us the values that, if implemented, will ultimately be the most "satisfying" in life, faith saves us energy which can be better spent in creatively developing ways of implementing that praxis. Apart from faith, every day would be like starting all over again in figuring out how to live our lives, resulting in devastating effects not only for freedom but for creativity.

Segundo's interpretation of Paul confirms this same truth on a more anthropological rather than cultural plane and, here again, the quality of "creativity" is fundamental. As Segundo points out, Paul's notion of "Christian liberty" so destroyed the security of many of his contemporaries (both religious and otherwise) that they preferred to return to the bondage of the law. As Segundo says, "that 'liberty,' in effect, required them to have to think for themselves, where previously they had prefabricated answers" (I: 411). Thus, throughout a human life, freedom "learns" creativity, or what Segundo refers to as evolutionary "flexibility."

> the more a person grows, in every sense, the more and more clearly he or she perceives that a particular attitude towards some value never constitutes once and for all the best solution with regard to the problem at hand. If his or her faith is to persist, it must more and more be based on the

---

[60]Indeed, in his analysis of faith and ideologies, Segundo often simply equates the words "freedom" and "faith" (Cf. 1982: I: 41).

[61]Here, as I have already mentioned, I differ from Segundo with respect to the meaning of the word "reality."

creative capacity to solve many problems, in accordance with the growing complexity of the reality with which he or she is faced (I: 99).

But if, for Segundo's analysis of human and social existence, faith implies freedom and creativity, it also implies love. As Segundo says,

> *Faith,* in the sense which Paul uses the term, consists in entrusting our destiny to God, thereby liberating us *from* the temptation to seek security in the law and *for* the work of achieving the most perfect possible love with the instruments provided by each age and circumstance (II: 122)

In keeping with the requirements of freedom and creativity, the love required "to reconstruct human beings and society from the roots of their relational base up" must be an *effective* love (II: 119), by which Segundo means that it must be expressed, for example, politically.

> Now then, the only thing that characterizes politics as a plane different from others is that it brings together the threads of all these others and weaves them together, in principle, for the common welfare with the proportionate power needed to ensure that unification. Thus, all the planes where the religious intervenes and provides orientation must ultimately open out to this more universal--political--dimension of love (II: 122).

Here, again, Segundo's interpretation of Paul is instructive. In Segundo's view, Paul gives faith meaning on two planes--the plane of the invisible (hope) and the plane of the manifest (freedom). Both are essential to faith. Just as, on the one hand, we cannot "see" our status as "children of God" and "inheritors of the world" (for that matter, we cannot "see" any transcendent data), so also, on the other hand, our historical existence is not thereby exchanged for an abstraction, and faith lives a quite visible existence. As Segundo says, "our work of 'cooperating' in 'God's building up' will be sized up by the 'quality' of its own inner dynamism and will pass, thanks to God's judgment, to the plane of the visible" (II: 557). But for Paul, as Segundo notes, this cooperation with God is precisely a work of "love"--a work that becomes our historical *project*, not a *test* to achieve salvation. At this point, it is not difficult to see why Segundo prefers Paul's notion of faith over what Segundo detects as Ignatius Loyola's constant worrying about salvation. Segundo says that "faith makes love possible by liberating the human being from anxiety over its own predicament and destiny" (II: 742).

One could, I believe, give a fuller and more complete account of these three interrelated and overlapping characteristics of human existence, each of which points up the depth and profundity of the concept of liberation as it applies today to human beings. I hope, however, that I have at least suggested the direction toward which an adequate christology must look in order to relate the significance of Jesus to the most critical problems and concerns of contemporary human beings if it is to have any practical relevance or credibility. We must now ask, however, just how Jesus himself can justifiably be claimed to be of decisive significance for human existence, given the brief analysis just sketched.

So far as the historical data about Jesus are concerned, I find a remarkable degree of unanimity between Segundo and Marxsen with regard to what may fairly be taken as the earliest traditions about Jesus apart from any influence of the events of the crucifixion and resurrection and which, therefore, may be considered the normative witness to which christological statements must be appropriate. Without oversimplifying all that could be said about these early traditions, referred to by Marxsen as the "Jesus-kerygma," I would like to explore just three examples mutually acknowledged by both Segundo and Marxsen as belonging to this early kerygma. Even though Segundo, as I have noted, misidentifies the subject of this kerygma as "the historical Jesus" and even though he goes on to predicate of Jesus a kind of radical political consciousness that, by the very nature of our sources, is impossible to confirm or deny, his own identification of these three elements as combining "to form what might be called a circle of meaning" (II: 127) about Jesus is not far off, it seems to me, from providing a reasonable summary of what the earliest witnesses had to say about Jesus' significance.

The first element in that "circle of meaning" is the summary of Jesus' teachings recorded in Mark 1:15--"The time is fulfilled, and the kingdom of God is at hand; repent, and believe in the gospel." Marxsen agrees that this is a central and uniquely representative statement of the Jesus-kerygma and says, "the key to the christological understanding of the Jesus kerygma may very well be offered by Mark 1:15" (1976: 147). The most striking feature of this brief statement, of course, is its reference to the "kingdom of God." Segundo believes the term is a "loaded" term, full of political content, and deliberately employed by Jesus to elicit political reaction (1982: II: 129). Marxsen, while recognizing the occasional political use of the term, claims that, so far as its background use in Jewish apocalypticism goes, "the dominant idea is that of the futurity of the kingdom, conceived of as a state of affairs" (1976: 147). Both Segundo and Marxsen are agreed, however, that Jesus' presence was interpreted by his original witnesses as a *kairos* which was ushering in a new state of affairs that demanded nothing short of radical change and conversion on the part of those to whom it was proclaimed and that it is Jesus' announcement of this imminent kingdom rather than his own personal relationship to God or divine status that is the focus of the Jesus kerygma.

But how do human beings participate in this kingdom? Marxsen stresses that while there is certainly much that the Jesus kerygma has to say about how people are to live *in* the kingdom, people yet "need do nothing more *for* the coming of God's kingdom, since it now works of its own accord, automatically" (148; Cf. Mark 4:26ff). When Marxsen says "more," here, he is referring to the attitude of those who, in Jesus' parable, "have been incorporated into the kingdom of God by selling everything in order to acquire a field or a pearl" (148; Cf. Matthew 13:44-46). Segundo would undoubtedly disagree with Marxsen's use of the word "automatically" here and, indeed, it does seem that Marxsen has overstated the case. What our attitude should be in terms of how the kingdom is received, on the one hand, and how the kingdom actually works on earth, on the other hand, are, it seems to me, two distinct things. As John Wesley puts the matter, "First, God works; therefore you *can* work. Secondly, God works, therefore you *must* work" (511). Segundo, for example, interprets Jesus, as he is testified to by the earliest witnesses, as proclaiming the gratuitousness of the kingdom without thereby claiming that the kingdom simply works automatically apart from human creativity. Precisely because the kingdom is to be an "earthly" kingdom, its gracious origin does not rule out but only affirms a high degree of causality and creativity on the part of human beings in bringing it about.[62]

> Jesus' listeners understood one thing perfectly: while the force behind the kingdom (or those poor) was the divine force, the reality of the kingdom was something that would have to be achieved on the earth, so that society as a whole would reflect the will of God: "Thy *kingdom* come. Thy will be done *on earth* as it is in heaven" (1982: II: 130).

But even if human actions both condition and are conditioned by the kingdom, it is still "God's" kingdom that is understood by the Jesus kerygma to be imminent. Indeed, for Segundo, because God is the "force" behind the kingdom, human participation in the building of the kingdom is freed from the oppressive fear and burden of trying to earn salvation or entry into the kingdom. Because of this, says Segundo, Jesus means for us "existence as *project*," not "existence as *test*." It is only insofar as we know that God is the source of salvation that we are *free* to live our lives *creatively* as a "project" of *love*, quite apart from the anxiety and fear that come from relying on our own efforts. In fact, as Segundo says, "if Jesus has any meaning and significance, it is that there is nothing to fear" (II: 556). Thus, in summary, Jesus confronts us, with an authentic freedom characterized, on the one hand, by its freedom *from* fear, anxiety, and legalism and, on the other hand, by its freedom *for* creatively loving others, understood as the historical project of the kingdom of God; and this freedom can be understood pre-

---

[62]Segundo, as I have aleardy pointed out, disagrees with much of European political theology at this point and also disagrees explicitly with Bultmann's definition of the reign of God as a "miraculous event, which will be brought about by God alone without the help of men" (Bultmann, 1951: I: 4; Cf. Segundo, 1982: II: 557).

cisely as "authentic" freedom because it is the freedom which only God can make possible.

The second element in Segundo's "circle of meaning" amplifies the meaning of the "proximity" of the kingdom and is based on Jesus' response to John the Baptist's query, "Are you he who is to come, or shall we look for another?" (Cf. Matthew 11:2-6; Luke 7:22-23). In answering this, Jesus turns John's question about *who* Jesus is into a question of *what* takes place when the kingdom is here, i.e., its "functions"--"the blind receive their sight and the lame walk, lepers are cleansed and the deaf hear, and the dead are raised up, and the poor have good news preached to them"). Marxsen confirms Segundo's point and says,

> John the Baptist's inquiry about who Jesus is shows that even the "miracles" of Jesus cannot be *proved* to be eschatological deeds. Moreover, John's question is not answered with a reference to Jesus, but with a reference to his "functions"; and then salvation is promised to the person who does not take offense at the one who is performing these functions (1976: 148).

Even here, however, what is clear is that it is precisely these "signs" that are associated in the minds of Jesus' interpreters as the "signs of the times." They confirm to all who "have eyes to see" that the reign of God is near.

The third element offered by Segundo is closely related to the second and focuses on Jesus' sermon on the mount (Matthew) or on the plain (Luke), and especially the opening set of Beatitudes in that discourse. Here Jesus clarifies the values of the kingdom and the relationship of these values to two groups--namely, "the poor" (for whom the kingdom is "good news") and the wealthy and powerful (for whom the kingdom is "bad news," requiring conversion and a change of values). Segundo claims that this relationship is not viewed by the earliest witnesses, however, as symmetrical. In other words, though it is the *values* of the second group that turns the gospel into "bad news," it is the *situation* of the first group that causes them to see the gospel as "good news."

> And the kingdom comes to change the *situation* of the poor and to put an end to it. That the poor possess the kingdom of God, in accordance with the first Beatitude, is not due to any merit of theirs, much less to any value that poverty might have. The reason is the opposite: the inhumanity of their situation. The kingdom is coming because God is "humane," because God cannot tolerate that situation and is coming to make sure that his will is accomplished on earth (1982: II: 160).

Thus, Jesus' followers understand themselves to be confronted by nothing less than what Marxsen calls "the will of God" (1976: 147), which, to be sure, is communicated primarily in terms of how we ought to love one another. So for example, we are asked to go the extra mile with our enemy and to include everyone as our neighbor. Because no one can earn or merit the kingdom of God, the poor enjoy a special place of honor in the kingdom and sinners are invited to fellowship as well. Thus, Jesus confronts us with an "authentic" love characterized by both its extension and inclusiveness and this love can be so qualified because it is the love which God both offers and demands.

Perhaps the strangest feature of what Segundo takes to be the core of the earliest teaching about Jesus (the "Jesus kerygma") which I have just summarized, is the role of God in that teaching. The reason it is strange, of course, is because, as I have pointed out over and over, Segundo is interested in presenting a "Jesus for atheists" and he claims that the function of the word "God" in christology, far from pointing to the meaning of ultimate reality for us, is a merely verbal device to lend a sense of "ultimacy" to Jesus' historical witness. Segundo believes that Jesus can be existentially meaningful whether or not God is a reality.

But just this claim is what, it seems to me, runs exactly counter to the most minimal claims of the earliest witnesses to Jesus, as even Segundo summarizes those claims. Unless the word "God" refers meaningfully to a reality, it is hard to understand how Jesus can be taken to have the kind of decisive significance that the above witnesses take him as having. If the meaning of Jesus for us is that we now need no longer fear or be anxious for our salvation because God is the "force" behind it, then surely the significance of Jesus cannot be appropriately interpreted apart from clarifying the meaning of who God is, understood by Jesus' followers as the one whose kingdom was breaking in. By the same token, if Jesus' inclusion of all in the kingdom is grounded on the premise that this is because *God* includes them, then who God is becomes a matter of great importance for interpreting Jesus' significance. For example, Segundo insists that the church cannot be about restoring brotherhood and sisterhood in society "if in the course of history God did not in one way or another give the dignity and function of 'brother' and 'sister' to every human being" (1982: II: 528). This, for Segundo is a fundamental "transcendent datum" of the Christian faith and, yet, apart from some clear and coherent idea of who God is, I can hardly see the force of such a statement. In other words, any interpretation of the significance of Jesus which claims not only to be appropriate to the earliest witnesses to Jesus but also credible to common human experience and reason must clarify just who this God is that, as re-presented by Jesus, is the ultimate ground in reality not only of our freedom and creativity but also of our love.

By way of offering just such a clarification, I rely, first, on the biblical witness as to the meaning of God for us and, second, on a metaphysical analysis of God understood as ultimate reality itself. The biblical witness, of course, does not so much speak of the structure of ultimate reality in itself but does talk about the meaning of God for us in terms of the "*imago dei.*" At face value, the *imago dei* presents itself as a good starting point for talking about the meaning of God for us because, by its very definition, it intends to tell the truth about both God and us, insofar as it affirms that humans are created in the image of God and that, therefore, both humans and God exhibit a similar structure of being. If we look briefly at the Genesis account from which the doctrine of the *imago dei* is taken, we discover three elements that are taken as intrinsic to human existence--namely, freedom, creativity, and sociality. Theologically, these elements are not the result of a "fall" but insofar as the "paradise" state of Eden points us not to some state of affairs "once upon a time" (Tillich) but to the way it essentially is with us, they refer to constitutive elements of our existence as human beings. What we find in Genesis, then, is that not only are Adam and Eve created as free human subjects, they are also created as creators, both in terms of their ability to procreate and to work (tending the garden). But if Adam and Eve are created as free and creative, they are also created for each other, together, as social beings. Thus, freedom, creativity, and sociality are deeply embedded in the very heart of human existence.

The question then arises, how can God, as decisively re-presented in Jesus, be said to function in our lives as the ground of the freedom, creativity, and love to which we are called, given the structure of human existence expressed in the concept of the *imago dei*? My own conviction is that a neoclassical metaphysics can assist greatly in answering this question insofar as it converges with the insights of the biblical witness and extends them by showing how all of reality itself exhibits the three-fold structure of existence discovered in the *imago dei*--freedom, creativity, and sociality--including, especially, God. A neoclassical metaphysics can also provide clarification of how, on the basis of this universal structure, God through Jesus calls us to an authentic freedom, an authentic creativity, and an authentic sociality (which we call "love"). Here again, however, I can only suggest the outline of how one might fairly go about providing just such a clarification.

We will recall, first of all, that metaphysical statements are confirmed by all experience and denied by no possible experience. Thus, sociality, creativity, and freedom, if they are to be considered metaphysical traits must be universal categories that apply to any and every actuality whatsoever. It is just that truth, however, which Charles Hartshorne has so carefully developed in his own writings. In the first place, sociality, or relatedness, is one of the most obvious and irrefutable categories that one can attach to what it means to be "human," though it has traditionally been a real problem when applied to deity. We know ourselves, of course, to be related; indeed, everything we do is tinged by influences from others and, to that degree, we are "dependent" on others. But can God also be said to be "social" and, therefore, dependent? Hartshorne demonstrates how it is possible not only to speak of God as social and conditioned by others, but eminently so--i.e., in a categorially different way than finite beings are related to one another. Hartshorne believes that we can and must conceive of God as "super-relative."

Hartshorne's argument proceeds from the metaphysical observation that the social category fits all actual or conceivable facts of observation, while non-social conceptions are at best required by no conceivable observations and contradicted by some (1953: 32-33). Sociality, thus, is a universal category that applies to any and every actuality whatsoever and may be defined as follows:

> the appeal of life for life, of experience for experience. It is "shared experience," the echo of one experience in another. Hence nothing can be social that is without experience (33).

It would be inconsistent to say that God is not social. He is a member of a society, as we all are, only God as the supreme social being rules the world society not from the outside as a dictator but, by being related perfectly to every member, as "the supreme conserving and coordinating influence" (40). Hartshorne says,

> This is not quite the traditional theological idea of God; though it is, I believe, the religious idea. For religion, as a concrete practical matter, as a way of life, has generally viewed God as having social relations with man, as sympathizing with him and gaining something through his achievements. God was interested in man, therefore could be "pleased" or "displeased," made more or less happy, by man's success or failure, and could thus be "served" by human efforts (40).

This conception of God, then, has the advantage of maintaining literally both God's non-relativity and God's relativity. Hartshorne expresses this thought as follows:

> The difference between ordinary and divine relativity can be expressed in many ways. One way is this: God is relative, but what we may call the extent of his relativity is wholly independent of circumstances, wholly nonrelative (1948: 82).

Thus, while all beings have some degree of "absoluteness" or independence of relationships (in that all beings are creative and free, as we shall see) and some degree of "relativity," God is the one being in whom both "absoluteness" and "relativity" are maximal.

Hartshorne's view of "sociality," it seems to me, provides a clear path for understanding how it is an aspect of the *imago dei*, descriptive of both creatures and deity. Indeed, even the creation account in Genesis itself expresses in a mythological way God's desire for social relations. But if, as Hartshorne claims, God is universally related, then on Hartshorne's model of sociality--"the experience of experience"--God may be said, first, to be supremely sympathetic and, secondly, supremely inclusive. But is this not the very God that Jesus represents so decisively to those who encountered him? Jesus, then, confronts human existence with a twofold possibility: first, that we understand ourselves as objects of God's supremely sympathetic and all-inclusive love and, second, that we respond to that love by structuring our praxis in accordance with that love. In the first place, to understand one's self as the object of God's love; to know that whatever else happens, one's life unfailingly contributes to the divine life, gives to our praxis a new meaning and sense of abiding significance. What we do matters. Furthermore, this understanding of ourselves as loved by God has tremendous implications for our understanding of freedom, as Schubert Ogden explains.

> Because God's love for us is completely boundless and is offered to any and every person who is willing to receive it, nothing whatever can separate one from life's ultimate meaning. For this reason, to accept God's love through faith is to be freed from oneself and everything else as in any way a necessary condition of a meaningful life. But for the very same reason, the acceptance of God's love through faith establishes one's freedom *for* all things as well as one's freedom *from* them. Because God's love is utterly boundless and embraces everything within its scope, anything whatever is of ultimate significance and thus the proper object of one's returning love for God (1982: 123).

In the second place, as Ogden indicates, to know one's self to be the object of God's unconditional love is to be free to love others as God has loved us.[63] This means, of course, that our love must, insofar as possible, be fully sympathetic and without bounds. Obviously, our relations are finite and our ability to sympathize with and include others is categorially different from that of God. Nonetheless, if the sociality at the base of our existence is to be "authentic" sociality, it must actualize itself in sympathetic, unbounded love. In this way, and this way only, can the contemporary reconstruction of the human being and of society move beyond the ever-increasing tendencies toward privatization, on the one hand, and massification, on the other, both of which threaten our existence in Christian love.

But if the *imago dei* presents us as social beings, it also depicts both God and human beings as creative. One of the central religious beliefs about God, of

---

[63]Segundo, like both Hartshorne and Ogden, affirms that "all love loves God" (1962a: 72). By this Segundo means to stress that the object of all authentic love is as divine as its origin. Nonetheless, this identification of the love of God and the love of neighbor seems to me to require a notion of God such as I have tried to explicate here but that is explicitly lacking in Segundo's theology.

course, is that he is creator; that God somehow stands behind and is the cause of all that is. Humans also create through work, sexuality, art, and play. Is, then, creativity a metaphysical trait? From what I have already demonstrated of Hartshorne's metaphysical system, God is not and never could be without a world. There is a certain necessity in creation, since God could not have been without some kind of world. That is not to say, however, that God had to create *this* particular world. Any world would have done. This or any other world is contingent, since everything about it might have been different.

From this, however, one cannot conclude that God might have refrained from creating. God does not choose to have a world; God has to have one. But God has the choice of creating a particular world with such and such general characteristics. If it is objected that this idea is contrary to the religious idea, in which God is creator *ex nihilo*, Hartshorne would argue that an alleged freedom not to act is without value. In other words, there are some impossibilities for God which do not thereby diminish God since they are logical impossibilities.

But even if we can affirm literally that both God and human beings create, there is still a radical asymmetry between the way God is creative of the world and the way human beings are creative of God. God always creates and is literally creative of every actuality whatsoever. In other words, God is an ingredient in the becoming of every being and provides an element of novelty to every entity whatsoever. Human beings, on the other hand, most certainly do create but might not have, since they might not have been at all. Furthermore, the scope of contribution which human beings make is severely restricted. Because of the obvious limitations on our own ability to impact and make a difference to others, we are creative of only *some* others. God, on the other hand, is creative of *all* others. Not unlike sociality, then, creativity may also be understood as a universal metaphysical principle.

> A theistic philosophy must take "create" or "creator" as a universal catego-
> ry, rather than as applicable to God alone. It must distinguish supreme
> creativity from lesser forms and attribute some degree of creativity to all
> actuality. It must make of creativity a "transcendental," the very essence
> of reality as self-surpassing process (1967: 26).

For Hartshorne, creativity, as characteristic of all reality, is an element in every experience. "To be is to create" (1983: 1), says Hartshorne. Each actuality is an emergent synthesis in which several causal influences are taken by the entity and "created" (there is always the freedom of the entity - no matter how small) into a new entity. In this way, everything is both creative of something else and self-creative, no matter what else it may be. In God's case, God is creative of everything, and everything contributes to God's self-creation. Thus, rather than being the only creator, God creates like we do, only in a supreme way.

God, if social, is eminently or supremely so. On the other hand, that which in the eminent form is called divine creation, in a milder or ordinary form must be exhibited by lesser beings such as man. Man certainly is social. If then ordinary sociality is ordinarily creative, eminent sociality will be eminently creative, divinely creative. And ordinary sociality is, in a humble sense, creative (1948: 29).

Here, it seems to me, Hartshorne's view of "creativity," like his view of "sociality," is one that opens up doors to understanding the meaning of God for us which we encounter in Jesus of Nazareth. If, as Hartshorne claims, both God and human beings are creative (in different ways, of course), first, as self-creative and, second, as creative of others, then may we not understand Jesus as confronting human existence, again, with a twofold possibility: first, that we understand ourselves as creative of God, ourselves, and others and, second, that we understand ourselves as created by God, ourselves, and others. In other words, no matter the entity, every actuality is an instance of the process of creative synthesis whereby the influence of another is accepted and whereby one becomes an influence for another.

Thus, in the first place, to understand ourselves as creative of God is, again, to give our praxis a real causal significance and not an apparent one only. Not only does what we do matter; things can be different. Insofar as we are creative of God, we contribute to the divine life and so to all of reality eternally. In the second place, to understand ourselves as created by God is to instill in our lives a proper sense of dependency, of recognizing the sheer gratuitousness of our existence and of living in worship and thanks to God. Of course, one can also speak confidently on these grounds about the difference that we make to others and the difference they make to us, and in both respects that difference is such as to raise our consciousness and responsibility in every historical project we undertake. Nonetheless, the meaning of God for us with which Jesus confronts us is the possibility of real novelty both in terms of our own individual lives and in terms of the transformation of our world. Jesus is taken as presenting the kingdom of God as something which God creates and which we simply receive, but also something which we create insofar as the life and work of the kingdom requires human participation and causality. In the final analysis, however, what must be said is that, if our own finite creativity contributes in any "authentic" way to the kingdom of God, that is to the extent that God becomes the ultimate source of novelty for our creativity. In this way, an authentic Christian existence can bring to the individual and social tasks of humanization and liberation a creative and effective faith that brings novelty to our world by drawing upon the creative life of God himself. The reality which we face today is such that we no longer understand ourselves as beings who are merely driven by evolution, but rather who now also drive evolution. So also, any authentic Christian praxis today must be a creative and flexible praxis in its expression of an "effective faith" which attempts to move beyond the ever-increasing tendencies toward destruction, on the one hand, and inflexibility, on the other, both of which threaten our existence in Christian hope.

Finally, the *imago dei* characterizes both human beings and the God who creates them as "free." For Hartshorne, of course, freedom as a metaphysical category is crucial to an adequate understanding of God and reality; both our freedom and God's freedom are basic to the whole process of creative synthesis. The coming to be of any actual entity implies the influence of others as well as the freedom of the entity that is becoming. Thus, freedom is essential to all experience and, as Hartshorne says, "we shall never understand life and the world until we see that the zero of freedom can only be the zero of experiencing, and even of reality" (1983: 6). Hartshorne, like Whitehead, holds that all entities at all levels of existence -- cosmic, human, animal, cellular, atomic, etc. -- experience and thus are, in some measure, free.

Within this coming to be, the influence of others is always a factor but it never rules out freedom. Thus, God's sociality does not undermine God's freedom.

> Since an object always influences, but cannot dictate, the awareness of itself, we influence God by our experiences but do not thereby deprive him of freedom in his response to us. This divine response, becoming our object, by the same principle in turn influences us, but here, too, without removing all freedom (1948: 142).

God, of course, influences every becoming while our influences are much more radically limited. Our influence upon God is real, though slight, while God's influence on us is great, though it does not override our freedom. Hartshorne understands God's "providence" in this way, not as a coercive power that dictates the course of events, but as God's own essential presence in every becoming.

> Thus God can rule the world and order it, setting optimal limits for our free action, by presenting himself as essential object, so characterized as to weight the possibilities of response in the desired respect. This divine method of world control is called "persuasion" by Whitehead and is one of the greatest of all metaphysical discoveries . . . (142).

A consequence of Hartshorne's view is that God the Creator is himself created, on the one hand, while creatures are not merely creatures who in no way create. This is true because "freedom is self-creation" (1983: 9).

For Hartshorne, then, freedom is a universal characteristic of reality as is creativity and sociality. Indeed, the three categories are inseparably related. But if, as Hartshorne claims, God influences us without overriding our freedom, then, certainly we may say that Jesus confronts us, first, with the possibility of understanding ourselves as truly liberated by God to implement effectively the faith we have chosen. Segundo echoes Hartshorne at this point:

> In effect, authentic *personal* love is always characterized by the fact that it assigns decisive importance to the freedom of the one who is loved, so that our own fulfillment and happiness depend on that person's free decisions. This, in turn, presupposes two things: first, that we leave something decisive and unfinished to the other's freedom; second, that we consider the risk and the pain of the inconclusive to be better for the other and for ourselves, respectfully depending on the other's decisions. Something conclusive cannot be decisive, it can only be painless and indifferent. The best of all possible worlds would mean the total loss of meaning and value for our existence (1982: II: 520).

In the second place, on the basis of the freedom which Jesus means for us, we not only *can* act, we *must* act. Here the two demons are passivity and bondage. If, as the Apostle Paul says, "it is for freedom that Christ has made us free," then just as we are released *from* bondage, so also we are free *for* others. This and only this attitude can convert the freedom at the core of our very existence into "authentic" freedom, despite the inevitable limitations not only on our freedom but on our abilities. What Jesus offers us, by re-presenting to us the ground of freedom, creativity, and love in reality itself, is the challenge and the assurance that an effective and creative use of freedom, guided by love, can fulfill our own existence. Insofar as we take up that challenge, empowered and confident in the possibilities thus presented to us, perhaps the urgency of human and social reconstruction can move beyond the ever-increasing tendencies toward passivity, on the one hand, and bondage, on the other, both of which threaten our existence in Christian freedom.

BIBLIOGRAPHY

I. Works by Juan Luis Segundo

Segundo, Juan Luis

1948   *Existencialismo, filosofía y poesía: ensayo de síntesis.* Buenos Aires: Espasa-Calpe.

1962a   *Función de la Iglesia en la realidad rioplatense.* Montevideo: Barreiro y Ramos.

1962b   *Etapas precristianas de la fe: Evolución de la idea de Dios en el Antiguo Testamento.* Montevideo: Cursos de Complementación Cristiana.

1963a   *Berdiaeff, une réflexion chrétienne sur la personne.* Paris: Editions Montaigne.

1963b   "The Future of Christianity in Latin America." *Cross Currents* 12, no. 2: 273-281.

1964a   *Concepción cristiana del hombre.* Montevideo: Mimeográfica "Luz."

1964b   *La cristiandad, ¿una utopía? I. Los Hechos.* Montevideo: Mimeográfica "Luz."

1964c   *La cristiandad, ¿una utopía? II. Los principios.* Montevideo: Mimeográfica "Luz."

1964d   "Pastoral latinoamerican: hora de decisión." *Mensaje* (Santiago) 4, no. 127 (March-April): 74-82.

1964e   "Problemas teológicas de Latinoamérica." Petrópolis, Brasil. Unpublished paper presented at one of the first international conferences of Latin American theologians during Vatican II.

1965   "La función de la Iglesia." *Diálogo* (Montevideo) 1, no. 1 (December): 4-7.

1966a   "La función de la Iglesia." *Diálogo* (Montevideo) 1, no. 2 (February): 5-10.

1966b   "El diálogo, Iglesia, mundo, reflexión." *Diálogo* (Montevideo) 1, no. 6 (October): 3-7.

1966c   "El diálogo, Iglesia-mundo." *Diálogo* (Montevideo) 1, no. 9 (November): 8-12.

1966d   "Lo que el concilio dice." *Diálogo* (Montevideo) 1, no. 10 (December): 3-13.

1967a   "The Church: A New Direction in Latin America." *Catholic Mind* (March): 43-47.

1967b   "Un nuevo comienzo." *Víspera* (Montevideo) 1, no. 2 (August): 39-43.

1967c   "América hoy." *Víspera* (Montevideo) 1, no. 2 (October): 53-57.

1967d   "Hacia una exégesis dinámica." *Víspera* (Montevideo) 1, no. 3 (October): 77-84.

1967e   "Hipótesis sobre la situación del Uruguay: Algunas posibilidades de investigación." In *Uruguay 67: Una interpretación*, Juan Luis Segundo, Pedro Almos, Dionisio J. Garmandia et al., 11-32. Montevideo: Editorial Alfa.

1967f   "¿Que nombre dar a la existencia cristiana?" *Perspectivas de Diálogo* (Montevideo) 2, no. 11 (January-February): 3-9.

1967g   "Intellecto y salvación." In *Salvación y construcción del mundo*, Gustavo Gutiérrez, et al., 77-86. Barcelona: Editorial Nova Terra.

1967h   "Universidad latinoamericana y consciencia social." Unpublished paper prepared by Segundo for an international conference of Catholic educators in Buga, Colombia.

1967i   "La condición humana." *Perspectivas de Diálogo* (Montevideo) 2, no. 12 (March-April): 30-35.

1967j   "La condición humana." *Perspectivas de Diálogo* (Montevideo) 2, no. 13 (May): 55-61.

1967k   "Camilo Torres, sacerdocio y violencia." *Víspera* (Montevideo) 1, no. 1 (May): 71-75

1967l   "La vida eterna." *Perspectivas de Diálogo* (Montevideo) 2, no. 14 (June): 83-89.

1967m   "La vida eterna." *Perspectivas de Diálogo* (Montevideo) 2, no. 15 (July): 109-118.

1967n   "Profundidad de la gracia." *Perspectivas de Diálogo* (Montevideo) 2, no. 19 (November): 235-240.

1967o   "Profundidad de la gracia." *Perspectivas de Diálogo* (Montevideo) 2, no. 20 (December): 249-255.

1968a   "Christianity and Violence in Latin America." *Christianity and Crisis* 28: 31-34.

1968b   "¿Dios nos interesa o no?" *Perspectivas de Diálogo* (Montevideo) 3, no. 21 (March): 13-16.

1968c   "Social Justice and Revolution." *America* 118, no. 17 (27 April): 574-577.

1968d   "Del ateísmo a la fe." *Perspectivas de Diálogo* (Montevideo) 3, no. 22 (April): 44-47.

1968e   "Padre, Hijo, Espíritu: Una historia." *Perspectivas de Diálogo* (Montevideo) 3, no. 23 (July): 71-76.

1968f   "El poder del hábito." *Perspectivas de Diálogo* (Montevideo) 3, no. 23 (July): 90-92.

1968g   "Padre, Hijo, Espíritu: Una sociedad." *Perspectivas de Diálogo* (Montevideo) 3, no. 24 (July): 103-109.

1968h   "Padre, Hijo, Espíritu: Una libertad I." *Perspectivas de Diálogo* (Montevideo) 3, no. 25 (July): 142-148.

1968i   "Padre, Hijo, Espíritu: Una libertad II." *Perspectivas de Diálogo* (Montevideo) 3, no. 26 (August): 183-186.

1968j   *Esa comunidad llamada Iglesia.* Buenos Aires: Carlos Lohlé. (*The Community Called Church.* Translated by John Drury. Maryknoll: Orbis, 1973.)

1968k   *Gracia y condición humana.* Buenos Aires: Carlos Lohlé. (*Grace and the Human Condition.* Translated by John Drury. Maryknoll: Orbis, 1973.)

1969a   "Has Latin America a Choice?" *America* 120, no. 8 (22 February): 213-216.

1969b   "¿Un Dios a nuestra imagen?" *Perspectivas de Diálogo* (Montevideo) 4, no. 32 (March): 14-18.

1969c   "¿Hacia una Iglesia de izquierda?" *Perspectivas de Diálogo* (Montevideo) 4, no. 32 (April): 35-39.

1969d   "Ritmos de cambio y pastoral de conjunto." *Perspectivas de Diálogo* (Montevideo) 4, no. 35 (July): 131-137.

1969e   "¿Autoridad o qué?" *Perspectivas de Diálogo* (Montevideo) 4, nos. 39-40 (December): 270-272.

1969f   "Introducción." *Iglesia latinoamericana, ¿protesta o profecía?*, 8-17. Buenos Aires: Búsqueda.

1969g   "Riqueza y pobreza como obstáculos al desarrolo." *Perspectivas de Diálogo* (Montevideo) 4, no. 32 (April): 54-56.

1970a   "Evangelización y humanización: Progreso del reino y progreso temporal." *Perspectivas de Diálogo* (Montevideo) 5, no. 41 (March): 9-17.

1970b   "Desarrollo y subdesarrollo: Polos telógicos." *Perspectivas de Diálogo* (Montevideo) 5, no. 43 (May): 76-80.

1970c   "La ideología de un diario católico." *Perspectivas de Diálogo* (Montevideo) 5, no. 44-45: 136-44.

1970d   "El posible aporte de la teología protestante para el cristianismo latinoamericano en el futuro." *Cristianismo y Sociedad* (Montevideo) 8, no. 22: 41-49.

1970e   "Wealth and Poverty as Obstacles to Development." In *Human Rights and the Liberation of Man*. Edited by Louis M. Colonnese, 23-31. South Bend: University of Notre Dame Press.

1970f   *De la sociedad a la teología*. Buenos Aires: Carlos Lohlé.

1970g   *Nuestra idea de Dios*. Buenos Aires: Carlos Lohlé. (*Our Idea of God*. Translated by John Drury. Maryknoll: Orbis, 1973.)

1971a   "La iglesia chilena ante el socialismo I." *Marcha* (Montevideo) (27 August): 1558.

1971b   "La iglesia chilena ante el socialismo II." *Marcha* (Montevideo) (4 September): 1559.

1971c   "La iglesia chilena ante el socialismo III." *Marcha* (Montevideo) (11 September): 1560.

1971d   "Education, Communication, and Liberation: A Christian Vision." *IDOC International: North American Edition* (13 November): 63-96.

1971e   *Los sacramentos hoy*. Buenos Aires: Carlos Lohlé. (*The Sacraments Today*. Translated by John Drury. Maryknoll: Orbis, 1974.)

1971f   *¿Qué es un Cristiano?* Montevideo: Mosca Hnos. S. A. Editores.

1972a   *Evolución y culpa*. Buenos Aires: Carlos Lohlé. (*Evolution and Guilt*. Translated by John Drury. Maryknoll: Orbis, 1974.)

1972b   *Acción pastoral latinoamericana: Sus motivos ocultos*. Buenos Aires: Búsqueda. (*The Hidden Motives of Pastoral Action*. Translated by John Drury. Maryknoll: Orbis, 1978.)

1973a   "Las élites latinoamericanas: problemática human y cristiana ante el cambio social." In *Fe cristiana y cambio en América Latina: Encuentro de El Escorial*, 203-212. Salamanca: Sigueme.

1973b   "Teología y ciencias sociales." In *Fe cristiana y cambio social en América Latina: Encuentro de El Escorial*, 285-296. Salamanca: Sigueme.

1973c   *Masas y minorías en la dialéctica divina de la liberación.* Buenos Aires: La Aurora.

1974a   "On a Missionary Awareness of One's Own Culture." *Jesuit Missions Newsletter*, no. 33 (May): 1-6.

1974b   "Reconciliación y conflicto." *Perspectivas de Diálogo* (Montevideo) 9, no. 86 (September): 172-178.

1974c   "Fe y ideología." *Perspectivas de Diálogo* (Montevideo) 9, nos. 89-90 (December): 172-182.

1974d   "Theological Response to Talk on Evangelization and Development." *Studies in the International Apostolate of Jesuits* (November): 79-82.

1974e   "Teología: Mensaje y proceso." *Perspectivas de Diálogo* (Montevideo) 9, no. 89-90 (December): 259-270.

1975a   "Conversión y reconciliación en la perspectiva de la moderna teología de la liberación." *Cristianismo y sociedad* 13: 17-25.

1975b   *Liberación de la teología.* Buenos Aires: Carlos Lohlé. (*The Liberation of Theology.* Translated by John Drury. Maryknoll: Orbis.)

1975c   "Condicionamientos actuales de la reflexión teológica en Latinoamérica." In *Liberación y cautiverio: debates en torno al método de la teología en América Latina.* Edited by Enrique Ruiz Maldonado, 99-101. Mexico City: Comité Organizador.

1976   "Statement by Juan Luis Segundo." In *Theology in the Americas*. Edited by Sergio Torres and John Eagleson, 280-283. Maryknoll: Orbis.

1977   "Perspectivas para una teología latinoamericana." *Perspectiva Teológica*, January-June: 9-25.

1978   "Derechos humanos, evangelización e ideología." *Christus* (November): 29-35.

1979a   "Preface." In *Theologies in Conflict: The Challenge of Juan Luis Segundo*, Alfred T. Henelly, xiii-xviii. Maryknoll: Orbis.

1979b   "Capitalism Versus Socialism: Crux Theologica." In *Frontiers of Theology in Latin America*. Edited by Rosino Gibellini, 240-259. Maryknoll: Orbis.

1980   "A Conversation with Juan Luis Segundo, S.J." In *Faith: Conversations with Contemporary Theologians*. Edited by Teófilo Cabestrero, 172-180. Maryknoll: Orbis.

1982   *El hombre de hoy ante Jesús de Nazaret.* 3 volumes. Madrid: Ediciones Cristiandad.

1983a   "Faith and Ideologies in Biblical Revelation." In *The Bible and Liberation*. Edited by Norman K. Gottwald. Maryknoll: Orbis.

1983b   *Teología abierta.* 3 volumes. Madrid: Ediciones Cristiandad.

1985   *Theology and the Church.* Translated by John W. Diercksmeier. Minneapolis: Winston Press.

1986   "Christ and the Human Being." *Crosscurrents* 36: 39-67.

1990   "Two Theologies of Liberation." In *Liberation Theology: A Documentary History*. Edited by Alfred T. Henelly, 353-366. Maryknoll: Orbis.

II. Other Works

Aristotle
      1958   *The Politics of Aristotle.* Translated with an Introduction, Notes, and Appendixes by Ernest Barker. New York: Oxford University Press.

Assman, Hugo
      1971   *Opresión-liberación: Desafío a los cristianos.* Montevideo: Tierra Nueva.

      1976   *Theology for a Nomad Church.* Maryknoll: Orbis.

      1984   "The Actuation of the Power of Christ in History." In *Faces of Jesus: Latin American Christologies.* Edited by José Míguez Bonino, translated by Robert R. Barr. Maryknoll: Orbis.

Barbour, Ian G.
      1971   "Teilhard's Process Metaphysics." In *Process Theology.* Edited by Ewert H. Cousins. New York: Paulist.

      1974   *Myths, Models, and Paradigms.* San Francisco: Harper and Row.

      1990   *Religion in an Age of Science.* New York: Harper and Row.

Bateson, Gregory
      1972   *Steps to an Ecology of Mind.* New York: Ballantine Books.

Baum, Gregory
      1971   *Man Becoming: God in Secular Experience.* New York: Herder & Herder.

      1975a   *Religion and Alienation: A Theological Reading of Sociology.* New York: Paulist Press.

      1977   "The Theological Method of Segundo's *The Liberation of Theology.*" *Catholic Theological Society of America Proceedings* 32: 120-124.

Berger, Peter L.
    1979   "A Politicized Christ: Continuing the Discussion." *Christianity and Crisis* 39: 52-54.

Bertram, Robert W.
    1988   "Liberation by Faith: Segundo and Luther in Mutual Criticism." *Dialog* 27, no. 4: 268-276.

Boff, Clodovis
    1987   *Theology and Praxis: Epistemological Foundations.* Translated by Robert R. Barr. Maryknoll: Orbis.

Boff, Leonardo, O.F.M.
    1974   "Salvation in Jesus Christ and the Process of Liberation." In *Concilium 96: The Mystical and Political Dimension of the Christian Faith*, Claude Geffre and Gustavo Gutiérrez, 78-91. New York: Herder and Herder.

    1978   *Jesus Christ Liberator: A Critical Christology for Our Time.* Translated by Patrick Hughes. Maryknoll: Orbis.

Brown, Robert McAfee
    1975   "Reflections on Detroit." *Christianity and Crisis* 35, no. 17: 255-256.

Bultmann, Rudolf
    1951-55   *Theology of the New Testament.* 2 volumes. Translated by Kendrick Grobel. New York: Scribner's.

    1969   *Faith and Understanding.* Translated by Louise Pettibone Smith. New York: Harper & Row.

    1982   "Jesus--History and Faith" (unpublished). Edited and translated by Schubert M. Ogden.

    1984   *New Testament and Mythology and Other Basic Writings.* Edited and translated by Schubert M. Ogden. Philadelphia: Fortress.

Calvert, D.G.A.
    1971-72   "An Examination of the Criteria for Distinguishing the Authentic Words of Jesus." *New Testament Studies* 18: 209-218.

Candelaria, Michael R.
    1990   *Popular Religion and Liberation: The Dilemma of Liberation Theology.* State University of New York Press.

Ching, Theresa Lowe, R.S.M.
    1989   *Efficacious Love: Its Meaning and Function in the Theology of Juan Luis Segundo.* Lanham: University Press of America.

Clark, Henry
    1981   "Process Thought and Justice." In *Process Philosophy and Social Thought.* Chicago: Center for the Scientific Study of Religion.

Clarke, Thomas E.
    1975   "Ignatian Spirituality and Societal Consciousness." *Studies in the Spirituality of Jesuits* (September): 127-150.

Cobb, John B., Jr.
    1969   *God and the World.* Philadelphia: Westminster.

    1971   "A Whiteheadian Christology." In *Process Philosophy and Christian Thought.* Edited by Delwin Brown, Ralph E. James, Jr., and Gene Reeves, 382-398. Indianapolis: Bobbs-Merrill.

    1975   *Christ in a Pluralistic Age.* Philadelphia: Westminster Press.

    1982   *Process Theology as Political Theology.* Philadelphia: Westminster.

Cobb, John B., Jr. and Franklin Gamwell (eds.)
    1984   *Existence and Actuality: Conversations with Charles Hartshorne.* Chicago: University of Chicago Press.

Collingwood, R. G.
    1968   *Faith and Reason: Essays in the Philosophy of Religion.* Edited by Lionel Rubinoff. Chicago: Quadrangle Books.

Comblin, Jose
    1976   *Jesus of Nazareth: Meditations on His Humanity.* Maryknoll: Orbis.

Cook, Michael L.
    1983   "Jesus From the Other Side of History: Christology in Latin America." *Theological Studies* 44: 258-287.

Coste, Rene
    1985   *Marxist Analysis and Christian Faith*. Translated by Roger A. Couture, O.M.I. and John C. Cort. Maryknoll: Orbis.

Crossan, John Dominic
    1991   *The Historical Jesus: The Life of a Mediterranean Jewish Peasant*. New York: Harper and Row.

Devenish, Philip E. and George L. Goodwin (eds.)
    1989   *Witness and Existence: Essays in Honor of Schubert M. Ogden*. Chicago: The University of Chicago Press.

Dussel, Enrique
    1976   *History and the Theology of Liberation*. Translated by John Drury. Maryknoll: Orbis.

    1981   *A History of the Church in Latin America*. Translated by Alan Neely. Grand Rapids: Eerdmans.

    1985   *Philosophy of Liberation*. Translated by Aquilina Martinez and Christine Morkovsky. Maryknoll: Orbis.

    1989   "Teología de la Liberación y Marxismo." *Cristianismo y Sociedad* 98: 37-60.

Flannery, Austin (ed.)
    1975   *Vatican Council II: The Conciliar and Post Conciliar Documents*. Collegeville, MN: Liturgical Press.

Flew, Antony and Alasdair MacIntyre (eds.)
    1955   *New Essays in Philosophical Theology*. London: SCM Press.

Freire, Paulo
    1970   *Pedagogy of the Oppressed*. New York: Seabury.

Gager, John G.
    1974   "The Gospels and Jesus: Some Doubts about Method." *Journal of Religion* 54: 244-272.

Galilea, Segundo
  1984   "Jesus' Attitude Toward Politics: Some Working Hypotheses." In *Faces of Jesus: Latin American Christologies*. Edited by José Míguez Bonino, translated by Robert R. Barr. Maryknoll: Orbis.

Gamwell, Franklin
  1984   *Beyond Preference*. Chicago: University of Chicago Press.

  1990   *The Divine Good: Modern Moral Theory and the Necessity of God*. New York: HarperCollins Publishers.

Geertz, Clifford
  1979   "Religion as a Cultural System." In *Reader in Comparative Religion: An Anthropological Approach*, 4th edition. Edited by W. Lesser and E. Vogt, 78-90. New York: Harper.

Gesché, Adolphe
  1987   "Foreword." In *Theology and Praxis: Epistemological Foundations*, Clodovis Boff, translated by Robert R. Barr, xiii-xvii. Maryknoll: Orbis.

Gonzalez-Ruiz, Jose-Maria
  1976   *The New Creation: Marxist and Christian?* Translated by Matthew J. O'Connell. Maryknoll: Orbis.

Griffin, David R.
  1973   *A Process Christology*. Philadelphia: Westminster Press.

  1981   "Values, Evil, and Liberation Theology." In *Process Philosophy and Social Thought*. Chicago: Center for the Scientific Study of Religion.

Gutiérrez, Gustavo
  1972   "Jesus and the Political World." *Worldview* (September): 43-46.

  1973   *A Theology of Liberation*, Edited and translated by Sister Caridad Inda and John Eagleson. Maryknoll: Orbis.

1974   "Liberation Movements and Theology." In *Jesus Christ and Human Freedom*. Edited by Edward Schillebeeckx and Bas van Iersel. New York: Herder and Herder.

1976   "Faith as Freedom: Solidarity with the Alienated and Confidence in the Future." In *Living with Change, Experience, Faith*. Edited by Francis A. Eigo, 15-54. Villanova: Villanova University Press.

1977   *Teología desde el reverso de la historia*. Lima: Centro de Estudios y Publicaciones.

1978   "Two Theological Perspectives: Liberation Theology and Progressivist Theology." In *The Emergent Gospel*. Edited by Sergio Torres and Virginia Fabella, 227-255. Maryknoll: Orbis.

1979a   "Liberation Praxis and Christian Faith." In *Frontiers of Theology*. Edited by R. Gibellini. Maryknoll: Orbis.

1979b   *La fuerza histórica de los pobres: selección de trabajos*. Lima: Centro de Estudios y Publicaciónes.

1984   *Beber en su propio pozo*. Salamanca: Sigueme.

1990   "Criticism will Deepen, Clarify Liberation Theology." In *Liberation Theology: A Documentary History*. Edited by Alfred Henelly. Maryknoll: Orbis.

Gutiérrez, G., J.L. Segundo, S. Croatto, B. Catao, and J. Comblin
1968   *Salvación y construcción del mundo*. Santiago: Nova Terra.

Haight, Roger, S.J.
1976   "Mission: The Symbol for Understanding the Church Today." *Theological Studies* (December): 620-649.

1985   *An Alternative Vision*. New York: Paulist.

1986   "The Liberation Theology of the Centre." *Grail: An Ecumenical Journal* 2 (September): 23-32.

Hartshorne, Charles

1941   *Man's Vision of God and the Logic of Theism.* Hamden, CT: Archon Books.

1948   *The Divine Relativity: A Social Conception of God.* New Haven: Yale University Press.

1953   *Reality as Social Process: Studies in Metaphysics and Religion.* Glencoe: Free Press.

1962   *The Logic of Perfection and Other Essays in Neoclassical Metaphysics.* La Salle: Open Court.

1963-64   "Man's Fragmentariness." *Wesleyan Studies in Religion* 56: 17-28.

1967   *A Natural Theology for Our Time.* La Salle: Open Court.

1976   "Beyond Enlightened Self-Interest." In *Religious Experience and Process Theology*, 301-322. New York: Paulist Press.

1983   *Creative Synthesis and Philosophic Method.* Lanham: University Press of America.

1989   "Metaphysical and Empirical Aspects of the Idea of God." In *Witness and Existence: Essays in Honor of Schubert M. Ogden.* Edited by Philip E. Devenish and George L. Goodwin. Chicago: University of Chicago Press.

Hartshorne, Charles and William L. Reese (eds.)

1953   *Philosophers Speak of God.* Chicago: University of Chicago Press.

Harvey, Van A. and Schubert M. Ogden

1964   "How New is the 'New Quest of the Historical Jesus'?" In *The Historical Jesus and the Kerygmatic Christ: Essays on the New Quest of the Historical Jesus*, edited and translated by Carl E. Braaten and Roy A. Harrisville. Nashville: Abingdon.

Hawks, James
    1990   "Juan Luis Segundo's Critique of David Tracy." *Heythrop Journal* 31: 277-294.

Hengel, Martin
    1983   *Between Jesus and Paul.* Translated by John Bowden. Philadelphia: Fortress Press.

Henelly, Alfred
    1977a   "Theological Method: The Southern Exposure." *Theological Studies* (December): 709-735.

    1977b   "The Challenge of Juan Luis Segundo." *Theological Studies* (March): 125-135.

    1978   "Apprentices in Freedom: Theology Since Medellin." *America* 27: 418-21.

    1979   *Theologies in Conflict: The Challenge of Juan Luis Segundo.* Maryknoll: Orbis.

    1989a   *Theology for a Liberating Church.* Washington, D.C.: Georgetown University Press.

    1989b   "Review of *Jesus of Nazareth: Yesterday and Today,*" *Religious Studies Review* 15: 45-47.

Herzog, Frederick
    1972   *Liberation Theology: Liberation in the Light of the Fourth Gospel.* New York: Seabury Press.

    1974   "Liberation Hermeneutic as Ideology Critique?" *Interpretation* (October): 387-403.

    1980   *Justice Church.* Maryknoll: Orbis.

Hewitt, Marsha A.
    1989   "Review of *Jesus of Nazareth: Yesterday and Today.*" *Religious Studies Review* 15: 47-51.

    1990   *From Theology to Social Theory: Juan Luis Segundo and the Theology of Liberation.* New York: Peter Lang.

Hooker, M.D.
    1970-71   "Christology and Methodology." *New Testament Studies* 17: 480-487.

Ignatius of Loyola
    1951   *The Spiritual Exercises of St. Ignatius.* Translated by Louis J. Puhl, S.J. Westminster, MD: Newman Press.

    1963   *Obras completas.* One-volume edition. Madrid: B.A.C. (Segundo cites from this edition).

Jiménez Limón, Javier
    1984   "Sobre la cristología de Juan Luis Segundo." *Christus* 49: 57-61.

Kasper, Walter
    1976   *Jesus the Christ.* Translated by V. Green. New York: Paulist Press.

Kroger, Joseph
    1985   "Prophetic-critical and Practical-strategic Tasks of Theology: Habermas and Liberation Theology." *Theological Studies* 46: 3-20.

Küng, Hans
    1976   *On Being a Christian.* Translated by E. Quinn. Garden City: Doubleday.

Lamb, Matthew
    1976   "The Theory-Praxis Relationship in Contemporary Christian Theologies." In *Catholic Theological Society of America: Proceedings of the Thirty-First Annual Convention,* 149-178. New York: Manhattan College.

    1978   *History, Method and Theology.* Missoula: Scholars Press.

Land, Philip
    1976   "Justice, Development, Liberation and the Exercises." *Studies in the International Apostolate of Jesuits* (June): 1-62.

Lane, Dermot
    1984   *Foundations For a Social Theology.* New York: Paulist
                Press.

Leech, Kenneth
    1981   "Liberating Theology: The Thought of Juan Luis Segundo."
                Theology 84: 258-266.

Leon-Dufour, Xavier
    1963   *The Gospels and the Jesus of History.* New York:
                Doubleday Image Books.

Lonergan, Bernard
    1972   *Method in Theology.* New York: Herder & Herder.

Lord, Elizabeth
    1989   "Human History and the Kingdom of God: Past
                Perspectives and Those of J. L. Segundo." *Heythrop
                Journal* 30: 293-305.

Löwy, Michael
    1989   "Marxismo y religión: el desafío de la Teología de la
                Liberación." *Cristianismo y Sociedad* 98: 7-22.

Machovec, Milan
    1976   *A Marxist Looks at Jesus.* Philadelphia: Fortress.

Mackey, James P.
    1979   *Jesus, the Man and the Myth: A Contemporary Christology.*
                New York: Paulist Press.

Maduro, Otto
    1989   "La desacralización del marxismo en la Teología de la
                Liberación." *Cristianismo y Sociedad* 98: 69-84.

Mahan, Brian and L. Dale Richesin (eds.)
    1981   *The Challenge of Liberation Theology: A First World
                Response.* Maryknoll: Orbis.

Marshall, Bruce
    1987   *Christology in Conflict.* New York: Basil Blackwell.

Marx, Karl
    1963   *Early Writings*. Edited and translated by T. B. Bottomore. New York: McGraw-Hill.

Marx, Karl and Friedrich Engels
    1975   "The German Ideology." *On Religion*. Moscow: Progress Publishers.

Marxsen, Willi
    1976   "Christology in the New Testament." In *The Interpreter's Dictionary of the Bible: Supplementary Volume*. Edited by Keith Crim, 146-156. Nashville: Abingdon.

    1989   "The Limit to the Possibility of Christological Assertions." In *Witness and Existence: Essays in Honor of Schubert M. Ogden*. Chicago: The University of Chicago Press.

    1990   *Jesus and Easter: Did God Raise the Historical Jesus from the Dead?* Translated by Victor Paul Furnish. Nashville: Abingdon.

McCann, Dennis P.
    1981a   *Christian Realism and Liberation Theology: Practical Theologies in Creative Conflict*. Maryknoll: Orbis Books.

    1981b   "Political Ideologies and Practical Theology: Is There a Difference?" *Union Seminary Quarterly Review* 36: 243-257.

McElvaney, William K.
    1980   *Good News is Bad News is Good News*. Maryknoll: Orbis.

McGovern, Arthur F.
    1980   *Marxism: An American Christian Perspective*. Maryknoll: Orbis.

Meland, Bernard (ed.)
    1969   *The Future of Empirical Theology*. Chicago: University of Chicago Press.

Merkle, Judith Ann
    1985   *The Fundamental Ethics of Juan Luis Segundo*. Toronto: University of St. Michael's College.

Metz, Johann Baptist
1969   *Theology of the World*. New York: Herder and Herder.

1989   "La pugna de la teología para la integración de la historia
            y de la sociedad." *Cristianismo y Sociedad* 98: 61-68.

Migliore, Daniel
1980   *Called To Freedom: Liberation Theology and the Future of
            Christian Doctrine*. Philadelphia: Westminster Press.

Míguez Bonino, José
1975   *Doing Theology in a Revolutionary Situation*. Philadelphia:
            Fortress Press.

1976   *Christians and Marxists: The Mutual Challenge to
            Revolution*. Grand Rapids: Eerdmans.

1979   "Historical Praxis and Christian Identity," In *Frontiers of
            Theology in Latin America*. Edited by Rosino Gibellini,
            260-283. Maryknoll: Orbis.

1984   *Faces of Jesus*. Maryknoll: Orbis.

Millas, Orlando
1989   "Los comunistas chilenos ante los procesos de renovación
            surgidos en el cristianismo." *Cristianismo y Sociedad* 98:
            85-92.

Miranda, José Porfirio
1974   *Marx and the Bible: A Critique of the Philosophy of
            Oppression*. Maryknoll: Orbis.

1976   *Being and the Messiah*. Maryknoll: Orbis.

1978   *El cristianismo de Marx*. Mexico City.

1982   *Communism In the Bible*. Translated by Robert R. Barr.
            Maryknoll: Orbis.

Moltmann, Jürgen
1959   *Religion, Revolution and the Future*. New York:
            Scribner's.

1976   "An Open Letter to José Míguez Bonino." *Christianity and Crisis* 29: 56-63.

Muñoz, Ronaldo
 1979   "The Historical Vocation of the Church." In *Frontiers of Theology in Latin America.* ed. Rosino Gibellini, translated by John Drury, 151-162. Maryknoll: Orbis.

Nessan, Craig L.
 1986   "Liberation Praxis: Challenge to Lutheran Theology." *Dialog* 25: 124-128.

Niemeyer, Gerhart
 1981   "Structures, Revolutions and Christianity." *Center Journal* 1: 79-99.

Norris, Richard A., Jr.
 1966   "Toward a Contemporary Interpretation of the Chalcedonian Definition." In *Lux in Lumine: Essays to Honor W. Norman Pittenger.* Edited by Richard A. Norris, Jr. New York: Seabury Press.

Norris, Richard A., Jr. (ed.)
 1980   *The Christological Controversy.* Philadelphia: Fortress Press.

O'Donnell, James G.
 1982   "The Influence of Freud's Hermeneutic of Suspicion on the Writings of Juan Luis Segundo." *Journal of Pscyhology and Theology* 10: 28-34.

Oestreicher, Paul (ed.)
 1969   *The Christian-Marxist Dialogue.* London: Macmillan.

Ogden, Schubert
 1961   *Christ Without Myth.* Dallas: SMU Press.

 1963   *The Reality of God.* San Francisco: Harper & Row.

 1967   "How Does God Function in Human Life?" *Christianity and Crisis* 27: 105-108.

 1969a   "Theology and Metaphysics." *Criterion* 9: 15-18.

1969b   "Present Prospects for Empirical Theology." In *The Future of Empirical Theology*. Edited by Bernard E. Meland. Chicago: University of Chicago Press.

1971   "The Task of Philosophical Theology." In *The Future of Philosophical Theology*. Edited by Robert A. Evans, 55-84. Philadelphia: Westminster Press.

1973   "The Gospel We Hold in Common--Or Do We?" Unpublished Manuscript - Faith and Order Conference.

1975   "The Criterion of Metaphysical Truth and the Senses of 'Metaphysics.'" *Process Studies* 5: 47-48.

1976a   "The Authority of Scripture for Theology." *Interpretation* 30: 242-261.

1976b   "Christology Reconsidered: John Cobb's 'Christ in a Pluralistic Age.'" *Process Studies* 6: 116-122.

1976c   "Sources of Religious Authority in Liberal Protestantism." *Journal of the American Academy of Religion* 44: 403-416.

1976d   "The Meaning of Christian Hope." In *Religious Experience and Process Theology*, 196-212. New York: Paulist.

1977   "Linguistic Analysis and Theology." *Theologische Zeitschrift* 33: 318-325.

1979a   *Faith and Freedom: Toward a Theology of Liberation*. Nashville: Abingdon.

1979b   *Christ Without Myth: A Study Based on the Theology of Rudolf Bultmann*. 2nd edition. Dallas: Southern Methodist University Press.

1980a   "Faith and Freedom: How My Mind Has Changed." *Christian Century* 97: 1241-1244.

1980b   "On the Trinity." *Theology* 83, no. 692 (March): 97-102.

1981   "Response to Dorothee Soelle." In *The Challenge of Liberation Theology: A First World Response.* Edited by Brian Mahan and L. Dale Richesin, 17-20. Maryknoll: Orbis.

1982   *The Point of Christology.* San Francisco: Harper & Row.

1983   "Concerning Belief in God." (unpublished).

1984a   "Rudolf Bultmann and the Future of Revisionary Christology." In *Rudolf Bultmann's Werk und Wirkung.* Edited by Bernd Jaspert, 155-173. Darmstadt: Wissenschaftliche Buchgesellschaft.

1984b   "Process Theology and the Wesleyan Witness." *Perkins Journal* 37 (Spring): 18-32.

1985   "The Metaphysics of Faith and Justice." *Process Studies* 14: 87-101.

1986   *On Theology.* San Francisco: Harper & Row.

1987   "'For Freedom Christ Has Set Us Free': The Christian Understanding of Ultimate Transformation." *Buddhist Christian Studies* 7: 47-58.

Olthuis, James H.
1986   "Evolutionary Dialectics and Segundo's Liberation of Theology." *Calvin Theological Journal* 21: 79-93.

Pannenberg, Wolfhart
1977   *Jesus - God and Man.* 2nd Edition. Translated by Lewis L. Wilkins and Duane A. Priebe. Philadelphia: Westminster Press.

Peel, David R.
1977   "Juan Luis Segundo's "A Theology for Artisans of a New Humanity": A Latin American Contribution to Contemporary Theological Understanding." *Perkins School of Theology Journal* 30: 1-9.

Persha, Gerald
1980   *Juan Luis Segundo: A Study Concerning the Relationship Between the Particularity of the Church and the Universality of Her Mission* (1963-1977). Maryknoll: Orbis.

Pittenger, W. Norman
1959   *The Word Incarnate: A Study of the Doctrine of the Person of Christ.* New York: Harper & Brothers.

1970   *Christology Reconsidered.* London: SCM Press.

1971a   "Bernard E. Meland, Process Thought and the Significance of Christ." In *Process Theology.* Edited by Ewert H. Cousins, 203-215. New York: Paulist Press.

1971b   "Process Thought: A Contemporary Trend in Theology." In *Process Theology.* Edited by Ewert H. Cousins, 23-35. New York: Paulist Press.

1974   "The Incarnation in Process Theology." *Review and Expositer* 71: 43-57.

1977   "Christology in Process Theology." *Theology* 80: 187-193.

Rahner, Karl, S.J.
1961-1988   *Theological Investigations*, 21 volumes. New York: Crossroad.

1978   *Foundations of Christian Faith: An Introduction to the Idea of Christianity.* Translated by William V. Dych. New York: Seabury Press.

1979   "Towards a Fundamental Theological Understanding of Vatican II." *Theological Studies* 40: 716-727.

Rahner, Karl, S.J. and Wilhelm Thüsing, S.J.
1980   *A New Christology.* New York: Crossroad.

Rahner, Karl, S.J. and Karl-Heinz Weger, S.J.
1981   *Our Christian Faith: Answers for the Future.* Translated by Francis McDonagh. New York: Crossroad.

Richards, Glyn
  1987   "Faith and Praxis in Liberation Theology, Bonhoeffer and
                    Gandhi." *Modern Theology* 3: 359-373.

Ricoeur, Paul
  1970   *Freud and Philosophy: An Essay on Interpretation.* New
                    Haven: Yale University Press.

Ringe, Sharon
  1985   *Jesus, Liberation, and the Biblical Jubilee: Images for
                    Ethics and Christology.* Philadelphia: Fortress Press.

Robinson, James M.
  1959   *A New Quest of the Historical Jesus.* London: SCM Press.

Scannone, Juan Carlos
  1979   "Theology, Popular Culture, and Discernment."   In
                    Frontiers of Theology in Latin America. Edited by Rosino
                    Gibellini, 213-239. Maryknoll: Orbis.

Schüssler-Fiorenza, Elisabeth
  1981   "Toward a Feminist Biblical Hermeneutics: Biblical
                    Interpretation and Liberation Theology." In *The Challenge
                    of Liberation Theology: A First World Response.* Edited by
                    Brian Mahan and L. Dale Richesin, 91-112. Maryknoll:
                    Orbis.

Schweizer, Eduard
  1968   *The Quest of the Historical Jesus.* New York: Macmillan.

  1971   *Jesus.* Atlanta: John Knox.

Sia, Santiago
  1985   *God in Process Thought: A Study in Charles Hartshorne's
                    Concept of God.* Dordrecht: Martinus Nijhoff Publishers.

Slade, Stanley David
  1979   *The Theological Method of Juan Luis Segundo.*   Ph.D.
                    Dissertation, Fuller Theological Seminary.

Sobrino, Jon, S.J.
  1975   "El Jesus histórico: Crisis y desafio para la fe." *Estudios
                    Centroamericanos* (April): 201-224.

| 1978 | *Christology at the Crossroads: A Latin American Approach.* Translated by John Drury. Maryknoll: Orbis. |

| 1987 | *Jesus in Latin America.* Maryknoll: Orbis. |

Soelle, Dorothee
| 1981 | "'Thou Shalt Have No Other Jeans Before Me' (Levi's Advertisement, Early Seventies): The Need for Liberation in a Consumerist Society." In *The Challenge of Liberation Theology: A First World Response.* Edited by Brian Mahan and L. Dale Richesin, 4-16. Maryknoll: Orbis. |

Sontag, Frederick E.
| 1980 | "Is There a Universal Human Experience?" *Religious Life* 49: 373-381. |

Strauss, David Friedrich
| 1977 | *The Christ of Faith and the Jesus of History: A Critique of Schleiermacher's The Life of Jesus.* Translated by Leander E. Keck. Philadelphia: Fortress Press. |

Stumme, Wayne (ed.)
| 1984 | *Christians and the Many Faces of Marxism.* Minneapolis: Augsburg. |

Sweeney, John, S.J.
| 1980 | "For the Builders of a New Ireland: The Theology of Juan Luis Segundo." *Furrow* 31: 783-789. |

Taborda, Francisco
| 1987 | "Artigos." *Perspectiva Teológica* 19: 293-319. |

Tambasco, Anthony J.
| 1981 | *The Bible for Ethics: Juan Luis Segundo and First World Ethics.* Washington, D.C.: University Press of America. |

Teilhard de Chardin, Pierre
| 1959 | *The Phenomenon of Man.* New York: Harper & Row. |

| 1960 | *The Divine Milieu.* New York: Harper & Row. |

| 1964 | *The Future of Man.* New York: Harper & Row. |

1965   *The Appearance of Man.* New York: Harper & Row.

1968   *Science and Christ.* Translated by René Hague. New York: Harper & Row.

Toulmin, Stephen
    1950   *An Examination of the Place of Reason in Ethics.* Cambridge: Cambridge University Press.

Tracy, David
    1975   *Blessed Rage for Order.* New York: Seabury Press.

Tripole, Martin Ralph, S.J.
    1981   "Segundo's Liberation Theology vs. an Eschatological Ecclesiology of the Kingdom." *Thomist* 45: 1-25.

Verkamp, Bernard J.
    1988   "On Doing the Truth: Orthopraxis and the Theologian." *Theological Studies* 49: 3-24.

Walker, Theodore Jr.
    1989   "Hartshorne's Neoclassical Theism and Black Theology." *Process Studies* 18: 240-258.

Weir, J. Emmette
    1982   "The Bible and Marx: A Discussion of the Hermeneutics of Liberation Theology." *Scottish Journal of Theology* 35: 337-350.

Wells, Harold
    1981   "Segundo's Hermeneutic Circle." *Journal of Theology for Southern Africa* 34: 25-31.

    1987   "The Question of Ideological Determination in Liberation Theology." *Toronto Journal of Theology* 3: 209-220.

Wesley, John
    1979   "On Working Out Our Own Salvation." In *The Works of John Wesley*, Volume VI, 3rd Edition. Kansas City: Beacon Hill Press.

Whitehead, A. N.
    1978   *Process and Reality.* Corrected edition. New York: Free Press.

Wilson-Kastner, Patricia
    1983   *Faith, Feminism, and the Christ.* Philadelphia: Fortress.

Wood, Charles M.
    1985   *Vision and Discernment: An Orientation in Theological Study.* Atlanta: Scholars Press.